MIDDLE EAST PEACE PLANS

MIDDLE EAST PEACE PLANS

EDITED BY
WILLARD A. BELING

ST. MARTIN'S PRESS
New York

Library of Congress Cataloging in Publication Data

Beling, Willard A.
    Middle East peace plans.

    Includes index.
    1. Jewish–Arab relations—1973–   —Addresses,
essays, lectures.   2. Israel–Arab War, 1973–   —Peace—
Addresses, essays, lectures.   3. Arab countries—Politics
and government—1945–   —Addresses, essays, lectures.
I. Title.
DS119.7.B379   1986   956'.048   85-30361
ISBN 0-312-53193-1

CONTENTS

ACKNOWLEDGEMENTS

This book derives from a series of lectures which were presented at the University of Southern California, under the sponsorship of the Middle East/North African Program during the spring semester of 1985.

A number of people played important roles in staging the lecture series and in preparing the book for publication. However, three stand out for their special contributions: Priscilla Tucker Schneidman, Douglas MacLellan and Dr Fariborz Rouzbehani.

INTRODUCTION

Willard A. Beling

Peace has become a major field in the literature of the Middle East, particularly since President Sadat's historic trip to Jerusalem in November 1977. Publications in the meantime fall into four main categories: those inspired by (i) Sadat's trip itself and the subsequent efforts for peace; (ii) the Camp David negotiations and agreement in September 1978; (iii) the Fahd Plan of August 1981 and the Reagan and Fez Plans which followed in September 1982; and (iv) alternative proposals offered by individual politicians and area specialists.

This volume attempts to provide a somewhat different dimension. It treats the peace proposals of the various actors who have a meaningful impact on the peace process. The principal actors in the area itself, of course, are Israel, the Palestine Liberation Organization (PLO) and the Arabs and, outside the Middle East, the United States, the Soviet Union and Western Europe (EEC). The essays examine the character of each plan, its commonalities/incompatibilities with others, and finally the prospects of its being implemented.

The volume's aim is not to moralize since it has no peace plan of its own, nor does it aim to 'sell' any plan. Indeed, its sole goal is to examine the plans, their diversity and the potential for acceptability or change. Is there any light at the end of the tunnel for peace in the Middle East? These essays answer this question, it is hoped, as well as anyone could.

Diverse National Interests: Diverse Positions

Although there are other influential factors, diverse national interests are ultimately responsible for the diverse positions on the Middle East. Therefore, it is not logical at all to expect a universally acceptable peace plan, much less one acceptable to the major antagonists in the conflict. Nevertheless, it should be noted in this regard that national interests are not static. They are formed by

1

domestic forces which themselves evolve and change. In effect, positions can change, indeed dramatically. They are not cast in concrete.

The Middle Eastern Actors

Israel and the Palestinians

The two major actors in the Palestinian conflict are the Palestinians and the Israelis. Popular identification of it as the 'Arab-Israeli' conflict has, of course, always clouded this fact. In the name of Arab nationalism, its self-avowed leader Abdel Nasser of Egypt had insisted that it was an 'Arab' issue. For their own purposes the Israelis also preferred this label for the dispute. The world media followed suit.

President Bourguiba of Tunisia always disagreed with Nasser on this point, insisting that it was really a Palestinian fight first and then Arab, in that order, and the latter's only if the Palestinians themselves took up the issue and sought Arab aid. The creation of the PLO in the early 1960s and the 1967 war were major turning points in this direction. Nevertheless, almost every actor involved in the peace process, including Israelis and Arabs themselves, ironically still often ignore the Palestinians while trying to resolve the Israeli-Palestinian conflict.

The formulas for peace of both Israelis and Palestinians were, of course, mutually exclusive from the beginning. They have not changed their respective positions very much in the meantime. Nevertheless, there has been a certain evolution: they are no longer completely polarized. One can recall when they barely acknowledged each other's existence. The other actors in the process have changed their positions far more.

The PLO has its own peace plans(s), which, in their most moderate format, have evolved (according to some observers) to the point of providing official recognition of Israel in exchange for a homeland. However, the fact that neither Israel nor the United States will recognize the PLO blunts the latter's hopes for its plans. Israeli's programme of settlements in the occupied West Bank may in the meantime, of course, eliminate the possibility of achieving peace on that basis. There may be no land left to exchange for peace with the Palestinians. In light of all the recent developments, Helena Cobban examines the PLO's plans for peace in Chapter 2.

While the PLO apparently has become more moderate, Israel apparently hardened its position under the Likud. But not really. Its position on Eretz Israel was always clear: neither Labour nor the Likud will give up the West Bank. There is consensus on this point. In effect, only the borders with its Arab neighbours are left to be negotiated. To this end, should not the Israelis logically prefer negotiating with 'Arabs' rather than Palestinians, with Hussein or Mubarak rather than Arafat? Peace with Arab neighbours will resolve their border problems, and within these borders the Israelis feel that they can handle the internal problems with the remaining Palestinians. Professor Don Peretz evaluates the prospects of peace from the Israeli perspective in Chapter 1.

Israel and the Arabs

On the other hand, there is no unanimity on peace plans among the Arab states. Sadat negotiated a peace treaty with Israel on a 'land for peace' basis, regaining the Sinai in the exchange. Lebanon also negotiated for peace but subsequently reneged on the deal. Neither Jordan nor Syria have moved to negotiate their borders with Israel and do not appear to be prone to do it in the near future.

As for the non-contiguous Arab states, peace with Israel really means a resolution of the Palestinian conflict. To be sure, there is an Arab peace plan, the so-called Fahd Plan, which other Arab states endorsed at Fez in September 1982. Nevertheless, it is essentially a Saudi rather than Arab peace plan. While recognition of Israel is avowedly anathema to these Arab states, the Fahd Plan implicitly allows for it. This is a major breakthrough. Nevertheless, it is very doubtful that diplomatic relations would really be established between Israel and all of the Arab states even if the Palestinian-Israeli conflict were resolved under the Fahd (Fez) Plan. Dr David Long examines in Chapter 3 the Fahd Plan in detail.

The Other Principal Actors in the Peace Process

The United States

It has been well known since President Truman's time, of course, that American domestic politics play a major role in shaping American policy toward the Middle East.[1] How much has American policy on the Palestinian issue changed in the meantime?

The United States is one of the principal actors, and after President Sadat's surprise visit to Jerusalem in 1977 and the Camp David Accords in September 1978, peace became the 'buzz' word in Washington, DC. While the White House had supported the peace process for years, it was never with the same level of expectation as in the Carter Administration. President Carter was committed to resolving the conflict. The Reagan Plan is an updated version of the Carter position. But does the present Administration have the same commitment to resolve the issue? In Chapter 4 Professor Quandt, who as a member of the Carter Administration was present at the Camp David talks, answers these questions.

It became quite clear after the Camp David talks that while the United States is important, it obviously is not the only actor in the peace process for the Middle East and may not even be a major one. In fact, there are several other important actors, each with its own idea (a) of what the peace should be and (b) how it should be achieved. National interest, of course, also determines their posture on the Middle East.

The Soviet Union

Whether one likes it or not, the Soviet Union is a principal actor in the Middle East peace process. Many in America, of course, demonize the Soviet Union's interest in the Middle East, that is, that it derives solely from anti-West and anti-capitalist biases, and so on. Indeed it does, but not entirely. Dr Sakharov shows in Chapter 5 how Soviet policy in the Middle East is affected as much by domestic politics as it is by strategic or ideological concerns.

Can the Soviet anti-Israeli stance therefore perhaps also be explained, at least in part, in terms of domestic politics *vis-à-vis* the very large Moslem population in the Soviet Union? Perhaps the Soviet decision against large-scale overt commitment to the Iraq-Iran conflict may also derive from a domestic concern. In effect, is the USSR aiding Iraq just enough to keep it from losing and Iran from winning? An Iranian victory over Iraq and the concomitant export of Khomeini's Islamic fundamentalism into the USSR could, of course, wreak havoc in the Soviet Moslem population.

Western Europe

The Western European nations have moved away from the American position on the Middle East since 1967 to develop their own. Interest groups with close religio-ethnic ties to the Middle

East do not appear to play as important a role in Western European policy-formulation as they do in the United States or the Soviet Union. Furthermore, the economic interests of Western Europe are quite different from both the USA and the USSR. Neither of the latter needs Middle East oil; Western Europe depends upon it.

Nevertheless, Western Europe's policy position must also be weighed by the ability to implement it. While both the United States and the Soviet Union can interfere directly in the Middle East, Western Europe cannot. It lacks the power. Therefore, although Western Europe can interfere indirectly in the Middle East in a variety of ways, Professor Adam Garfinkle questions in Chapter 6 its impact on the peace process. In essence, is Western Europe's pro-Arab switch significant in the peace process for the Middle East?

The Lebanese and Iran-Iraq Crises: Peripheral but Related Conflicts

The Lebanese Conflict

It would be simplistic, of course, to blame Lebanon's crises solely on the Palestinian issue. In fact, all sorts of social, political and economic factors triggered Lebanon's problems. Nevertheless, the influx of Palestinian refugees into Lebanon, compounded with the PLO presence, have been major factors. Certainly, they triggered the Lebanese military responses against the PLO and the Israeli invasion. They also created rather strange Lebanese political alliances.

History has shown that Lebanon cannot stand alone against its enemies on the outside or, for that matter, on the inside. Unfortunately for Lebanon, it had lost the client-state relationships that had maintained it since its creation after World War I, first losing French and then American support. To this end, both the Maronites and the Shi'ites in Lebanon looked to Israel for support against the PLO, and the Israelis invaded Lebanon in 1982. But while the invasion resolved the PLO issue it created other problems, and all sides became unhappy with this relationship.

Unfortunately, Lebanon now appears to have become so tied to the Israeli-Palestinian issue that it can only re-emerge as a united nation when regional peace is achieved, and then, perhaps, only under a client-state relationship. It is difficult at this point to identify with whom. Dr McLaurin sorts out the possibilities in Chapter 7.

The Iraq-Iran Conflict

Dr Rouzbehani points out in Chapter 8, of course, that while the current Iraq-Iran conflict is a long-standing *local* boundary dispute, its shock waves are far from local. The conflict has no inherent relationship, for example, to the Arab-Israeli conflict. Nevertheless, its resolution/non-resolution does have a real bearing upon the Arab-Israeli conflict — so perceived at least by several of the actors in the Arab-Israeli peace process. It is also perceived to impact significantly upon the strategic interests of the United States and the Soviet Union, indeed, also upon Soviet domestic interests.

The United States, a friend of Khomeini's enemy the Shah, became in the logic of the Middle East also his enemy. Adding injury to insult, the United States now shows ill-concealed sympathy toward Iraq in the Iraq-Iran conflict. These factors alone make the American presence in the Middle East anathema to Khomeini. The fact that the United States is also Israel's guarantor adds fuel to the fire since, in contrast to the Shah, the Ayatollah Khomeini is very anti-Israel. Finally, Iran seeks to drive both the United States and Israel from Lebanon, where the United States is viewed as the Maronites' and Israel's ally against fellow Shi'ite Moslems.

The Iraq-Iran conflict's relation to the Israeli-Palestinian issue is, of course, obvious to both the Israelis and Americans. Therefore, Israel aided Iran (until the United States asked them to desist) against the *Arab* Iraqis, their mortal enemy. The United States, of course, also recognizing Iraq's role in the Arab-Israeli dispute, has used a different tactic to the same end, in essence, bleeding both Iran and Iraq to the point of keeping both (a) from radicalizing the Persian Gulf region and (b) from messing in the Arab-Israeli issue.

Conclusion

Peace for the Middle East is obviously not an absolute. It is a highly subjective concept, meaning different things to different people: (a) because of the religious connotations associated with the area; and (b) because in international politics, of course, peace for the Middle East also reflects the national interests of all the actors involved in the peace process, whatever that national interest really is or is perceived to be. In effect, the peace plans are highly diverse.

The following essays examine the nature of the peace plans of the principal actors, their incompatibility with the other plans, and the potential for change. Certain change has already occurred. The Soviet Union, for example, and Western Europe have changed their positions. However, without major changes in the positions of the major actors of the area itself there does not appear to be much hope for peace in the Middle East. The essays examine these prospects.

Note

1. Hans Morganthau noted that on the domestic level we find group interests, represented by ethnic and economic groups, who tend to identify themselves with the national interest, in essence arguing that their own interest is the national interest. See his 'Another "Great Debate": The National Interest of the United States', *American Political Science Review, 46* (1952), 961–88; and 'The National Interest and Moral Principles in Foreign Policy: The Primacy of the National Interest', *American Scholar*, vol. 18, no. 2 (Spring 1949), 207–12.

PART ONE

THE MAJOR ACTORS IN THE PEACE PROCESS

1 ISRAELI PEACE PROPOSALS

Don Peretz

Although the key issues in the Arab-Israeli dispute have remained much the same since Israel was established in 1948, there have been major modifications in the parameters of a peace settlement, modifications that are related to changes in the balance of power between Israel and the Arab states. They correspond with Israel's growth from a minor, relatively weak nation to the dominant military power of the region.

Since the beginning of conflict between the Zionist and Arab nationalist movements, even before Israel was established, most Zionists perceived that the key issues were less substantive than ideological, i.e. the issues they perceived were Arab recognition of a Jewish State and its right to a secure existence in Palestine. After the Arab defeat in the first Arab-Israeli war of 1947–9, the Arab states in particular and the international consensus in general perceived the major questions to be Israel's borders, the fate of Jerusalem, and the rights of Arab refugees who fled Israeli-held territory during the first war. Whereas Israelis argue that the dispute over borders, Jerusalem and refugee rights is a result of Arab refusal to accept the Jewish State, international consensus as expressed in numerous United Nations resolutions and in the policies of Western nations including the United States, is that an accommodation on substantive issues will lead to recognition of Israel by the Arab states and peace in the region.

Israel's policies with regard to peace, its government peace plans and those of the various groups within Israel reflect the tension between these two perspectives — the perspective that regards the conflict as one over substantive issues and that which underscores ideology. Official government policies and peace proposals, both those of Labour and Likud, emphasize ideology in that they regard the key to peace, not in concessions by Israel, but in prior Arab acceptance of the Jewish State. All governments have consistently emphasized that a weak Israel will never be accepted, therefore Israeli power is the key to peace regardless of concessions on borders, refugees or Jerusalem. The willingness of the Israeli

11

government to consider such substantive issues is more the result of outside pressures, such as those from the US, than of the conviction that concessions will soften Arab hostility and lead to peace.

All official peace proposals therefore, emphasize Israel's security position *vis-à-vis* its Arab neighbours. Differences between the two major Israeli political parties reflect differing perceptions of what Israel must do to maintain its position as the dominant power in the region. Likud's approach also gives central consideration to its territorialist ideology in which the national boundaries will include all of historical Israel. Since Likud became a powerful political force after Israel acquired additional land in 1967, territorialist ideology has acquired as much significance as security in developing official peace plans.

Pre-1967 Plans

First let us examine how Israel's changing role in the Middle East has altered its perception of the acceptable in peace plans. Before the state was established in May 1948, its leaders accepted the UN partition plan which allocated some 6,000 of Palestine's 10,000 square miles (26,000 km²) to the new Jewish State, although it gave the state no authority in Jerusalem, which was to become internationalized. Israel at the time was weak militarily and in no position to insist that it control all of mandatory Palestine as was the desire of mainstream Zionism.

There were factions at both the left and right of the political spectrum which opposed the partition compromise. Until partition was adopted by the UN General Assembly in November 1947, the left-wing Hashomer Hatzair, predecessor of today's Mapam party, strongly advocated a binational solution in which all of Palestine would remain united as an Arab-Jewish state rather than one divided between the two peoples.[1] However, between November 1947 and the declaration of independence in May 1948, all but a tiny faction of the binationalists disappeared from the political scene; most of them eagerly accepted the opportunity to establish a Jewish state.

At the other end of the spectrum, the right-wing heirs of Vladimir Jabotinsky's Zionist Revisionist movement continued to reject any form of partition as a solution. Until now his heirs in the

Herut party and in the larger Likud movement, insist that at a minimum all of mandatory Palestine is the Jewish State. Some even insist that all of the Hashemite Kingdom of Jordan and even parts of adjoining nations cannot be bargained away for peace.[2] The left wing of the Zionist movement finally accepted the peace plans of mainstream Zionism, but the right-wing territorialists, growing in strength from a relatively minor Zionist faction to the government of Israel between 1977 and 1984, still oppose any form of partition.

The UN Partition Plan remained the basis of official peace plans for less than a year. By the end of 1948 it was clear that Israel would no longer implement it. As a result of its military victory it extended the area under control of the Jewish State from 6,000 (15,500 km[2]) to 8,000 square miles (20,700 km[2]), ending the strange configuration of the UN scheme which divided Palestine into an international enclave, three Arab and three Jewish zones. Israeli-held territory was now consolidated and received quasi-international recognition through the 1949 UN-sponsored armistice agreements between Israel and Egypt, Jordan, Syria and Lebanon. For all practical purposes the partition plan was dead.

Despite occasional proposals like those of Count Folke Bernadotte and Anthony Eden to revive the Plan as a basis for peace negotiations, and Arab insistence that Israel withdraw to the partition borders before engaging in peace talks, the Israel government no longer considered the Plan valid. Within a few years all distinctions between the partition borders and the armistice lines had disappeared. Eventually, international consensus also accepted the armistice lines as formal if unratified borders, and all discussion of return to partition ended. The exception was Jerusalem.

The international consensus refused to recognize Israel's annexation of the city's Jewish quarters, and until now, Israel's closest ally, the United States, has not recognized annexation. A separate consulate-general responsible directly to Washington rather than to the US embassy in Tel-Aviv underscores the State Department's reluctance to accept Israel's sovereignty over the city.

Although Israel refused to renounce annexation of Jerusalem, it made various proposals intended to accommodate international concerns and the various religious interests in the city. When the Jerusalem question was debated at the UN in 1949, Israel proposed a form of 'functional internationalization' in which it would conclude an agreement with the UN guaranteeing protection of the

Holy Places in Israeli-controlled Jerusalem, and providing for a resident UN representative in the city to observe implementation of the agreement.[3] A year later the proposal for 'functional internationalization' was reintroduced with increased status for the UN resident representative. He would be 'a sovereign authority of the UN' with full control over the Holy Places, 'including protection, free access, and repairs'. A certain degree of extra-territoriality would be conceded by Israel to the UN representative who would have 'the sole power of decision in disputes between the different religious communities in Jerusalem'.[4]

After annexing the whole of Jerusalem, both its Jewish and Arab (former Jordanian) sectors in June 1967, Israel informed the UN that the process of integration was irreversible and not negotiable. The Holy Places would be under the control of those interested in them, but no mention was made of extending any authority to a UN representative as in the 1949 and 1950 proposals.[5]

The 1948 war created another issue which became central in the search for peace — the Palestine Arab refugee question. Should the 725,000 Arabs who had left their homes be repatriated to Israel or resettled in the Arab countries? Should Israel pay compensation for their abandoned property, and if so should it be on individual or global basis?[6]

To many non-Israelis the refugee question appeared to be the key to a settlement; thus the US government during the 20 years between 1947 and 1967 urged a series of peace plans on Israel in which refugee resettlement would be combined with repatriation and compensation. However, Israel consistently argued that return of the refugees would undermine national security, dilute the Jewish character of the state, and subvert its economy. It had little faith that concessions on the refugees would diminish Arab hostility; therefore the government offered only token concessions to American pressure. These included reunion within Israel of Arab families separated by the 1948 war, unfreezing blocked Arab bank accounts, and laying the groundwork for evaluation of Arab property so that a formula for compensation might be devised in the future.[7]

In a larger context, attempts were made to divert consideration of specific issues like borders and Jerusalem with offers of broad-ranging peace plans sketched in general terms, such as regional co-operation in the development of markets and exploitation of raw materials, regional irrigation schemes based on inter-state agreements, exchange of knowledge and co-operation of all governments in the region 'so as to turn the deserts . . . into flourishing gardens'. If the Arab states accepted Israel, it would extend land, sea and air communication rights, including use of ports and institution of telephone, radio and postal connections. Social and health problems would be tackled jointly, and scientific and cultural exchanges would be fostered 'reminding both peoples of the common elements in their own traditions'. These plans would be based on treaties of peace to replace the armistice agreements, ending the Arab boycott and blockade.[8]

A later plan included an offer to accept a Middle East arms embargo provided 'all armaments be removed from the region — by its total disarmament, accompanied by guarantees of the territorial integrity of all countries in the area and the signing of peace treaties . . . or both Israel and the Arabs should be equally armed'. In 1959 Prime Minister Ben Gurion proposed an agreement

> leading to full disarmament and the abolition of the armed forces in Israel and in Egypt, Saudi Arabia, Iraq, Jordan, Syria, and Lebanon, on condition that constant and unhampered mutual control of this agreement is assured, and that the borders and sovereignty of all these States shall not be affected.[9]

Post-1967 Perceptions

Victory in the 1967 war and acquisition of Sinai, Golan, Gaza, the West Bank and East Jerusalem radically altered the Middle East balance of power and the parameters of Israel's peace plans. A new conception of secure borders emerged based on the Jordan River rather than the armistice lines, which were now perceived as obsolete as the UN partition borders. Jerusalem disappeared from the agenda as a negotiable item after the *de facto* annexation of the former Jordanian sector. The problem of the 1948 refugees, whose numbers had almost doubled due to natural increase, was overtaken by a new exodus from the West Bank.

Israel's victory also changed perceptions of feasible parameters for peace in neighbouring Arab states and in the international arena. United Nations Security Council Resolution 242 became the new basis for negotiations and the foundation upon which Israel, the US, the UN and moderate Arab states now constructed their respective frameworks for peace. The resolution called for Israel to withdraw its 'armed forces from territories of recent conflict'; termination of belligerency and 'respect for and acknowledgement of the sovereignty, territorial integrity and political independence of every state in the area and their right to live in peace within secure and recognized boundaries free from threats or acts of force'; and 'a just settlement of the refugee problem'.[10]

Since 1967, disagreements between Israel and the Arab states and between Israel and the international community have not been over the principles in Resolution 242, but in interpreting their meaning. International adoption of the resolution means that several previously accepted principles for settlement have been discarded. They included establishment of an international regime for Jerusalem, return of Arab refugees to Israel within its pre-1967 frontiers, and use of the 1947 UN Partition Plan as the starting point for determining boundaries.

Within Israel itself the gap that existed before 1967 between militant nationalists and moderates has greatly diminished because the government now controls the territory claimed by nationalists, but which prior to 1967 they were willing to forgo in exchange for peace. Even political factions most prone to make territorial concessions for peace like the Rakah Communist Party and the various peace organizations ancillary to it, no longer discuss a settlement in terms of a large refugee return to Israel proper, internationalizing Jerusalem or return to the UN Partition Plan.

Since 1967 the future of the West Bank has overshadowed all other issues in the development of peace plans, both those of Israel, of the Arabs, and of others engaged in the peace process. The West Bank question encompasses the issue of Jerusalem, the refugees, the dilemmas of Palestinian nationalism and Palestinian national rights, relations with Jordan and with Egypt. The future of Gaza will also probably be determined by the outcome of any negotiations over the West Bank. The importance of the West Bank issue became even greater after the 1979 Egypt-Israel peace treaty was signed and Israel returned all of Sinai to Egypt. True, the question of Golan remains, but difficult as it is, it would be easier to resolve once the future of the West Bank were decided.

Likud's Plans

Because Likud and Labour constitute some two-thirds of the

electorate, their plans for the future of the West Bank should be given primary consideration. Devising peace plans has been simpler for Likud than for Labour because Likud was formed in 1973 with a programme to keep territory captured in 1967. There is little dissent within Likud, for the territorial issue is the glue that holds the party together. Labour, on the other hand, is an amalgamation of groups with diverse programmes and perceptions about Israel's territorial rights and the scope of acceptable bargaining items in peace negotiations.

Likud's position on the West Bank has never been in doubt. It is clear cut and unambiguous. Judea and Samaria (the biblical terms used by Likud for the West Bank) are integral parts of Israel and are not negotiable in a peace settlement. According to Menachem Begin, former leader of the Likud, Israel did not have to annex the West Bank because

Judea and Samaria are an integral part of our sovereignty. It's our land. It was occupied by Abdullah against international law, against our inherent right. It was liberated during the six-day war when we used our right of national self-defense, and so it should be . . . You annex foreign land. You don't annex your own country. It is our land. You don't annex it.

Begin's interpretation derives from the historic Revisionist position that all of mandatory Palestine and Transjordan are by international law and historic right integral parts of the Jewish State.[11]

Under Begin, Likud's peace plan did include certain rights for the Arab inhabitants of the West Bank. These were outlined in his 26-point proposal presented to the Knesset in December 1977, the substance of which were included in the Camp David autonomy proposals of September 1978. Begin initially offered to terminate the military government in the West Bank (Judea and Samaria) and Gaza, replacing it with administrative autonomy 'by and for' the Arab inhabitants, who would elect an eleven-member administrative council with its seat in Bethlehem for a four-year period. The council would be responsible for education, religious affairs, finance, transportation, construction and housing, industry, commerce, agriculture, health, labour and social welfare, refugee rehabilitation, justice and local police. However, primary responsibility for security and public order would remain with Israel.[12]

West Bank and Gaza residents would be offered the choice of

either Israeli or Jordanian citizenship. Those choosing to be Israelis would be entitled to vote for and be elected to the Knesset. Those opting for Jordanian citizenship would have the same rights within Jordan. A joint committee of Israelis, Jordanians and the administrative council would determine which existing legislation would remain in force and which would be abolished.

Residents of Israel would be entitled to acquire land and settle in the West Bank and Gaza, and Arabs in these areas who became Israeli citizens would be entitled to the same rights in Israel. Immigration, including immigration of Arab refugees, would be regulated 'in reasonable numbers' by a committee representing Israel, Jordan and the administrative council. Residents of the autonomous areas and Israel would both have freedom of movement and economic activity within the total area of Israel and the autonomous regions. A special proposal would be drawn up to guarantee freedom of access by Christians, Moslems and Jews to their respective holy shrines. Finally,

> Israel stands by its right and its claim of sovereignty to Judea, Samaria and the Gaza district. In the knowledge that other claims exist, it proposes for the sake of agreement and the peace, that the question of sovereignty be left open.[13]

The Camp David Framework agreement on the West Bank and Gaza integrated the substance of these proposals calling them 'transitional arrangements' which were to provide a five-year autonomy period to the Arab inhabitants. No later than three years after initiating the autonomy arrangements, negotiations would open to determine the final status of the territories, leading to a peace treaty between Israel and Jordan.[14]

Upon conclusion of the 1979 peace treaty between Egypt and Israel negotiations were begun to implement the Camp David autonomy framework. It soon became evident that the Begin government's interpretation of autonomy differed greatly from Egypt's and from the United States', under whose auspices the negotiations were conducted. The essential difference was that Begin intended autonomy for *Arab residents* of the West Bank and Gaza, but not for the territory, a notion derived from Jewish experience in Eastern Europe during the latter part of the nineteenth and early twentieth centuries. The term 'autonomism' was then coined 'to designate a theory and conception of Jewish nationalism in the Disapora' in which 'personal autonomy' would be granted to Jewish communities living within the Tsarist and Austro-Hungarian empires. Areas of jurisdiction such as religion, culture and personal-status matters would be turned over to local communities. The basic objective of 'personal autonomy' was to preserve the religious, legal, social and cultural self-sufficiency of the (Jewish) community within the sovereign (non-Jewish) state or its subdivisions. Another analogy might be the millet system during the Ottoman empire.[15]

Major differences of principle with Egypt included Israel's total rejection of a Palestinian state, an option which Egypt left open. Every major party in Israel still rejects the concept of an independent Palestinian state in the West Bank and Gaza or the separation of Jerusalem from Israeli sovereignty. Opponents of a Palestinian state argue that it would be a security threat to Israel; Likud reinforces the security argument with its version of territorial Zionism, i.e. that the region is an integral and inseparable part of Israel. Begin consistently emphasized that the 'full autonomy' mentioned in the Camp David agreements in no way implied territorial or political separation of these areas from Israel:

> The Green line [the 1949 armistice demarcation line separating Israel from the former Jordanian West Bank] no longer exists — it has vanished forever. There is no line any more. We want to coexist with the Arabs in *Eretz Israel* . . . under the autonomy scheme they will run their own internal affairs and we will ensure security . . . Jews and Arabs coexist in Judea and Samaria as they do in Jerusalem, Ramle, Jaffa, and Haifa.[16]

Begin stated that autonomy was an interim measure to provide opportunity for a peace agreement with Egypt. Peace with Egypt would give Israel more freedom of action in the West Bank and Gaza. Autonomy, therefore, was not a goal, but a means or 'a price that Israel is paying to gain peace and normalization with Egypt'.[17] Postponing a final decision on the West Bank and Gaza, according to Brigadier General Aryeh Shalev, would facilitate gaining 'a geopolitical situation more favorable (to Israel)'. During the transition period Israel could create 'facts' in the territories, and perhaps influence the US toward accepting its position, i.e. after the transition period, the territories would become part of the Jewish State. Furthermore, within a few years Israel would be able to demand application of Israeli law in the territories.

Begin's agreement to return the Sinai peninsula to Egypt as part of the peace accord was, according to some Israeli observers, motivated by his assumption that he would be given greater consideration in determining the future of the West Bank and Gaza.

After returning Sinai to Egypt, Likud's peace proposals focused on the future of the West Bank and Gaza. Further discussion of the Golan and East Jerusalem was foreclosed by steps to incorporate them into Israel. During 1981 the Golan issue ended when the Knesset passed legislation imposing Israeli law on the region, in effect annexing it, and the East Jerusalem question was closed with the passage of another annexation bill. The peace treaty with Egypt and the two annexation bills removed all territorial issues from Likud's peace agenda. All that was left to negotiate was the status of Arabs in Judea, Samaria and Gaza.

The principles governing the Arab status were included in Begin's 1977 plan, and in the Camp David agreements as interpreted by Likud in its 1981 and 1984 election platforms. They called autonomy arrangements 'the guarantee that under no condition will a "Palestinian" state arise on the territory of the Western Land of Israel'. The autonomy agreed on at Camp David 'is not a state, is not sovereignty, and is not self-determination. The Arab nation was given its self-determination by means of the existence of twenty-one independent Arab states'.[18] The plan emphasized that 'There will be no negotiations with this murderous organization [PLO], which directs its weapons, supplied to it by the Soviet Union . . . against men, women, and children'. Jewish settlement would be continued and increased in the occupied territories as a right and as an integral part of national security.

Begin's agreement to the Camp David peace accords and his subsequent peace proposals created a split in his Herut party when two of its most militant Knesset members left to establish the ultranationalist Tehiya (Renaissance) movement. When the 1979 peace treaty was placed before the Knesset, 18 of its 120 members voted against. Seven of the negative votes were from the Likud bloc and another six from within Begin's coalition government. Among those opposed to the treaty were Begin's successor as Herut leader and as prime minister, Yitzhak Shamir (now foreign minister), Moshe Arens, minister of defence in the Shamir government, and Ariel Sharon, Begin's former defence minister.

By 1981 Tehiya emerged as an established party whose major

programme was a demand for immediate annexation of all remaining occupied territories. It was Tehiya's initiative that started the Knesset move for the annexation of Golan, and its continued pressure on the Begin government that reinforced a policy of more rapid and intense Jewish settlement in the West Bank. Tehiya called for the immigration of a million Jews by 1995, a large number of whom would be settled in the occupied areas. As for the population there, 'the Arab minority possessing Jordanian citizenship', they would be permitted to become permanent residents 'with equal rights and obligations' except for military service and participation in Knesset elections, and would be free to vote in Jordanian elections. Arab refugees would be absorbed 'in their country east of the Jordan [River], parallel to the absorption of Jews from Arab lands in the State of Israel and the right of the remaining Jews in those lands to immigrate to the Land of Israel'.[19]

By 1984 Tehiya was able to increase its strength to five Knesset members, becoming the country's third-largest party after Labour and Likud. However, it emerged from the eleventh Knesset election as the third largest party largely as a result of fragmentation among other factions, especially the Orthodox religious parties, which until 1984 had been the third-largest Knesset bloc.[20]

The NRP Plan

Until the 1981 election the National Religious Party (NRP) was the dominant faction within the religious bloc, and had been the junior partner in nearly every government since the state was established. Before the 1967 war the NRP and its predecessors, Mizrachi and Poeli Mizrachi, generally supported the foreign policies and peace plans devised by the Labour-led coalitions. Within the cabinet the party usually backed 'moderate' foreign-policy positions, such as those advocated by former foreign ministers Moshe Sharett and Abba Eban. The party 'rarely, if ever, allowed its religious nationalist ideology . . . to condition its choices throughout the 1948–67 period'. It was a 'consistent advocate of moderate solutions to the series of crises that arose'. Even on Jerusalem it followed a pragmatic approach 'with an eye to the practical consequences of the issue with minimal reference to abstract or absolute notions or values'.[21]

The consensus on 'practical' approaches to problems of war and

peace began to erode by the early 1960s as a new, younger generation of religious NRP leaders began to assert themselves emphasizing messianic nationalism. The rise of nationalist fervour in the
NRP youth factions corresponded with the attrition of traditional
Labour Zionist ideology and its emphasis on pioneering and
socialism.

The NRP youth faction was strongly influenced by Rabbi Kook,
the first Ashkenazi Chief Rabbi during the mandate, who emphasized the link between religion and nationalism and the central role
of the Land of Israel in religious-nationalist thinking. After Israel
had acquired Judea, Samaria and Gaza in the 1967 war, the
Orthodox youth action was greatly strengthened because its emphasis on the centrality of the land was no longer theoretical but a
question of practical policy. The faction's lead in urging settlement
of the West Bank placed it in conflict with older NRP leaders as
well as with the leaders of the government coalition to which NRP
belonged. Many NRP youth belonged to the Whole Land of Israel
movement established by diverse secular as well as religious supporters of annexation. By 1969 the youth faction induced the NRP
to adopt a platform calling for large-scale Jewish settlement in the
'liberated areas' which were 'promised by the God of Israel' to the
Jewish people.

Increasingly, the NRP position converged with Herut's, emphasizing 'God's promise' and the justification of Torah and Jewish
law to support annexation. NRP now asserted that an essential condition for remaining in the coalition government was a commitment from the Labour Alignment not to withdraw from Judea and
Samaria.

By 1974 many of the NRP youth were dissatisfied with Labour's
ambivalent policies in the occupied territories. Some perceived
Israel's territorial concessions in the 1974 disengagement agreement
with Egypt as an indication of future concessions in other occupied
areas. In an effort to either push the government into action or to
confront its ambivalent policies, several of the NRP youth formed
Gush Emunim (Bloc of the Faithful) in 1974, and Gush Emunim
now became the vanguard in efforts to challenge government
policies by establishing new Jewish settlements, if necessary without government authorization.[22]

The influence of the youth faction was even stronger in forming
the 1973 election platform than in 1969. The new platform proclaimed that developments since 1967 were 'the beginning of the

realization of the will of divine Providence in the process of the full redemption of the people of Israel in the land of its fathers'.[23] The basic principles which should guide Israel's representatives in peace negotiations, according to NRP included: 'Our religious right to the Promised Land', and 'ensuring security borders for the country'. The party rejected 'any plan which entails forgoing parts of the historic Land of Israel, our patrimony, and [we] will not accept such a plan'. The party commended NRP members who had personally settled in Judea and Samaria, especially those who had established Kiryat Arba on the outskirts of Hebron even though the new Jewish town was originally set up in the face of government opposition. The platform emphasized that 'There shall be no sovereignty over all of Jerusalem except for Israeli sovereignty'. All of the 'liberated territories' would be integrated into Israel's economy.[24] The Arab inhabitants would be guaranteed civil rights and their religious and cultural autonomy would be safeguarded. Since 1973 the peace plan of the NRP has remained unchanged.

After Likud's 1977 election victory and Begin's ascent as prime minister, the NRP abandoned its long association with Labour to join the new right-wing coalition. By now its approach to peace was much more in accord with Likud's than with Labour's. There was also a closer harmony of interests, not only on peace plans but in a wide range of domestic issues, as demonstrated by Begin's willingness to grant the religious parties much greater influence in matters of personal status and in education.

Gush Emunim, although not officially sanctioned, was treated much more sympathetically by the Begin government, and through its connections with the NRP youth faction was represented in cabinet discussions on matters related to Judea and Samaria. Although four of the NRP Knesset members voted against the 1979 peace treaty, Begin accepted the NRP interpretation of the autonomy provisions in the agreement.

The NRP sustained a serious setback in the 1981 election, losing half of its 12 Knesset seats. Two were captured by the new Tami party established by Oriental Jews within NRP who broke with the party because they were not given a large enough share of political spoils. Other former NRP voters shifted to Likud and Tehiya. The 1982 invasion of Lebanon sparked another crisis when many NRP members openly voiced doubts about the operation. Some objected to the relative lack of civilian control, some to the high level of civilian casualties, and others to the deterioration of Israel's image.

NRP criticism focused on Defence Minister Ariel Sharon's management of the war and the extent to which it was believed he had misled the cabinet. After the massacres of Palestinian refugees by Phalangist militia forces in the Sabra and Shatilla camps, there was talk that the NRP alliance with Likud was 'outliving its usefulness'.[25]

By 1984 NRP was reconsidering negotiations with Labour for a partnership in a new coalition. The unpopularity of the war in Lebanon seemed to reopen options for new peace plans in the orthodox camp. Zevulun Hammer, a leader of the youth faction, stated that he 'could think of ten possible options regarding the future of Judea and Samaria after implementation of autonomy'.[26] He now rejected outright annexation because it 'would foreclose all the possibilities of a solution'. However, he still insisted that Jewish settlement should continue.

> If I don't want to rule a million Arabs this does not mean that I am giving up parts of the Land of Israel. A distinction must be made between the right to settle and the dominion of another people. For this reason, autonomy was the best solution.

Hammer and others within the youth faction seemed very shaken by events in Lebanon. 'Lebanon has proved that there is no solution to Israel's problems by military means alone. Israeli annexation of the West Bank would foreclose all possibilities of a solution of the Palestinian problem'. A startling new perspective was revealed by his comment that 'The Land of Israel is not the only factor in my view of the world. We must also think of the people who live on this land'.[27]

By 1984 the NRP had lost its status as the dominant faction in the religious camp and[28] Israel's third-largest political party, the essential component in either a Labour or Likud coalition. While the religious bloc as a whole maintained its strength with just under 12 per cent of the vote, it fragmented during the election into five disparate factions divided along ethnic, as well as on policy lines. The NRP now had only four Knesset seats; one reason for its continued decline was an integral rift between hawks and doves. Several hawkish members also left the party in 1984 to establish, with other Orthodox factions, the new Morasha Party, which captured two Knesset seats. After the election the five religious parties were divided, with the NRP inclined toward Labour, and

Morasha, Aguda Israel and Shas backing Likud. When the new government was formed, all four joined the coalition, leaving only Tami with its single Knesset seat in the cold.

A new development in the religious camp after Lebanon was the increased support for Nevetot Shalom, an organization of religious doves formed earlier to oppose Gush Emunim, but which failed to attract a following substantial enough to check the growth of militant nationalism.

Labour's Plans

Devising peace plans has been much more difficult for Labour than for other political groups in Israel because of Labour's diverse constituency and the many factions that comprise the bloc. From 1968 to 1984 three Labour factions, Mapam, Rafi and Achdut Avoda were united in the Labour Party; affiliated with the party in the Labour Alignment was Mapam.[29] This 15-year alignment required each of the four members to dilute its ideological orientations. They represented a spectrum of views on peace ranging from supporters of annexation to those in the left-wing Mapam who agreed to return most territory conquered in the 1967 war in exchange for a binding and secure contractual peace settlement. The Alignment's proposals for peace were also constrained by its attempt to absorb a wide constituency of voters including Orthodox Jews and secularists, militant nationalists and humanist universalists, oriental and Ashkenazi Jews, each with its own particular vision of peace.

As Begin's nationalist-territorialist ideology gained strength during this era, Labour's support steadily declined from a total of 63 Knesset seats in the sixth election during 1965, to 33 by the ninth election in 1977. After the 1967 war Labour governments had found it difficult to divest the occupied territory, the historical heart-land of Israel demanded by the nationalists for the preceding half-century. Labour's ten-year rule over the West Bank and Gaza was consequently indecisive, and characterized by ambiguous policies and peace plans.

Initial policy for the occupied territories was shaped by Defence Minister Moshe Dayan, for all practical purposes the sovereign authority in the West Bank and Gaza. His approach was to create 'new facts' in the territories which Israel held by 'right and not on sufferance'. Establishing 'new facts' envisaged Jewish settlement of the occupied areas and creation of the infrastructure required to support the settlers. Road networks were greatly extended and integrated with Israel. Water supply in the West Bank was placed under Israeli control, the electricity grid was connected with Israel's, agricultural land and production were controlled and meshed with Israel's agricultural economy. Israeli business and commercial enterprises were encouraged to extend operations in the new areas. Government assistance to Jewish enterprises in the West Bank included cheaper prices for raw materials, lower interest rates on loans, government sureties and tax relief to foster investment. Special subsidies were granted to Israeli Jewish investors who could find Arab West Bank partners.[30]

A major threat of Labour's policy was to encourage planned but controlled Jewish settlement, primarily in the sparsely settled Jordan Valley and other regions with few Arab inhabitants. At first Jewish settlement was organized according to a plan devised by Deputy Prime Minister Yigal Allon (later foreign minister), in which a ring of Jewish settlements would be established around the Arab-inhabited regions of Jenin, Nablus and Ramallah as their centre. Although the Allon plan was never officially adopted because of divisions within the government, it was followed closely as the basis for Jewish settlement during Labour's reign over the occupied territories. A basic premise was that the Arab population would govern itself with as little interference as possible from Israeli authorities, but all strategic points in the West Bank would remain under Israeli military control. To support Labour's plan, scores of military bases were set up and quasi-military outposts established by Jewish settlers.[31]

Alon's plan and Dayan's 'new facts' doctrine did not go unchallenged within the ranks of Labour. A small dovish wing of the party openly advocated withdrawal from all or most of the territories as the only way to preserve Zionism. They were greatly concerned about growing Jewish dependence on Arab workers imported from Gaza and the West Bank. While only about 5 per cent of Israel's total workforce, the Arab transients provided a fifth of all workers in such vital sectors as construction and agriculture in 1961. Even leftist-oriented collectives were using Arab labour for less desirable farm jobs, menial factory chores and in service industries. Finance Minister Pinchas Sapir warned that higher wages, improved working conditions and social services would not diminish anti-Zionism or the growth of Palestinian nationalism among the 'guest' workers. To preserve Israel as a Jewish state it would be necessary to maintain political separation from the occupied territories and to sever the economic bonds. Dayan's policies, warned Sapir, were an opening wedge to the 'dezionisation' of Israel.[32]

An attempt was made to paper-over these divisions by adopting the Galili plan on the eve of the 1973 election. This four-year scheme for the West Bank reiterated programmes for extensive investment in infrastructure and assistance to Israeli business. The Israel Land Authority was authorized to 'acquire land and real estate in the territories for the purposes of settlement, development and land exchanges . . . through every effective means'.[33] Differences within the cabinet over the private acquisition of Arab lands were resolved by establishing a special committee to grant permits 'on condition that the purchases are transacted for the purpose of constructive projects and not for speculative purposes, and within the framework of government policy'. The plan also called for a Golan Heights industrial centre and regional centres in the Jordan Rift, in Jerusalem and in Sinai. In essence the Labour plan differed little in its practical implications from those of the religious parties or Likud. The major difference was that Likud and the religious parties called for outright annexation.

By election time in December 1973 the Galili plan was further modified with a 14-point programme calling for peace and co-operation with the peoples of the Middle East and supporting the Geneva peace conference (of Israel and several Arab states). The new plan emphasized that 'Israel will not return to the lines of June 4, 1967, which were a temptation to aggression', but it did call for 'territorial compromise'. Rather than emphasizing Jewish settlement rights in the West Bank, the new proposals discussed Israel's position until peace treaties could be signed. During this period, 'Israel will continue to maintain the situation as determined at the time, with priority for security considerations'.[34]

The ambiguity of Labour's plans for peace was underscored by divisions within the Alignment over interpretation. Finance Minister Sapir insisted that the Galili plan had been 'repealed', while Dayan stated that it was still party doctrine. The Labour Party's Secretary-General asserted that new proposals merely 'overlay' the previous ones. Mapam interpreted the Alignment's new election platform as 'truly dovish', cancelling out the Galili plan and Dayan's oral doctrine on plans for the West Bank.

One significant change in 1973 was Labour's recognition of the Palestinians. This new recognition seemed to reverse Prime Minister Golda Meir's insistence only a year before that there was 'no such thing as a Palestinian'. Mapam called for Palestinian self-determination; it believed 'that the Palestinian problem exists and we caused it to come about . . . Our very existence was a catalyst for the crystallization of the Palestinian entity'. However, Mapam agreed with the Labour Party that the solution could not be a separate Palestinian state but realization of Palestinian national aspirations in a common framework with Jordan, to include Gaza.[35]

By 1977 there were few differences between the official platforms of the Labour Alignment and Likud. Most public opinion and major political parties took it for granted that the West Bank, Gaza and Golan, or large parts of them, would remain under Israeli control. Differences among the principal parties likely to become members of any government coalition were over methods of dealing with Arab residents of the occupied territories, forms of administration, and the rights of inhabitants. Labour still hinted that minor territorial compromises might be made. According to the Israeli political scientist Asher Arian,

> The only real debate between (and sometimes within) the major camps was when it would be tactically advisable to mention territorial concessions. The major dove position in Israel is not 'bring the boys home by Passover', but rather a willingness to concede the possibility of territorial concessions in exchange for certain political and diplomatic moves on the part of the Arabs.[36]

With Likud's victory in 1977 public support for Begin's version of peace increased. The West Bank, including Jerusalem, Gaza and the Golan, were now excluded as negotiable items. The peace treaty with Egypt only reinforced Begin's determination not to give up more land, especially since he regarded the return of Sinai to Egypt as a *quid pro quo* for Israel's retention of the rest of the occupied territories. The Likud coalition government perceived Begin's autonomy plan discussed above as the greatest compromise that Israel could make in the occupied areas.

The Labour Alignment, in opposition from 1977 to 1984, was highly critical of Begin's version of autonomy. The plan to remove the borders between Israel and all territory west of the Jordan

River (the West Bank and Gaza) was incompatible with Zionist objectives, argued Abba Eban, former Labour foreign minister. The Begin scheme would threaten 'a permanently assured Jewish majority and a sufficient measure of world recognition to enable the new state to function within the international system'. Unless the predominantly Arab West Bank were separated from Israel, it would be necessary to impose Israel's authority on a disproportionate number of non-Jews. 'Partition [of Palestine] reduced the imposition of Israeli rule on an Arab population to the degree compatible with Israel's security and a viable territorial expanse'. The 'sharp duality' of national identities created by history west of the Jordan River made the establishment of any unitary governmental structure in the area 'artificial, coercive and morally fragile', Eban insisted.[37]

Furthermore, he stated, attempts to establish a 'united Land of Israel' subverted the Camp David agreements and reduced Israeli diplomacy 'to incoherence'. 'To proclaim that "there will never be a boundary west of the Jordan" is to say that Israel may one day become the only nation governing a foreign people permanently against its will and consent'.[38]

A Labour Party committee was set up to devise new approaches. It recommended autonomy as a temporary measure leading to negotiations with Jordan, followed by a permanent arrangement based on territorial compromise. Defensible borders would be established through security zones in the Jordan Rift, the Etzion Bloc of Jewish settlements near Hebron, and the southern Gaza Strip. Full Israeli 'control' but not 'sovereignty' would be maintained in these zones. Beyond the security zones a single Jordanian-Palestinian entity would be negotiated over a period of time to be determined in the talks with Jordan. This scheme, stated Labour Party Chairman and former Chief-of-Staff Haim Bar Lev, assured that 'autonomy with some areas under our full control is a lesser evil than autonomy over the whole of the West Bank'.[39]

The basic principles of Alignment peace plans were re-emphasized in the 1981 and 1984 election platforms. Accommodation with Jordan over the future of the West Bank became the central focus, with emphasis on replacement of the 4 June 1967 frontiers by 'defensible borders'. Security borders were to be differentiated from political boundaries. This meant

The Israeli government will insist that, in time of peace, the security deployment of the IDF forces and of settlements in certain areas, including: the Jordan Valley with the northwestern shore of the Dead Sea, Gush Etzion, the environs of Jerusalem, and the southern Gaza strip will be included within the sovereign territory of Israel.[40]

The Jordan River is Israel's eastern security border. No foreign army will cross the western bank of the Jordan. The territories to be evacuated by the IDF west of the Jordan will be demilitarized; in addition to such demilitarization, Israel will insist on vital security arrangements.

Jewish settlement in these specified zones 'is vital for the security of the state'. Although a Labour government would not establish new Jewish settlements in densely populated West Bank Arab areas, 'no [existing] Jewish settlement will be uprooted, and the settlements will be allowed to remain in place'.

Labour's 1984 platform criticized Likud's West Bank policies and administration, asserting that Begin's 'domination of Judea, Samaria and Gaza has already undermined the democratic and moral foundations of Israeli society'. The Alignment rejected Likud's policy of 'not one inch' as subversive of peace and liable to transform Israel 'from a state with a clear Jewish majority into a bi-national state, contradicting the Zionist and democratic nature of the state of Israel and weakening it internally'.

The Alignment stated willingness to 'transfer broad powers and responsibilities on civilian matters to the local authorities and to civilian elements' in the occupied areas. While maintaining 'complete authority', the Alignment promised to respect the 'rights of the citizens' and to show concern for their well-being. Labour would 'insist on the protection of individual rights, the maintainance of law and order, and the equality of all residents before the law'. To establish permanent Israeli rule over the Arab inhabitants of the territories, stated the platform, was inconsistent with 'maintainance of a democratic society guaranteeing equal rights for all its citizens'. Labour denounced the emergence of a Jewish underground terrorist group that sought retaliation against Arabs in the territories for their attacks on Jewish settlers, and promised to 'firmly and decisively . . . uproot every instance of the[ir] violation of the law'. 'These phenomena which run counter to all Jewish and human ethics grew out of the annexation policy [of Likud], a mystical nationalistic ideology, and the rejection of any compromise solution'.

Labour agreed with Likud not to recognize the PLO 'and any other organizations based on the Palestinian Covenant which denies the State of Israel's right to exist'. Nor would Labour agree to 'establishment of another Palestinian state in the territory between Israel and Jordan (east of the river)'. Rather, the Alignment insisted that the Palestinian problem be resolved

> within a Jordanian-Palestinian framework. The Jordanian-Palestinian state will include the territory of Jordan, most of whose residents are Palestinians, and well-defined, densely populated areas in Judea, Samaria, and Gaza which will be evacuated by the IDF forces with the establishment of peace . . .

provided, of course, that the evacuated areas remained demilitarized and subject to Israeli security control. These arrangements would be negotiated by representatives of Jordan and 'authorized representatives of the Palestinian Arab residents of Judea, Samaria, and the Gaza strip . . . and [other] Palestinian individuals . . . who recognize Israel and reject terrorism'.

Other components of the Labour Alignment 1984 peace plan called for renewal of diplomatic representation and negotiations with Egypt, reinforcement of UN Security Council Resolutions 242 and 338, and security arrangements for northern Israel which would not depend on continued occupation of Lebanon. Likud was criticized for extending the goals of the 1982 invasion from security in the north to 'political goals not necessitated by Israel's security needs, and which were, moreover, unattainable'. Pursuit of these illusive goals only prolonged the war and created an 'internal rift among the [Israeli] people and exacted a heavy price in blood'.

Labour failed to gain sufficient votes to form its own coalition in the July 1984 election. Instead, a National Unity Government (NUG) was created with Likud as an equal partner and seven other parties as members. Although Labour Party leader Shimon Peres became prime minister, his deputy and minister for foreign affairs was the Likud leader, former Prime Minister Yitzhak Shamir. Peres thus had to water down the Alignment's election peace plans. Furthermore, dovish elements associated with Labour were much weakened after the election when Mapam broke up the alignment and its six Knesset members became part of the opposition.

Another dovish member of the Labour Party also defected to the opposition, leaving the Labour Party with only 37 Knesset seats to Likud's 41. The defection of Mapam and one Labour Party dove was compensated by three small Knesset factions which associated themselves with the Labour Party.

The agreement which served as the basis for the NUG made only vague reference to peace plans.[41] It mentioned withdrawal from Lebanon but without a timetable, the development of relations with Egypt on the basis of the 1979 peace treaty and the Camp David peace proposals, and resumption of the autonomy talks with Egypt broken off in 1982. Arab residents of the West Bank and Gaza were promised a voice in determining their own future. Jordan would be invited to enter the peace negotiations, but in the event of internal disagreement within the Israeli government over territorial concession new elections would be held. The NUG agreement emphasized Likud and Labour opposition to establishment of a Palestinian state 'between Israel and the Jordan River', and to negotiations with the PLO. However, Likud's goals were thwarted by the stipulation that 'During the period of the unity government, no sovereignty, Israel or other, will be applied to Judea, Samaria and the Gaza District'. New Jewish settlements would have to be agreed on by the members of the NUG. (Rather than the score or more which Likud had promised, Labour agreed to establish only four or five.)

Conclusion

The core of most Israeli peace plans is still the West Bank and Gaza and the question of the Palestinians. While there are minority factions in the Knesset including the Progressive List for Peace and the Communist-controlled Democratic Front for Peace and Equality that advocate establishment of a Palestinian state on the West Bank alongside Israel, all the dominant parties, parties likely to become members of a government coalition, reject the concept of a Palestinian state or recognition of the PLO. Israeli public opinion, especially among youth, has moved closer to the territorial nationalists since 1977, leaving the doves within Labour increasingly isolated and with a diminishing constituency. True, the election platforms of Labour and Likud indicated polarization between a 'no concession' nationalism and the traditional moderation of

Labour. But even had Labour formed a new government after the July election, it would have faced serious constraints in implementing its foreign-policy platform by the diversity of perspectives within its own ranks. Being forced to establish a NUG with Likud after the election and the split between Mapam and the Labour Party only decreased the possibilities of implementing these peace plans.

Some Israelis have argued that it would be no more difficult to evacuate the West Bank and Gaza as part of a peace settlement than it was to evacuate Sinai. But the comparison seems ill founded. Security arguments can be found to justify evacuation of the remaining occupied territories, but they are overridden by common perceptions which see Gaza, the West Bank and the Golan as threats to Israel if they ever return to Arab hands, even if demilitarized. The West Bank, including Jerusalem, is especially difficult because of the historico-religious connotations of the region, because over a hundred Jewish settlements have been established there, and because a generation of Israelis has grown up thinking of Judea and Samaria as integral parts of the Jewish state. In the race between territorial and non-territorial Zionism, the nationalists appear to be winning. Their perceptions of Israel as beleaguered and isolated, bereft of any true friends in the world, is much more common than the vision of socialist internationalism, of Israel as a centre of humanism and universalism that was once common.

Nurit Gertz, an Israeli political scientist, has observed that Begin's myth 'posits the world as a great wasteland peopled by only two protagonists: "them" and "us"'. Begin and Ariel Sharon, a likely successor to Begin in the future, aspire to establish Israel as a great nation

> in which 'we', the few and weak, took our destiny into our hands and triumphed over 'them', the many and mighty . . . Thus, not only in the war in Lebanon, but also in Israel's relations with the entire world Begin (and his successors) tend to see only 'us' (pre-Holocaust Jews, a downtrodden and outcast victim) and 'them' (Arabs, Nazis, or the like).[42]

Those who espouse this vision of Israel's fate are unlikely to 'surrender' more territory, or make significant new concessions for peace.

'We' versus 'them' perceptions as a major constraint on radical new peace proposals are reinforced by a natural conservativism among Israeli policy-makers whose approach to peace is often reactive and defensive. Aaron S. Kleiman, an Israeli commentator on international relations, observes that these attitudes have led to a reluctance by Israel to make specific proposals unless the Arab states altered basic attitudes toward Israel, i.e. unless the Arab states first recognized Israel. The perception of the Arab states and of Arab attitudes as monolithic toward Israel was common until Sadat's surprise visit to Jerusalem in 1977. The Arab world, from the Maghreb to the Euphrates, came to be viewed in monochromatic terms of black or white, as comprising a solid enemy front yet one incapable of surmounting internal controversies in order to concert fully the effort against Israel. The defensive attitude of suspicion, of constant vigilance but not direct involvement in Arab affairs, did not require any initiative on the part of Israel. Instead, Israeli leaders found refuge in adhering to certain standard conceptions. Arab hostility was one of these. It represented the only permanent 'given' in policy deliberations. Similarly, the Arabs could be trusted at the crucial moment to sow inter-Arab disunity. Signs of this growing rigidity were also to be discerned in the legalistic argument, given official sanction, that the conflict was confined exclusively to sovereign states (Israel and the neighbouring Arab countries), leaving the Palestinians without any *locus standi* in the political dispute or its resolution.

Despite the euphoria generated by Sadat's initiative in 1977 and the peace treaty with Egypt in 1979, many Israelis still cling to the belief that the 'Arabs will never make peace', or the 'world is against us', or 'there is little use in taking initiatives'. Although peace is a lofty aspiration of nearly all Israelis, security has far greater priority and it is seen as the key to peace. Continued Arab refusal to recognize Israel or to negotiate directly is proof to most Israelis that their future is still insecure, and that peace initiatives requiring tangible concessions such as territory or the grant of equal rights to Arabs in occupied territories are at best placebos to calm the conscience of the US government. At worst they are seen as nothing but wasted effort.

Notes

1. See *The Case for a Bi-National Palestine. Memorandum Prepared by the*

Hashomer Hatzair Workers' Party of Palestine, Tel Aviv, March 1946.

2. See Walter Laqueur, *A History of Zionism* (New York: Holt, Reinhart & Winston, 1972), Chapter 7, 'In Blood and Fire: Jabotinsky and Revisionism'.

3. See H. Eugene Bovis, *The Jerusalem Question, 1917–1968*, Hoover Policy Study No. 1 (Stanford, California: Hoover Institution Press, 1971), pp. 75–136.

4. Ibid., pp. 85, 138.

5. Ibid., p. 138.

6. See Don Peretz, *Israel and the Palestine Arabs* (Washington, DC: The Middle East Institute, 1958).

7. Ibid.

8. See *Towards Peace, Information Briefing No. 22*, Division of Information, Ministry of Foreign Affairs (Jerusalem: January 1974), p. 10.

9. Ibid., p. 19.

10. See *The Camp David Summit*, Department of State Publication 8954, Near East and South Asian Series 88, September 1978, p. 9.

11. Comments during *Issues and Answers* on 22 May 1977, cited in Bernard Reich, 'Israel's Foreign Policy and the Elections' in Howard R. Penniman (ed.), *Israel at the Polls: The Knesset Election of 1977* (Washington, DC: American Enterprise Institute, 1979), p. 272.

12. See Aryeh Shalev, *The Autonomy — Problems and Possible Solutions*, Paper No. 8, Center for Strategic Studies, Tel Aviv University, January 1980, Appendix E, pp. 211–14.

13. Ibid., point no. 24, p. 213.

14. *The Camp David Summit.*

15. See *Encyclopaedia Judaica*, vol. 3 (Jerusalem: MacMillan Co., 1972), article on 'Autonomism'.

16. *Jerusalem Post (JP)*, 30 April 1979.

17. Aryeh Shalev, *The Autonomy*, p. 55.

18. *New Outlook* (Tel Aviv), vol. 27, no. 5/6 (233/234) (June/July 1984), 28–9.

19. Ibid., 29.

20. See Don Peretz and Sammy Smooha, 'Israel's Eleventh Knesset Election', *The Middle East Journal*, vol. 39, no. 1 (Winter 1985), 86–103.

21. Stewart Reiser, *The Politics of Leverage: The National Religious Party of Israel and Its Influence on Foreign Policy*, Modern Series: Number Two, Center for Middle Eastern Studies (Cambridge, Mass: Harvard University Press, 1984), p. 30.

22. Ibid., p. 41. See also David J. Schnall, *Radical Dissent in Contemporary Israeli Politics: Cracks in the Wall* (New York: Praeger, 1979), Chapter 9, 'Gush Emunim: Messianism and Dissent'.

23. *New Outlook*, vol. 27, no. 5/6, 30.

24. Ibid.

25. Stewart Reiser, *Politics of Leverage*, p. 70.

26. Ibid., p. 71.

27. Ibid.

28. Mapai was the dominant Labour faction and core of the Labour bloc in 1965. Rafi was a faction led by Ben Gurion that broke from Mapai in 1964 but rejoined with Mapai and Achdut Avoda to merge into a new Labour Party in 1968. Achdut Avoda, the left wing of the Labour Party, had been part of Mapam until 1953, then became a separate party and later joined the new Labour Party in 1968. Mapam, still a leftist-oriented Labour faction, joined the Labour Party to form the Labour Alignment between 1968 and 1984.

29. *JP Weekly (JPW)*, no. 470 (27 October 1968); *Ma'ariv*, 17 April 1969; *Ha'aretz*, 11 November, 18 December 1968.

30. Yigal Allon, 'The Anatomy of Autonomy', *Jerusalem Post Magazine*, 31 May 1979.

31. *JPW*, no. 669 (21 August 1973).

32. Ibid.

33. Ibid.

34. *New Outlook*, vol. 16, no. 9 (146); vol. 17, no. 1 (147), December 1973–January 1974, 47.

35. Robert R. Penniman, *Israel at the Polls*, article by Asher Arian, 'The Electorate: Israel 1977', 71.

36. *JP*, 8 June 1979.

37. Ibid.

38. *JP*, 22 February 1979.

39. *New Outlook*, vol. 27, no. 5 (233/234), June/July 1984, 24–5.

40. *JP*, 12 September 1984, 'National Unity Government Agreement (Abridged)'.

41. Nurit Gertz, 'The Few Against the Many', *The Jerusalem Quarterly*, no. 30 (Winter 1984), 100.

42. Aaron S. Klieman, 'Zionist Diplomacy and Israeli Foreign Policy', *The Jerusalem Quarterly*, no. 11 (Spring 1979), 107.

2 PALESTINIAN PEACE PLANS

Helena Cobban

Introduction

Before 1968 there were few in the Palestinian Arab community who sought any kind of peace with the Jewish community living in the ancient homeland that both groups claimed. That year saw the explosive rise of a new breed of Palestinian activists — members of the guerrilla groups (predominantly Fateh) who have dominated the nationalist movement ever since. With their rise to prominence, the guerrilla leaders started groping for new ways to redress their community's ills, and one of the major facts with which they had to come to terms was the persistence of the Jewish community's existence in Israel/Palestine. In 1968 Fateh first committed itself to the goal of establishing a single, unitary state in all of Israel/Palestine in which Jews and Arabs would live together under a determinedly secular system. Six years later, when this goal appeared unrealizable or at least still extremely distant, the Fateh leaders formulated the idea of working for the interim goal of a two-state solution. Under this formula, a Palestinian Arab mini-state would be established in the West Bank and Gaza alongside the Israeli state, which would withdraw to its 1948 borders. More recently, in 1983 and 1984, a number of Palestinian leaders have spoken openly of the possibility of this state entering into some kind of confederation with Jordan.

This chapter will deal with the circumstances in which each of these changes was made, and will seek to assess the hopes of some variant of the mini-state or confederation plan being implemented.

Historical Background (pre-1967)

In the period before the establishment of the State of Israel in 1948 there were few voices in the Palestinian community publicly arguing for any kind of permanent, institutional reconciliation with the local representatives of the Zionist movement. Most of the

37

handful of Palestinians who did not put forward such proposals were members of the tiny Communist movement, or its affiliated or derived groups. In 1947, for example, Palestinian Communists, who generally worked closely with their Jewish counterparts, were vocal in their support for the UN Partition Plan of that year, which proposed the establishment of separate Jewish and Arab states in different areas of mandate Palestine.

By contrast, the vast majority of politicians in the Palestinian mainstream considered the Jewish immigration into Palestine as a threatening and intrinsically hostile development. Their debates were therefore not about whether or how to forge a settlement with the Zionists, but about how to combat them. Mistakenly considering the regional balances of force to be in their favour, the Palestinian leaders opposed the 1947 Partition Plan, holding out for the establishment of a Palestinian Arab state in the whole of Mandate Palestine.[1]

During the fighting of 1948 the Jewish community proved itself capable not only of defending the areas allotted to the Jewish state in the 1947 Plan, but also of extending Jewish control over several of the areas which the Plan had allotted to the Arab state (Galilee, the Triangle, the Little Triangle, etc.). The remaining parts of the Arab state as envisaged in the Partition Plan were taken under Egyptian and Jordanian control: Thus, no Palestinian Arab state came into existence.

The Palestinian leadership, under Hajj Amin al-Husseini, had seen its own forces and those of its Arab allies humiliatingly defeated on the battlefield. Husseini was almost totally discredited. Furthermore, since the mass exodus of Palestinians from the areas in Jewish hands had caused practically the entire Palestinian social structure to collapse, his demise was not followed by the emergence of any other Palestinian leadership for nearly two decades after 1948. Palestinian society in the new diaspora was demoralized, fragmented, angry, and in a mess. No-one who hoped to be politically active in it could think of proposing creative solutions to the question of co-existence with Israel.

The collapse of Palestinian civil society led to a situation in which, from 1948 to 1967, the 'Palestinian question' became the almost exclusive preserve of the rulers of various Arab states. Not surprisingly, these rulers manipulated such Palestinians as came under their control for their own (often pressing) *raisons d'état*. For example, in 1954 Egypt's President Gamal Abdel-Nasser deployed many of his own troops and security police in the Gaza and Sinai regions in order to prevent infiltration by Palestinian refugees back to their former homes inside Israel. The following year, however, it suited his purposes briefly to sponsor the activities of a tightly controlled group of Palestinian infiltrators/saboteurs. Then, in the aftermath of the 1956 war with Israel, he once again sought to seal the borders. All this time he was vocal in proclaiming his support for 'the Palestinian cause', though he still argued that 'Arab unity' (i.e. the aggrandizement of his own regional influence) was a prerequisite for 'the liberation of Palestine'.

First Emergence of a Palestinian Political Strategy, 1967–73

The 'Palestinian Question' remained in the cynical hands of the Arab regimes until 1967. The Arab-Israeli war of that year had two after-effects which are significant for the present study. The first was the discrediting of the Arab regimes and the concomitant crystallization of an authentically Palestinian leadership amongst the diaspora Palestinians. The second was the fact that this new leadership relatively rapidly started groping for some kind of solution to their people's problem which might take account of the reality of the substantial Jewish population in their former homeland.

The Palestinian leadership which emerged after 1967 was dominated by an organization called 'the Palestinian Liberation Movement', or 'Fateh'. The Fateh leadership had first coalesced in the early 1960s from a number of groups and individuals who argued the need for Palestinian self-activity, independent from the activities of the Arab regimes.[2] Throughout Fateh's early years a fairly wide debate over tactics and strategy had continued inside the movement, though it always contained a strong element of a basically militaristic bent; after late 1964 this element became dominant inside it. Starting on 1 January 1965, Fateh sustained a constant low-level infiltration of guerrilla sabotage groups into Israel. Until June 1967 this activity was organized with only some limited help from Syria, and that only intermittently. The other three Arab regimes whose land bordered Israel (Egypt, Jordan and Lebanon) remained firmly opposed to the Fateh guerrillas' activities.

In the new circumstances which resulted from the 1967 war, the

Fateh leaders sensed the possibilities of new forms of action. The first was the idea of fomenting a broad popular uprising against the Israeli occupation by the residents of the West Bank and Gaza. For many reasons this possibility rapidly proved a chimera. The second was the rapid escalation of guerrilla activity directed across the Israeli army's new frontlines (in practice, this activity was launched mainly along the Jordan River front). The third was the idea of complementing the group's continued commitment to clandestine military activity with political activity in the public sphere.

By the end of 1967 Fateh's ruling Central Committee had already taken the significant step of modifying its formulation of its ultimate political goal. Hitherto, Fateh had not proposed any alternative to the goal most commonly espoused in the Palestinian refugee communities: that of 'the liberation of Palestine'. This concept of 'liberation' was almost exactly analogous to that used by other anti-colonialist liberation movements: the native land would be liberated from foreign control, and the liberation movement would no more give special consideration to the fate of the colonialists than had the Algerians to the French *colons*, or the Chinese to their former Japanese occupiers.

In the latter months of 1967, however, the Fateh Central Committee replaced this goal of 'the liberation of Palestine' with a new formulation, that of the establishment of a 'secular, democratic state' in Palestine. The implication was that the Palestinians, whether Moslem or Christian, could live side by side with the Jewish population within this unitary state. On 1 January 1968 this new step was made public.[3] However, the Israeli government was still buoyed by its recent military victory over the Arab states; it was in no mood at all to respond to any such initiative from a little-known group of Palestinian outsiders. The Fateh leaders, for their part, did little to follow up on their initiative by trying actively to engage the support of sections of the Israeli public for their new idea. They paid much more attention, over the years which followed, to the ever problematic questions of their relations with the Arab regimes who controlled their daily operating environment, and with rival Palestinian contestants for the mantle of national leadership, than they did to the concept of affecting relations within the Israeli body politic.

Back in 1964 President Nasser had created his own, extremely regime-oriented Palestinian organization. This was the 'Palestinian Liberation Organization', PLO. After Nasser's humiliation in the

1967 fighting, the pro-Nasser leadership of the PLO was also discredited; and a key component of the Fateh leaders' political strategy after 1967 was their takeover of the otherwise moribund PLO apparatus. This takeover was achieved in co-ordination with Nasser, and was symbolic of a new alliance between the Arab regimes and their former detractors in the Fateh leadership.

In July 1968 and February 1969, the PLO's quasi-parliamentary ruling body, the Palestinian National Council (PNC) held its fourth and fifth congresses, both in Cairo. At the fourth congress, Fateh and the handful of other guerrilla groups with which it was allied were able to change the PLO Charter to a clearer reflection of their own views — though the formulation of the PLO's officially stated goal was still not changed from 'the liberation of Palestine' to 'the secular, democratic state'. But the guerrilla groups were successful in changing one key Article (number 6), which dealt with the question of the Jewish population in Israel/Palestine, to eliminate any reference to a troubling loyalty test. The original 1964 formulation of this Article had been, 'Jews of Palestinian origin are considered Palestinians, providing they are willing to commit themselves to live in order and peace in Palestine'; now it simply stated that 'The Jews who had normally resided in Palestine until the beginning of the Zionist invasion will be considered Palestinians'.[4]

The immediate political effects of Fateh's takeover of the PLO did not represent a straight-line move towards moderation. The new 'Young Turks' who were taking over the PLO inserted a new Article in the PLO Charter (number 9) which stressed that, 'Armed struggle is the only way to liberate Palestine. Thus it is the overall strategy, not merely a tactical phase'.[5] The conflict thus exemplified, between the militarist strand in Fateh thinking and its leaders' hopes of forging an effective political strategy, was to continue to plague both Fateh and the PLO for many years to come.

Development of the Palestinian 'Geneva Strategy' 1973–7

In October 1973 another Middle East war occurred, which once again altered the environment in which the Palestinian nationalists were operating.

Inasmuch as the 1967 war had led to the humiliation and discrediting of the key Arab regimes, the capabilities which the Egyptian and Syrian leaders evinced in October 1983 led —

regardless of the paucity of their final results on the battlefield —
to these regimes' rapid political rehabilitation in Arab eyes. At the
international level, meanwhile, the shock which the war had caused
to the international system was sufficient to catalyse the United
States into a speedy stepping-up of its efforts to mediate the Arab-
Israeli conflict. US diplomacy achieved a series of bilateral agreements (first Israeli-Egyptian, then Israeli-Syrian, then Israeli-
Egyptian again) between January 1974 and September 1975. These
agreements finally resulted, on both the Egyptian and the Syrian
fronts, in a partial Israeli pullback from the positions they had
occupied before the 1973 war. The net 'achievement' of these two
regimes, in thus partially 'liberating' occupied Arab land then
stood in strong contrast to the notable failure of the guerrilla
strategy the Fateh-dominated PLO had pursued since 1968, to
'liberate' even a square inch of occupied land. Now, it was the
guerrillas whose strategy was, by and large, discredited.

Some of the more astute thinkers in the Fateh leadership appre-
ciated this irony, and started to consider ways of rectifying their
movement's policies. Other Fateh leaders were still dominated by
the traditional weight of the militarist strand in the movement's
thinking. The debate between these two wings was, however,
muted, in the face of the weighty new reality of Egypt's and Syria's
new strength. Because Fateh and the PLO still existed mainly in the
environment of the Arab diaspora, this environment was the first
factor they felt they had to come to terms with before they could
consider their own strategies strictly on their Palestinian merits.
The debate between the 'politicos' and the 'militarists' within Fateh
and the PLO, which probably should have taken place seriously at
this stage, instead became translated into a contest between those
who favoured following Egypt and Syria into a political process
with Israel and those who favoured the hard-line rejectionism of
distant Iraq. This was not the same thing; and the fact that the pro-
Egypt and Syria section in the PLO won out over the pro-Iraq
section in 1974 still left many dedicated 'militarists' in the mainstream of the group which was nominally trying to prosecute a
peaceful political strategy.

The political strategy in question was that announced at the
Twelfth Session of the PNC, held in Cairo in June/July 1974. This
session adopted a ten-point programme, the second clause of which
read:

2. The PLO will struggle by every means, the foremost of which is armed struggle, to liberate Palestinian land and to establish the people's national, independent and fighting sovereignty on every part of Palestinian land to be liberated. This requires the creation of further changes in the balance of power in favor of our people and their struggle.[6]

This clause still contained the now routine tribute to the role of 'armed struggle'. But it also gave the first clue to the idea that the PLO might accept the creation of a Palestinian entity — under certain circumstances, which were not yet present, and still only pending the hypothetical establishment of the secular democratic state in all of Palestine — on *less than the whole of the territory of mandate Palestine*. This idea was further spelt out at the PNC's Thirteenth Session, held in March 1977 when the reference was now, more explicitly, to the establishment of an 'independent national state on the soil of the homeland'.[7] Once again, this Palestinian mini-state, which would be established alongside Israel within the area of mandate Palestine, was still portrayed as an interim step along the path to the (increasingly hypothetical) unitary secular, democratic state.

The major strategy of the PLO leaders who had proposed the mini-state concept was that by establishing a firm claim to Palestinian sovereignty over the West Bank and Gaza they could line up alongside the Syrians and Egyptians in the still-promised, comprehensive Geneva peace talks. In pursuit of this strategy, PLO Chairman Yasser Arafat made his historic appearance at the United Nations General Assembly in New York in November 1974. From its podium he spoke eloquently about the injustices his people had suffered, and referred at some length to 'My dream . . . that I may return with my people out of exile, there in Palestine to live . . . in one democratic state where Christian, Jew and Moslem live in justice, equality, fraternity and progress'.[8] But although the idea of the mini-state was already part of official PLO policy by then, Arafat's only reference to it was short and hurried. 'I appeal to you to enable our people to establish national independent sovereignty over its own land', he said toward the end of the speech.[9] He neglected totally to expand upon the idea of two states living alongside each other within the territory of mandate Palestine, and thus missed a great opportunity to develop this theme at any length before his worldwide audience.

The PLO leaders' move towards this concept had not been achieved without considerable internal discussion. On the one hand, the mini-state idea received tremendous backing from those 1.2 million Palestinians who lived under direct Israeli occupation in the West Bank and Gaza. By 1974 Arafat and his colleagues in the PLO leadership were beginning to consider this constituency as increasingly important for their movement. The Palestinians of these two areas constituted, after all, over one-third of the entire Palestinian people; and Arafat himself came from an old Jerusalem family, and had been the main instigator of the uprising which Fateh had tried (and failed) to organize inside the West Bank in the autumn of 1967.

Arafat's appearance at the United Nations received an extremely enthusiastic welcome from the Palestinians of the occupied areas, who took to the streets in mass demonstrations of joy at his sign that the occupation might soon be lifted through political negotiations. These marches then led to a cycle of arrests and countermarches which lasted for several weeks in some West Bank towns.[10]

However, the Palestinians of the occupied territories were some way distant from Beirut, where the PLO was still headquartered in 1974. Most of the members of the guerrilla groups which dominated the PLO there came, by contrast, from the refugee populations whose dream was still to return to their families' former homes in Haifa, Jaffa or elsewhere within the 1948 State of Israel. These Palestinians would not have nearly as much to gain from the establishment of a mini-state as would those who already lived within its future boundaries.

Throughout the summer of 1974, the pro-Iraq group inside the PLO fanned the opposition to the mini-state idea; and in September that year these critics (significantly, at a meeting held in Baghdad!) grouped themselves into the 'Rejection Front'. In a joint communiqué issued after the Baghdad meeting, the Rejection Front leaders and their hosts from Iraq's ruling Baath Party announced that they agreed on the need to condemn, 'the deviationist trends in the Palestinian arena aimed at enticing the Palestinians to participate in the liquidationist settlements'.[11]

From 1974 until 1978, the Rejection Front kept up continuous pressure on the PLO leadership to prevent it moving towards any explicit or implicit acceptance of Resolution 242. Rejection Front literature also heavily criticized the mini-state concept, arguing that this would then 'liquidate' the Palestinian refugees' claim to return to homes and properties inside Israel's 1948 boundaries.

The rejectionists were successful in preventing the PLO from modifying its explicit opposition to Resolution 242, which had always been based on the fact that the resolution made no mention of the Palestinian question in political terms, referring instead only to, 'a just settlement of the refugee problem'. And since this resolution had always been explicitly defined as one of the basic principles according to which any re-convened Geneva talks should be held, the PLO leaders found themselves hamstrung in their pursuit of their 'Geneva strategy'. They made various attempts to finesse this issue between 1974 and 1977, in the hopes that they might thereby receive a seat at a reconvened Geneva conference. In any event, these efforts were unsuccessful: after a brief spurt of diplomatic activity to this end in mid-1977 the process was abruptly interrupted by Egyptian President Sadat's surprise visit to Jerusalem. Once Sadat's peace initiative had launched its own, very different kind of peace process, it rapidly overtook the whole idea of a Palestinian 'Geneva strategy'. The PLO leadership nevertheless remained committed to the mini-state concept.

Ideas About the Mini-state Concept

What, in fact, was in the minds of the PLO leaders when they spoke of a Palestinian mini-state in the West Bank and Gaza? One prominent member of Fateh's 11-member Central Committee, Jaffa-born Salah Khalaf, has put it in the following terms:

> one must understand that every Palestinian aspires above all to a haven, however miniscule, to a consulate he can appeal to when he considers himself injured or threatened . . . The day we succeed in establishing a state in the liberated territories of the West Bank and Gaza, the first thing we'll do is deliver identity papers.[12]

Another, much more detailed explication of the mini-state concept has been produced by Walid Khalidi, a respected Palestinian Harvard professor who, while in no way officially affiliated to the PLO, has on occasion acted as one of Arafat's trusted outside advisors. In July 1978 Khalidi published an article in *Foreign Affairs* outlining his view of what a Palestinian state might look like.[13] Arguing that such a state must embody full Palestinian sovereignty if it is to win the endorsement of the PLO, as well as the support of Arab opinion and the majority of Arab states, Khalidi nevertheless concedes that 'there is no reason why the concept of Palestinian sovereignty should not accommodate provisions designed to allay legitimate fears of neighbors on a reasonable and preferably reciprocal basis' (p. 701). Suggesting that the proposed state might declare its non-aligned status, especially in the defence and military fields, according to 'some variant of the Austrian model', Khalidi explains that

> This does not mean that the state need be demilitarized. Nor would it preclude its membership in the United Nations, the Arab League and other international organizations. Nor would it prevent it, again like Austria, from having a foreign policy.

> The closest relations of the Palestinian state would naturally be with Arab League members . . . But its most intimate relations are likely to be with Jordan . . . Naturally, relations with Jordan would have to be on an inter-state basis of equality. But this does not preclude a consensual evolution of relations towards greater intimacy. (p. 73)

Khalidi included in his article two alternative, and admittedly hypothetical, models of how the armaments of such a state might compare with those of its neighbours. (These models were based on the state disposing of respectively one-half or one-third of Jordan's current arms levels in certain basic categories. At both levels, the arms levels were considerably lower than the Israeli levels.) He also produced a proposal for the linking, in a 'great municipal council', of separate Israeli and Palestinian boroughs in West and East Jerusalem — each of which might be, in its own right, the sovereign capital of its own state.

Khalidi's schema addressed head-on the remaining questions of those Palestinian refugees who did not already live in the area of the proposed state. 'As many refugees as possible need to be settled in East Jerusalem, on the West Bank and in the Gaza Strip', he wrote. But he pointed out that most refugees still have claims outstanding for their homes and properties within 1948 Israel, and that a key, long-standing UN resolution still calls on Israel to allow them the choice between return and compensation. 'While Israel may not be expected to welcome inundation by all those who will want to return, its acceptance of a mere handful will offer no solution', he judged. He added that, 'The balance of the Diaspora refugees who cannot return to pre-1967 Israel [because of Israeli objections] or to the Palestinian state [because of lack of absorptive capacity] will still have the options of compensation and Palestinian citizenship' (pp. 705–6). Countering arguments that a Palestinian state might pose a military threat to Israel, he points out that, in addition to the possibility of various international guarantees for the new *status quo*, and the existence of arms levels which would presumably be far inferior to those of Israel, the state would also suffer the territorial disadvantages of discontinuity, encirclement, accessibility to Israel, and remoteness from outside sources of supply (p. 710).

Professor Khalidi's picture, however detailed, could only remain a chimera so long as the hard political strategy required to put a Palestinian mini-state in place was lacking. As already, by the time his article was published in 1978, it was. By then, President Sadat's unilateral peace initiative with Israel was well on its way, and the PLO leaders' 'Geneva strategy' was totally off the agenda.

Palestinian Impasse, 1978–82: Reagan Plan Stimulates New Political Activities, 1982–4

In September 1978 the Egyptian, Israeli and American leaders finally concluded the Camp David agreements, which established that Egypt and Israel should conclude speedy negotiations in order to arrive at a peace treaty. At the Palestinian level, the Camp David agreements prescribed that talks should continue among the three countries until they could agree on a formula through which the Palestinians of the occupied territories might exercise their autonomy.

The text of the Camp David agreements themselves stated that they should be viewed as model for other, similar agreements between Israel and its other Arab neighbours. Had Jordan, Syria and Lebanon followed Egypt's lead, and had the autonomy talks led to a formula acceptable to the Palestinians, then Camp David might indeed have been a significant step on the path to a comprehensive settlement. As it was, neither of these conditions were fulfilled. Once the peace treaty effectively removed Egypt (Israel's weightiest Arab neighbour, by far) from the list of potentially hostile Arab forces, the Israeli government felt well able to dig in its heels on the autonomy issue. The PLO leaders, for their part, refused to take part in the autonomy talks so long as the Israelis made it clear that any 'autonomy' which resulted would be extremely circumscribed, that it would apply to the people of the occupied territories rather than touching on any questions of sovereignty over the land therein, and that Israel itself would resubmit its claim to sovereignty over this land at the end of the envisaged five-year interim period.

Meanwhile, as hopes for achieving an acceptable political settlement of the Palestinian question receded, the militarists gained new strength inside the PLO, this time with the support of Syria rather than Iraq. In 1982, a few weeks after the final phase of the Egypt-Israel peace process had been completed, with the last stage of Israel's withdrawal from Egyptian territory, the Israelis felt able to turn to their northern front, where the PLO still had its last semi-autonomous base of operations in Lebanon. In a hard-fought campaign which lasted two and a half months, Israeli units pushed their way up to Beirut, where they encircled the PLO forces and their leaders in the West of the city. The United States waged an intensive campaign to secure an end to the siege of West Beirut. By mid-August, US negotiator Philip Habib had succeeded in reaching an agreement whereby the PLO forces would leave Beirut, while the Israelis undertook not to move into the vacuum they left behind. Two days after the PLO evacuation was completed, US President Ronald Reagan produced a new peace plan for the Middle East — the first ever to bear the official imprimatur of the President of the United States. In his plan, Reagan spelt out that,

> The United States will not support the establishment of an independent Palestinian state in the West Bank and Gaza, and we will not support annexation or permanent control by Israel.
>
> . . . It is the firm view of the United States that self-government by the Palestinians of the West Bank and Gaza in association with Jordan offers the best chance for a durable just and lasting peace.[14]

Shortly after publication of the Reagan Plan, the Arab Heads of State — whose gatherings by then traditionally also included PLO

Chairman Arafat — met in Fez, Morocco, where they too enun-
ciated their plan to resolve the conflict with Israel. The Fez Plan
(which was closely modelled on the seven-point peace plan Saudi
Arabia's King Fahd had proposed the previous year) called for
'The creation of an independent Palestinian state with Jerusalem as
its capital'. In a veiled reference to Israel, the plan also said that the
UN Security Council should guarantee peace 'among all the states
of the region including the independent Palestinian state'.[15]

The PLO leaders, now scattered in a new diaspora throughout
the Arab world and stripped of their last possibilities of any
military option, had to examine the Reagan and Fez Plans to gauge
how to react to them. In February 1983, the PNC convened its Sixteenth Session of the PNC in Algiers. The PLO leaders were determined, at this session, to make a decisive point to the Israelis, and
others, that the military defeat of 1982 had not splintered Palestinian national unity. The cost of this gesture was that the militarists,
whose strength had been growing since 1978, and who had put up a
good performance against overwhelmingly superior Israeli forces
during the fighting of 1982, had to be welcomed and listened to at
the session; although Arafat's intention was also that this PNC
would boost him on the road back to political settlement. The
Council's final resolutions reflected the tension which resulted.
They stated that 'the PNC considers the Fes [Fez] summit resolutions as the minimum for political moves by the Arab states'. But in
a tortured attempt to reconcile the widely differing views concerning the Reagan Plan, the Council resolved that 'The PNC
rejects the considering of this plan as a sound basis for a just and
lasting solution of the cause of Palestine and the Arab-Zionist
conflict'.[16]

The PLO thus emerged from the Algiers PNC without the mandate some of its leaders had been seeking, to pursue an active investigation of the Reagan Plan. Nevertheless, the leaders did have a
mandate to continue the political talks with Jordan which had been
continuing since 1977, and which would be an essential precursor to
any future moves towards the Reagan Plan. These talks would
centre around how far the two sides could move towards the idea of
a confederation, which the Reagan Plan had seemed to favour. At
the Algiers PNC, the PLO leaders had been able to obtain support
for that part of its political programme which stated that 'the PNC
deems that future relations with Jordan should be founded on the
basis of a confederation between two independent states'.[17]

The following April, however, the Jordanian/PLO talks ran into serious difficulties after the Fateh leadership put severe restraints on the concessions Arafat would be able to offer King Hussein; and King Hussein, in seeming frustration with the whole process, then broke them off. Once again, the search for a political settlement to the Palestinian question had been stalled. And there, essentially, matters have stood until the present (January 1985). 1983 and 1984 were filled, for the Palestinians, with yet more long months of internecine fighting between different wings of their exiled nationalist movement, as the Syrians have poured support into the vocal militarist minority which continues to oppose the present PLO leadership's ongoing commitment to an investigation of the peace prospects.

By November 1984 the PLO leaders — reportedly at the prompting of the Jordanians — had resolved to try to proceed with their political-diplomatic campaign, regardless of the sniping from the Syrian-backed opposition. That month, Arafat succeeded in convening the Seventeenth Session of the PNC in Amman, Jordan, despite the protests of the opposition. In an opening address to the Council, King Hussein called on the PLO to join with Jordan in a joint search for peace, on the basis of Resolution 242. He also called for the convening of an international conference to resolve the Arab-Israeli conflict, advocating that the PLO attend the conference 'on an equal basis with the other parties'.[18]

The discussion concerning Hussein's offer was the major theme of the Council, but it did not result in any firm answer being given to the Jordanian monarch. Instead, the Council's resolutions recorded that the PNC called on the PLO Executive Committee to 'study these proposals in light of the goals of the Palestinian struggle' and to 'continue a dialogue and coordination with Jordan'.[19] The resolutions did reaffirm the PNC's endorsement of the Fez Plan; but, turning to other recent Middle East peace plans, the final resolutions said that

> The PNC emphasizes its rejection of the Camp David accords, autonomy, and U.S. President Ronald Reagan's plan, and the plans and resolutions which do not guarantee our right to repatriation, self-determination, and establishment of an independent Palestinian state.[20]

Conclusion: Lack of a Peace Strategy

The PLO's greatest lack at the moment is not the lack of a peace plan. The PLO leaders have shown themselves quite capable of making significant and innovative suggestions as to what a future peace settlement with Israel might look like, in reference both to its broad outlines, as described in this chapter, and to some of its most sensitive details. In October 1982, for example, veteran Fateh Central Committee member Khaled al-Hassan even spoke of the possibility of some of the Jewish settlements established during the years of Israeli occupation of the West Bank and Gaza being allowed to remain under the new, Palestinian authority, 'perhaps in return for the rehabilitation of some of our villages inside 1948 Israel'.[21] The lack, then, is not so much in thinking about the peace *plan* in terms of its goals, as in the failure to find a workable peace *strategy* in order to attain them.

This failure to find a peace strategy was caused in great part by the circumstances in which the Palestinian movement developed. From 1948 onwards the major motive force of the movement came not from those Palestinians who were under direct Israeli rule — the 150,000 Palestinians who remained in the State of Israel after its foundation lived there as a socially shattered, politically tightly controlled minority within the avowedly Jewish state. Rather, the movement's motive force came from those Palestinians living — most of them as refugees — under the control of the Arab states which bordered Israel. The prime environment in which the Palestinian movement had to develop was thus the Arab environment, rent as it was throughout the decades which followed 1948 by deep-seated ideological and inter-state rivalries.

In 1967 a substantial additional group of Palestinians was brought under Israeli control in the West Bank and Gaza. Since then, around one-half of all Palestinians have lived under Israeli rule. Yet the nationalist movement has continued to be based in the diaspora (and any nationalists who raised their heads inside the occupied territories were systematically deported into the diaspora by the Israelis, in direct contravention to the Geneva conventions). The conditions under which the movement had to operate in the diaspora contributed substantially to the emergence, growth and persistence of the blindly militaristic strand within it.

The Fateh/PLO leadership, to its credit, has tried to combat this strand, although its efforts have been hampered by its own past espousal of the importance of armed struggle. But it meanwhile remains extremely unlikely that the militarists' influence can ever be totally neutralized within the foreseeable future. So the PLO leaders will continue to be faced with their present choice between that part of their constituency which is under Syrian control and protection, which continues to oppose ongoing political moves with Jordan, and to a lesser extent Egypt, and that part of their constituency which lives under Israeli control and which favours political movement towards the end of the occupation.

Thus far, the PLO leadership has not evinced any clear-cut strategy for making this choice. (Nor, in the face of Israel's outright rejection of the Reagan Plan, and the Americans' own seeming indifference to its fate, have they seen much real incentive for doing so.) But it is on this whole question of formulating a workable peace *strategy* that the fate of the various peace plans the Palestinians have put together will have to rest.

Notes

1. For further details on the Palestinian politics of this period, see Ann M. Lesch, *Arab Politics in Palestine, 1917–1939: The Frustration of a National Movement* (Ithaca, NY: Cornell University Press, 1979), or Y. Porath, *The Emergence of the Palestinian Arab National Movement*, vol. I. *1918–1929* and vol. II. *1929–39* (London: Frank Cass, 1974 and 1977).

2. For details of the developments referred to in this and the following paragraph, see Chapters 2 and 3 of Helena Cobban, *The Palestinian Liberation Organization: People, Power and Politics* (Cambridge, England and New York: Cambridge University Press, 1984).

3. For the text of this Fateh statement, see *International Documents on Palestine, 1968* (Beirut: Institute for Palestine Studies; henceforth this annual series is referred to as *IDP*). For a fuller explanation of how at least some of the Fateh leaders came to envisage the secular democratic state, see Muhammad Rashid (Nabil Shaath), *Towards a Democratic State in Palestine* (Beirut: PLO Research Center, 1970).

4. Leila S. Kadi, *Basic Political Documents of the Armed Palestinian Resistance Movement* (Beirut: PLO Research Center, 1969), p. 137.

5. Ibid., p. 138.

6. *IDP, 1974*, p. 449.

7. *IDP, 1977*, p. 349.

8. Walter Laqueur and Barry Rubin (eds), *The Israeli-Arab Reader: A Documentary History of the Middle East Conflict* (New York: Viking Penguin, 1984), p. 516.

9. Ibid., p. 517.

10. Ann M. Lesch, *Political Perceptions of the Palestinians on the West Bank and the Gaza Strip* (Washington, DC: Middle East Institute, 1980), p. 60.

11. *IDP, 1974*, p. 513.

12. Abu Iyad, *My Home, My Land* (New York: Times Books, 1981), p. 224.

13. Walid Khalidi, 'Thinking the Unthinkable' in *Foreign Affairs* (New York),

vol. 56, no. 4 (July 1978), 695–713.

14. Laqueur and Rubin (eds), *Israeli-Arab Reader*, p. 661.

15. *New York Times*, 10 September 1982.

16. The entire text of the political programme ratified at the Sixteenth PNC, including the resolutions adopted by it, was published in English in *Foreign Broadcast Information Service* (henceforth, *FBIS*), Middle East Section, 23 Feb. 1983, pp. A14–16, and 24 Feb. 1983, p. A1; excerpts appear in Laqueur and Rubin (eds), *Israeli-Arab Reader*, pp. 679–83.

17. Laqueur and Rubin (eds), *Israeli-Arab Reader*, p. 681.

18. *FBIS-MEA-84-228*, p. A17.

19. *FBIS-MEA-84-233*, p. A3.

20. Ibid., p. A5.

21. Author's interview with Khaled al-Hassan, New York, October 1982.

3 SAUDI FOREIGN POLICY AND THE ARAB-ISRAELI PEACE PROCESS: THE FAHD (ARAB) PEACE PLAN

David E. Long

Psychological and Ideological Bases of Saudi Foreign Policy

Despite great changes in Saudi foreign policy over the last few years, notably its willingness to become more directly involved in intra-Arab politics and in the Arab-Israeli peace process, Saudi Arabia's basic approach to foreign affairs has been singularly constant in the more than 50 years since the Kingdom was founded in 1932. Its Najdi (central Arabian) heritage and its guardianship of the Moslem holy places have provided the bases for a uniquely Arab-Islamic world view on which all its foreign policies have been based.

Najd, as central Arabia is called, was until the present century one of the most inhospitable, impenetrable places to live on earth. Subject to climatic extremes of its desert environment, it was also subject to constant wars and uprisings among its fiercely independent tribes. Nevertheless, Najd experienced no extended period of foreign domination as did its neighbours to the north, south, east and west.[1] Thus, Najdis never developed an inferiority complex against Western imperialism as many other Arabs did.

On the contrary, Najdis have maintained an extraordinary sense of self-identity. Isolated in the vast desert reaches of central Arabia, the proud desert aristocrats of Najd consider themselves to be among the purest-blooded Arabs. With a strong sense of who they are, they had no need to rediscover their Arab identity in the pan-Arab reawakening of the late nineteenth and early twentieth centuries. Their sense of Arab identity, based more on lineage than on history, is therefore substantively different and much more cohesive than can be found almost anywhere else in the Arab world.

Najdi isolation also produced another psychological effect on Saudi foreign-policy perceptions. The peoples of central Arabia developed a strong sense of encirclement because, throughout much

54

of their history, they have indeed been surrounded by enemies. In earlier times the circle included the Hashemite Kingdoms of Jordan and Iraq, whose rulers had descended from Sharif (later King) Hussein of the Hijaz. Hussein had been defeated and driven into exile by the Saudis in the 1920s. Later, the encirclement syndrome focused on the radical status of the Middle East, the Horn of Africa and South Asia, and on Israel. Thus, although the identity of the enemies changes over time, the sense of encirclement endures.

Najd's Islamic revival predated the pan-Islamic movement by a century or more. Isolated though it was politically and geographically, Najd was not cut off from the contemporary thought and ideas of the Islamic world of its day. In the first part of the eighteenth century, a Najdi religious scholar-revivalist, imbued with zeal from the writings of a Hanbali Islamic jurist, Ibn Taymiya, began preaching for a return to the fundamentals of Islam.[2]

As so often happens, his message was ill received in his home town and he was forced to leave. The amir of a nearby town, Muhammad bin Saud of Dir'iyyah, welcomed him, however, and became his patron. This amir became the founder of the royal house of Saud. The revivalist, Muhammad bin Abd al-Wahhab, gave his name to what detractors initially referred to and eventually everyone came to know as the Wahhabi revival.[3] The spiritual-political alliance of the descendants of these two men has become the ideological glue holding together the Amirate of Najd and its lineal descendant, the Kingdom of Saudi Arabia.

Wahhabism has had a major influence on Saudi foreign policy by placing an indelible Islamic imprint on Saudis' perceptions of the world about them. Unencumbered by reactions to Western imperialism that they never experienced, and hence by Western political theory, Saudis have retained a strong sense of classical Islamic theory of international relations. Classical Islam envisages a bipolar world — one of monotheists who live under God's law in the Dar al-Islam, and of atheists who live outside the law in the Dar al-Harb. Monotheist religions recognized by Islam include Judaism, Christianity and Zoroastrianism, which with Islam are called Peoples of the Book.

It is not difficult to see how the bipolar world of classical Islam can be adapted to view the bipolar world of today. Dar al-Islam roughly coincides to the Free World, albeit predominantly under 'Christian' (i.e. US and Western European) protection rather than

Islamic protection. One major conceptual problem exists, however, involving the conflict with Israelis who are People of the Book. To the degree that Saudis attempt to rationalize this paradox, they consider secular Zionism rather than theological Judaism as the enemy. In practical terms, this may be a distinction without a difference.

The Saudi acquisition of the Moslem holy places, Mecca and Medina, occurred with the occupation of the Hijaz in the 1920s. Today almost two million Moslems annually visit these sites during the Hajj or Great Pilgrimage season. Responsibility for the holy places has reinforced the Saudi sense of responsibility as defenders of the faith and preservers of the Moslem way of life throughout the Islamic world. This sense of responsibility has become a major objective in Saudi foreign policy.

Before leaving the behavioural aspects of Saudi foreign policy, it is important to emphasize that they do not constitute a blueprint or a master plan for charting operational policies. For the most part, their influence is more implicit than explicit, and more sub-conscious than conscious. They do, however, indicate a broad sense of direction within which the country's foreign-policy establishment attempts to move.

The Emergence of Saudi Arabia as a Regional Power

Until the 1970s Saudi Arabia played a relatively passive role in regional Arab affairs. The Arab world in general was a vastly different place in the 1960s from what it is today, and so was Saudi Arabia. Egypt's President Nasser so dominated the regional political stage that inter-Arab politics were largely restricted to reactions to his initiatives. Capturing the imagination of Arabs everywhere with his electrifying charisma, Nasser had the power to threaten the domestic legitimacy of nearly any Arab leader who differed with him. The Saudi regime enjoyed more legitimacy than most, but felt threatened nevertheless. In 1961, a group of disgruntled Saudi princes 'defected' to Cairo.[4] The following year, the Yemeni civil war broke out. Lasting eight years, it quickly devolved into a confrontation between Egypt (the United Arab Republic), backing the Yemeni republicans, and Saudi Arabia, backing the Yemeni royalists.

In response to the Egyptian-Yemeni threat, the Saudis for the first time began to plan seriously for a small but credible modern military capability. To counter the appeal of Nasser's pan-Arabism, they tried to create a broader pan-Islamic consensus. Two of the vehicles used in promoting this policy were the Moslem World League, founded by King Saud, and the Islamic Foreign Ministers Conference, created under the leadership of King Faisal.

At the same time, Saudi Arabia tended to shy away from international Arab fora, particularly summit conferences. Weak politically and militarily, a target of criticism for its pro-Western ties from Arab radicals and of importuning from non-oil-producing Arab states, radical and conservative alike, the Saudis attempted to maintain as low a profile in Arab politics as possible.

Two factors helped Saudi Arabia emerge from the shadows of Arab politics to centre stage: war and oil. The Arab-Israeli war of June 1967 completely humiliated the Arabs and its titular leader, President Nasser. Although Nasser politically survived the defeat and lived three more years, his claim to primacy in pan-Arab politics never fully recovered, and his forward, expansionist foreign policies came to an end. Following the war, Saudi-Egyptian relations improved, and when Nasser was succeeded by President Anwar Sadat in 1970, the stage was set for a complete rapprochement. The process was further helped by the resolution of the Yemeni civil war the same year.

During the 1967 war, the Saudis consciously avoided committing their still embryonic armed forces, realizing full well the adverse psychological and political effects of a major humiliation on the battlefield. The war, however, did increase the Saudi leadership's awareness, spawned in the period of Saudi-Egyptian confrontation during the Yemeni civil war, that the Kingdom must develop a bona fide military capability. To this end, increased attention was placed on military development programmes begun with US assistance in the mid-1960s.[5]

The war also convinced King Faisal that he would probably not have the luxury of sitting out a subsequent Arab-Israeli conflict without at least token participation on the Arab side. To this end, the 1967 war drove home another lesson to the Saudis. Although always supportive of the Arab cause, the Saudis had remained on the periphery of the Arab-Israeli problem. As a result of the Israeli capture of East Jerusalem, however, Saudi opposition to Israel took on an added ideological dimension. The Aqsa Mosque on the Temple Mount is the third holiest site in Sunni Islam after Mecca and Medina. As guardians of the Arabian holy places, the Saudis feel a special responsibility for the return of East Jerusalem and its Moslem holy places to Arab (i.e. Islamic) sovereignty.

Still, the Saudis did not feel themselves to be, nor did they wish to be, a confrontation state. Ironically, since it became an issue in the Israeli withdrawal of Sinai 15 years later, the Israeli occupation of two Egyptian-administered Saudi islands, Tiran and Sanafir, gave rise to Saudi fears that the Kingdom could be drawn directly into open conflict.

The October 1973 Arab-Israeli war and its aftermath catapulted Saudi Arabia into the middle of Arab politics. For almost a year before the war King Faisal had been trying to warn the West, particularly the United States, that unless some progress was made on an Arab-Israeli settlement, the Arabs would be forced to use economic pressures. Short of war, it is hard to gauge whether King Faisal would have in fact resorted to an oil embargo at this time. (An Arab oil embargo had been called following the 1967 war, but due to the buyers' market at the time, it was ineffectual and short lived.) Faisal certainly exhibited reluctance to do so prior to the 1973 war — sufficient reluctance for many observers to conclude that he would not. Even during the war he hesitated, until the United States announced, on 16 October, its intention to provide 2.2 billion dollars in military aid to Israel. The king, having been assured that the United States would be even-handed during the war, felt personally betrayed. The following day, he announced an Arab oil embargo against the United States and the Netherlands.[6]

Oil, then, was a major catalyst for Saudi Arabia's emergence as a leader of the moderate Arab states. The stage was set when the traditional buyers' oil market changed to a sellers' market in the early 1970s. The primary catalyst was the shift by the United States from a net oil exporter to a net importer. This shift in the market enabled the oil-producing countries to gain control of their own oil resources and also of the ability to set price and production rates, formerly in the hands of the major international oil companies. Saudi Arabia's position as the leading oil-exporting country thus gave it political and economic leverage far out of proportion to its small population and its embryonic defence establishment.

Saudi Arabia and the Peace Process

Saudi Arabia's growing role in regional politics and its growing stake in world economic issues served to increase the sense of urgency that Saudi leaders felt for reaching an Arab-Israeli peace settlement. Israel, which had largely ignored Saudi Arabia prior to the energy crisis of 1973–4, increasingly viewed Saudi oil power as a threat potentially more devastating than Arab military force. The Saudis felt, therefore, that they probably could no longer avoid participation in any resumption of Arab-Israeli hostilities, nor rule out an Israeli pre-emptive strike. Israeli reconnaissance activity over northeast Saudi Arabia reinforced that concern. Moreover, the longer the Arab-Israeli conflict went unresolved, the more radicalized the Arab world was likely to get. It became a major goal of King Faisal, therefore, to unite the Arab world under the moderates, not in order to gain military superiority, which he considered out of the question, but to enter peace negotiations from a position of strength. Only through unity could the Arabs obtain recognition of Palestinian territorial and political rights requisite, in his view, for a settlement.[7]

Unfortunately, tragedy struck. In March 1975 King Faisal was shot and killed by a deranged nephew over a family matter. Thus was struck down one of the leading statesmen of the Arab world. With quiet dignity and single-minded determination, King Faisal had presided over his country's foreign relations as its first and virtually only foreign minister. (Faisal had held his office from its inception in 1932 to his death, with the exception of a brief period, 1960–2, when he had retired to private life.) At the time of his death he was respected as a major world leader by friend and foe alike.

The policies begun by Faisal were continued under his successor, King Khalid. During Khalid's reign Crown Prince Fahd took over much of the day-to-day operations of the government. The first test came soon after Faisal's death. The Saudis were greatly disturbed at the Sinai II Agreement, signed in September 1975. From their point of view it split the moderate-led Arab unity they were seeking by placing Syria and Egypt at odds.[8] Over the next year Saudi diplomacy was aimed at healing that rift. Saudi patience appeared to pay off, for on 18 October 1976 Egyptian President Sadat and Syrian President Assad agreed to attend a mini-summit in Riyadh, along with PLO leader Arafat and Lebanese President Sarkis, to discuss a ceasefire in the Lebanese civil war.[9]

The Saudis were jubilant. Having in their view restored an Arab consensus for negotiating a peace settlement, they then looked to the United States to pressure Israel into acceptance of Palestinian rights of self-determination. From the Saudi perspective, only the United States could extract sufficient Israeli concessions on Palestinian rights to make peace possible.

Saudi optimism, whether realistic or wishful thinking, was dashed on 21 November 1977 when President Sadat flew to Jerusalem. Saudi diplomacy lay in shambles. Arab unity was once more sundered; all, in the Saudis' view, for nothing. Sadat, they were convinced, had given up in advance his one bargaining chip, recognition of Israel, and had nothing left with which to negotiate a meaningful peace settlement.

The United States and others counselled restraint — to allow time for developments from Sadat's bold initiative. By the following summer, however, it appeared to the Saudis that indeed the Egyptian-Israeli peace talks would come to nothing. Because the Saudis feared that the most Sadat could obtain from Israel without US pressure was a separate peace — a return of Sinai for a separate Egyptian-Israeli peace treaty with no resolution of the core issue, Palestinian rights of self-determination — the breakdown of the Sadat initiative did not particularly bother Riyadh. The Saudis saw a separate peace with Egypt as an Israeli ploy to split the Arab world and deny Egyptian military support to the Arab cause. Without Egypt, the Arabs had no credible military threat, and without one, the Saudis saw no chance of acquiring enough political leverage against Israel to achieve a just settlement.

Thus it was that when President Carter invited President Sadat and Prime Minister Begin to Camp David in September 1978, the Saudis were in a relaxed mood. From their point of view, one of three outcomes would probably result from Camp David: (i) the United States would pressure Israel into the requisite concessions on Palestinian rights to achieve a comprehensive settlement, a desirable but unlikely prospect; (ii) the United States would refrain from pressuring Israel but would state its own position on the necessity for returning the West Bank and Gaza to Arab sovereignty as a Palestinian homeland according to the Saudi interpretation of the United Nations Security Council Resolution 242 of 22 November 1967, a lesser gain but slightly more likely; (iii) the Sadat initiative would die a quiet death, unlamented in the Arab world, and proving to the entire world that even Sadat's dramatic visit to Israel was not enough to move Israel toward recognizing legitimate Palestinian rights, and hence toward peace.

The Camp David Accords were for the Saudis, therefore, a complete disaster. The Sadat initiative did not die, but neither, in their view, were Palestinian rights recognized. Instead, the Accords signed on 17 September created a framework for peace negotiations which was viewed in Riyadh as the realization of their worst fears.[10] Egypt was indeed making a separate peace with Israel in return for Sinai, and the only provision for Palestinian self-determination was limited autonomy under Israeli control for the inhabitants of the West Bank and Gaza during a five-year transition period. No specific provisions were made for the Palestinian diaspora, including those still in refugee camps, and the entire question of the final disposition of the occupied Arab territories was begged until after the transition period. More importantly, Israel not only retained its claim to sovereignty over East Jerusalem with its Moslem holy places, a major element in Saudi foreign policy, but the Begin government also maintained its claim to sovereignty over the entirety of the old Mandate of Palestine as *Eretz Ysrael*.

US and Egyptian assurance that the Camp David Accords were merely the first step on a long road toward a final settlement were received with scepticism in Riyadh. The Saudis were convinced that Israel intended the Camp David Accords to be the penultimate step toward peace, requiring just a few more cosmetic changes but no real concessions on Palestinian rights.

Nevertheless, the Saudis reserved judgement, largely at the urging of the American ambassador, John West. They assured the United States that they would attempt to moderate the debate at the Baghdad Arab Summit in November 1978, called to discuss the Camp David Accords. Fahd did prevent a complete Arab break with Egypt; but the United States, apparently unwilling to accept the fact that Saudi opposition to the Accords was sincere and not forced upon it by the Arab hardliners, was upset with Saudi diplomacy.

The final Arab break with Egypt came in April 1979 at a second Baghdad Summit following the signing of the Egyptian-Israeli peace treaty of 26 March. Even then, the Saudis did not cut off all ties with Egypt, allowing Egyptian workers to remain in the Kingdom, maintaining airline connections, and promising not to cancel prior aid commitments, principally the bulk of a 500 million-dollar Egyptian purchase of 50 F-5 E aircraft. After Sadat delivered a personal diatribe at the Saudis in a speech on 1 May, however, the Saudis withdrew the funding offer.

The Saudis' conviction that all Sadat had obtained was a separate peace was reinforced as the Palestinians' autonomy talks called for in the treaty quickly reached an impasse. From the Saudi perspective, the Camp David Accords was a dead issue. Thus it was that on 7 August 1981 Crown Prince Fahd announced an eight-point plan for a comprehensive settlement of the Arab-Israeli problem.

The Fahd Plan, as it came to be called, was drafted without any consultation with the United States. Although the Saudis were still convinced that only the United States could pressure Israel to make sufficient concessions on Palestinian rights to achieve peace, and although they felt that close co-operation with the United States was still in order, they believed that the Americans had arrived at a dead end with the Camp David process. With Saudi self-confidence rapidly increasing as they adjusted to their new status as a major oil power, the Saudis believed it was up to them to try and break the deadlock. The Fahd Plan called for:

1. Israeli withdrawal from all Arab territory occupied in 1967, including East Jerusalem.
2. The removal of Israeli settlements established on Arab lands since 1967.
3. Guaranteed freedom of worship for all religions in the holy places.
4. Affirmation of the right of the Palestinian people to return to their homes, and compensation to those who decide not to do so.
5. United Nations control of the West Bank and Gaza Strip for a transitional period not exceeding a few months.
6. The establishment of an independent Palestinian state with Jerusalem as its capital.
7. Affirmation of the right of all states in the region to live in peace.
8. The United Nations or some of its members to guarantee and implement these principles.[11]

Point 7 was clearly the most noteworthy part of the entire plan. 'Affirmation of all states in the area of the right to live in peace', was in Saudi eyes a clear signal of its willingness to recognize the

existence of Israel in the context of a settlement. Israel and its supporters, which rejected the Fahd Plan out of hand, questioned this
assumption since the Saudis refused to be more specific. From the
Saudi perspective, however, being more specific would place them
in the same position as Sadat in Jerusalem — conceding in advance
their main bargaining chip.

This formula failed ultimately to win Arab consensus. From the
start the Saudis had been careful to create a consensus of support
for the plan. PLO chairman Yasser Arafat, who may have had a
hand in drafting the plan, welcomed it as a basis for negotiations,
calling for 'coexistence' between the Arabs and Israel.[12] Syria and
Iraq, both recipients of Saudi aid, also initially appeared to go
along with the plan. At the pre-Arab summit foreign ministers'
conference in Fez, Morocco, on 22 November, however, the two
states backed out. Syria also pressured the PLO to renounce the
Fahd Plan. When the full Arab summit was convened on 25
November, King Hassan of Morocco, who was chairman, quickly
adjourned the meeting to save the Saudis from a loss of face.

Even had there been a favourable vote at the November 1981
Arab summit, the Fahd Plan was far from assured of success.
Although nothing in the plan specifically ran counter to the Camp
David Accords, Israel quickly condemned it, and put the United
States on notice that any US support of the Fahd Plan would be
interpreted as weakening the Camp David Accords. Egypt, though
less negative, also insisted that the Camp David Accords were the
only agreed-upon basis for negotiations.

The failure of the Fahd Plan to win Arab consensus did not spell
the end of the Saudi initiative, however. In the summer of 1982
Israel invaded Lebanon, using as the pretext a terrorist attack on an
Israeli diplomat in London.[13] In response to the invasion the United
States, for the first time, stated its own position on an Arab-Israeli
settlement. In a major address on 1 September 1982 President
Reagan stated that, whereas the United States had to that time
simply tried to be a mediator, 'some clearer sense of America's
position on key issues is necessary to encourage wider support for
the peace process'.[14]

Called the Reagan Plan, the position he outlined called for
autonomy of the inhabitants of the West Bank and Gaza, 'in
association with Jordan'. It also called on Israel to cease further
settlement in the occupied Arabs territories.[15] Israel rejected the
Reagan Plan out of hand. The Arab reaction was more positive. At

the Arab League summit meeting at Fez, Morocco, on 5–8 September 1982, an eight-point counter-proposal was adopted which was essentially a modified version of the Fahd Plan. The provisions agreed upon at Fez were:

1. Israeli withdrawal from all occupied Arab territories including East Jerusalem.
2. Dismantling the Israeli settlements in the Arab territories.
3. Guarantees of freedom of worship for all religions and rites.
4. Affirmation of Palestinian rights of self-determination, and exercise of those rights under their sole representative, the PLO.
5. A transition period of a few months during which the West Bank and Gaza would be supervised by the United Nations.
6. The establishment of a Palestinian state with Jerusalem as its capital.
7. A United Nations Security Council guarantee for the peace and security of all states in the region including a Palestinian state.
8. A United Nations Security Council guarantee for the implementation of the above principles.[16]

While neither the United States nor the Arabs would fully accept the other's peace proposals, the two proposals did appear to be a starting point for negotiations, provided Israel would agree. In 1983 little happened on the peace front, and the tragic events of Lebanon preoccupied everyone's time and energies. In 1984 the Israeli and US elections further delayed progress.

Following the two sets of elections, with a Labour-led government in Israel and President Reagan re-elected for a second term in the United States, the Saudis believed that the time was again right for seeking progress on the peace process. In mid-February 1985 King Fahd visited Washington, the first Arab Chief of State to visit President Reagan during his second term. In the meetings between the king and the president, 11 and 12 February, the two leaders agreed that the search for a just, stable and lasting solution to the Arab-Israeli conflict was their primary concern. In the joint communiqué, announced the following day, the Fez principles and the Reagan Plan as bases for negotiations were reconfirmed:

The King expressed his belief that the Arab consensus defined in the communiqué issued at Fez in September 1982 provided a just basis for negotiations leading to a comprehensive peace. The

President expressed his appreciation for the Fez consensus, positive elements of which have been recognized by the United States. He reaffirmed his continuing commitment to the positions for peace which he announced on September 1, 1982, and renewed his pledge that the United States will support those positions in direct negotiations involving the parties most concerned.[17]

Unless or until a wholly new initiative is presented by one or several of the parties, the Fez principles continue to represent Arab consensus on how to resolve the Arab-Israeli conflict. As the country mainly responsible for leading the Arabs toward that consensus, the Saudis will continue to play a major moderating role in the process toward peace.

Notes

1. A Turko-Egyptian force under Ibrahim Pasha captured the Saudi capital, Dir'iyyah, in 1818, staying for four years. Aside from causing the capital to be moved about 29 km south to Riyadh, the occupation left little imprint at all.

2. Islam resembles Judaism more than Christianity in that it is essentially a juridical system. Of the four recognized schools of jurisprudence in Sunni Islam — Hanafi, Maliki, Shafi'i, and Hanbali — the latter is generally considered the most conservative. It is the school of law followed by Saudi Arabia and neighbouring Qatar.

3. The followers of the Wahhabi revival prefer to be called Muwahhidin ('Unitarians'), stressing their monotheism, rather than Wahhabis, which could connote denigration of reverence to God through reverence of a mortal.

4. The princes were Tallal, Badr, Fawwaz, and Saud bin Fahd.

5. The perceived need for a credible military capability was further reinforced by the establishment of a radical, Marxist regime in Aden in 1967, and the announcement by Britain the following year of its intention to withdraw its protective umbrella from the Gulf by 1971.

6. See William B. Quandt, *Saudi Arabia in the 1980s* (Brookings, 1980), p. 50.

7. The terms *moderate, radical* and *progressive* are generally inadequate and often misleading when discussing Arab politics. Domestic political ideology, for example, can differ markedly from foreign-policy positions. In the context of the Arab-Israeli problem, most Arabs would probably accept roughly the same terms: recognition of Palestinian territorial and political rights in the occupied territories. The dichotomy is between those, generally Western oriented, who feel a sense of urgency in getting a settlement, and those who do not, believing that time is on their side.

8. Quandt, *Saudi Arabia*, p. 112.

9. David Holden and Richard Johns, *The House of Saud: The Rise and Rule of the Most Powerful Dynasty in the Arab World* (New York: Holt, Reinhart & Winston, 1981), p. 445.

10. For the text of the Accords, see 'The Camp David Summit, September 1978',

Department of State Publication 8959, Near East and South Asian Series 88, September 1978.

11. Richard M. Preece, 'The Saudi Peace Proposals' (Washington, DC: Congressional Research Service, Library of Congress, 24 November 1981), p. 4.

12. Ibid., p. 7.

13. The Israeli strategy and rationale behind the invasion — principally to smash the PLO as a viable political and para-military organization — was detailed in an article by Menachem Milson a year earlier. See Menachem Milson, 'How to Make Peace with the Palestinians', *Commentary*, vol. 17, May 1981, 25–35.

14. United States Department of State, *The Quest for Peace: Principal United States Statements and Documents Relating to the Arab-Israeli Peace Process, 1967–1983* (Washington, DC: Government Printing Office, 1983), p. 107.

15. Ibid.

16. *The Middle East Journal*, vol. 37, no. 1 (Winter 1983), 71.

17. The text of the communiqué was released by the Department of State, 13 February 1985.

PART TWO

OTHER PRINCIPAL ACTORS IN THE PEACE PROCESS

4 AMERICAN PROPOSALS FOR ARAB-ISRAELI PEACE

William B. Quandt

The Arab-Israeli war of June 1967 was a watershed event for the United States in recent Middle East history. From that date onward, each American president has been involved, to varying degrees, in the search for an Arab-Israeli peace settlement.

Throughout this period the United States has been comparatively consistent in the vision it has held of the key elements of a negotiated settlement. But each administration has brought to the task of peacemaking a different sense of urgency, and each has differed over the tactics most suitable to the circumstances of the time. None the less, the underlying continuity in American policy with respect to the preferred elements of Arab-Israeli peace is striking.

The Historical Legacy

The United States has been deeply involved in the diplomacy of the Arab-Israeli conflict since the 1967 war, but this has not always been the case. Three distinct periods can be identified in American thinking toward the Arab-Israeli dispute since the creation of the state of Israel in 1948.

In the first phase the United States was actively involved in supporting the creation of the state of Israel, in encouraging the negotiation of the armistice agreements of 1949, and in trying to translate those armistice agreements into the basis for a permanent peace. Numerous efforts were made in the early 1950s, many of them still not fully known to the public, to bring about an Arab-Israeli peace settlement. By 1955 American officials were reaching the conclusion that little real progress could be made through these channels, and that, instead of resolving the Arab-Israeli conflict, the most they could hope to do was to contain it and prevent further explosions.

The second phase of American diplomacy, from about 1955 to

1967, was designed to stabilize the existing *status quo*. The key elements in this approach were a balanced diplomacy, in which the United States sought to maintain contacts with key Arab states while at the same time supporting Israel, and a selective policy of arms transfers to bolster the regional balance. During this period, however, there were no grandiose American peace plans, and the primary focus of attention was on organizing the region to resist Soviet inroads. In so far as American diplomacy concerned itself with the Arab-Israeli conflict, it was through incremental efforts to resolve issues such as the sharing of the water of the Jordan River and a partial solution to the status of Palestinian refugees. On the whole, American diplomats seemed to feel that the conflict could not be solved through negotiations, but that it could be contained, and eventually it might fade from the scene as a new generation came of age with new attitudes.

The third phase of American diplomacy toward the Arab-Israeli conflict was ushered in by the 1967 war. The June war caught most Americans by surprise. Even in official circles in Washington it had not been anticipated, and it did not fit the prevailing view that the *status quo* was comparatively stable. In the aftermath of the war President Lyndon Johnson and his aides were aware that the Middle East region was highly volatile and dangerous. There had been overtones of possible US and Soviet military intervention in the midst of the war, and this had alarmed Washington, particularly because the United States was deeply involved in the Vietnam war at the same time and could not have easily managed a military confrontation in the Middle East simultaneously.

The Aftermath of the 1967 War

The 1967 war quickly banished the complacency among American officials that had prevailed in the previous decade. It also led to an immediate judgment that the United States should support Israel's retention of the territories occupied in the 1967 war until the Arab parties were prepared to offer peace, recognition and security to Israel. This was a fundamental and basic judgment that has shaped American policy ever since 1967. In its simplest form, this meant that the United States was supporting an overall Arab-Israeli peace based on the exchange of territory for recognition of Israel.

It is important to note that the Johnson Administration, in

adopting this policy, was deliberately trying to avoid the precedent set by President Eisenhower in 1956–7. When Israel had gone to war against Egypt in October 1956 and had occupied the Sinai Peninsula, the United States had opposed Israeli action and had obliged Israel's armed forces to withdraw from Sinai in early 1957 without any significant concessions from the Egyptians. One reason for this was that President Eisenhower did not believe that Israel's war against Egypt in 1956 had been justified. President Johnson in 1967, however, along with most Americans, felt that Israel had been obliged to go to war by the reckless attempts of President Gamal Abd al-Nasser of Egypt to change fundamentally the *status quo* in the region. Therefore, the prevailing American attitude in 1967 was that Israel had been justified in going to war and should be allowed to retain the territory acquired in that conflict until the Arab parties were willing to make peace.

In the months following the June 1967 war, the United States played an active role in the United Nations in order to promote its concept of how a peace settlement should be reached. The result of these efforts was United Nations Security Council Resolution 242, adopted on 22 November 1967. It incorporated two key elements. First, it called for 'withdrawal of Israeli armed forces from territories occupied in the recent conflict'; and secondly, it called for the

> termination of all claims or states of belligerency and respect for the sovereignty, territorial integrity and political independence of every State in the area and their right to live in peace within secure and recognized boundaries free from threats or acts of force.

In short, it called on Israel to withdraw if and when the Arab parties offered peace, recognition and security.

The American view at the time of Resolution 242 was that the occupied territories would provide Israel with a tangible bargaining chip with which to extract major concessions from the Arab side. The Arab parties, in 1967, were locked into an intransigent position of 'no peace, no negotiations, and no recognition'. As a result, the American position led to full support of Israel up until such time as an Arab party might step forward and credibly offer peace.

From the time that Resolution 242 was adopted, the United States interpreted the resolution in somewhat different ways from both the Israelis and the Arabs. A crucial sentence in the resolution calls for withdrawal of Israeli forces from territories occupied in the recent conflict. The American interpretation of that sentence was that withdrawal by Israel need not be exactly to the 1967 lines. Particularly in the region of the West Bank, there should be some possibility of minor border adjustments. But the United States never interpreted this sentence as opening the way for major changes in territorial control. This was expressed repeatedly by President Johnson, when he said that the future borders should not reflect the weight of conquest, and subsequent presidents reiterated this view when they spoke of minor border adjustments, and sometimes even noted that these should involve only mutually acceptable changes in the 1967 lines. None the less, the American position was clear that the borders might be adjusted to some extent. The Arab interpretation, by comparison, was that Resolution 242 required complete Israeli withdrawal from all of the territories occupied in 1967. Finally, the Israelis interpreted Resolution 242 as allowing for substantial changes in territorial control.

While the United States has never been in full accord with either Israel or the Arabs on the interpretation of Resolution 242, there has been an essential consistency since 1967 in the American interpretation of the resolution. All American administrations have accepted the 'land for peace' trade-off embodied in Resolution 242, and have essentially interpreted this to mean that Israel should withdraw from most, if not all, of the territory it occupied in 1967 in return for full recognition and full peace from the Arab states on Israel's borders. As time has gone by, the concept of peace itself has been expanded upon, beyond the legalistic termination of the state of belligerency, so that since 1977 all American officials have spoken of 'real peace', or a peace that would involve diplomatic relations, trade, free movement of people, and other attributes of states living at peace.

The immediate American concern after the 1967 war was, not surprisingly, with the consequences of that conflict. In brief, the primary territorial preoccupation was with the Sinai, the West Bank and Gaza, and the Golan Heights. Missing from Resolution 242 was any detailed discussion of the long-festering Palestinian problem. In fact, the Palestinians were not even mentioned by name in Resolution 242, and the only reference that can be interpreted as dealing with problems of the Palestinians is a vague injunction to find a just settlement of the refugee problem.

It is on this question of the Palestinians and their future that American thinking has evolved most clearly in the period since 1967. From an initial preoccupation with finding a resolution of the refugee problem, primarily through resettlement and compensation, American thinking gradually came to envisage a political role of some sort for the Palestinians in a peace settlement. But this was slow in coming, and was never dealt with in great detail, in part because of the great political sensitivities within the United States surrounding this issue.

American officials have consistently maintained that Resolution 242 is not 'self-implementing'. In other words, it is only an outline of an agreement, the details of which should be worked out by negotiations. The United States has been unwilling to consider imposing a peace settlement on the parties to the conflict. The prevailing view has been that unless the parties to the conflict were to make concessions and commitments to one another, no settlement imposed by outsiders would have much chance of lasting. Rather than seek to impose a new *status quo* that might last for a few years, the United States instead has argued that a negotiated peace should be sought, even if the process might be longer and more difficult. Again, behind the thinking of many Americans was the realization that any attempt to impose a settlement against Israel would evoke strong and adverse reactions in the American domestic environment.

The Role of Mediator

In the American view, the essential burden of the peace process would be on the parties to the negotiations. Therefore, the United States never felt that it was essential to take positions on all the details of a future peace plan. In essence, anything the parties themselves could agree upon the United States would be willing to support. Problems arose, however, when the gap between the parties was too great. Then the United States might be called upon to suggest ways of resolving the differences. In the end, this would mean that the United States would be expected to express judgments about what might be acceptable as a compromise between the Israeli and Arab positions. Despite a considerable reluctance to be drawn into the details of an Arab-Israeli peace settlement, the United States found that, as the only mediator acceptable to both sides of the conflict, it was soon suggesting ways of bridging the gaps.

In order to have some credibility as a mediator, the United States tried to position itself so that it would appeal to some Israeli interests and some Arab interests. With respect to the elements of Resolution 242, the American interpretation on the extent of Israeli withdrawal tended to approximate the Arab interpretation, although it was not identical. Because of this similarity of views, the Americans hoped to retain some credibility with the Arab side. At the same time, however, the Americans were strongly in favour of the Israeli interpretation of peace, recognition and security. These would have to involve more than simply a signature on a piece of paper. There would have to be tangible content to commitments of peace, and there would have to be extensive and reliable security arrangements before Israel would be expected to withdraw. On this point, then, the United States hoped to develop credibility with the Israeli side of the negotiations.

On the question of the Palestinians, the US has been reluctant to express its views clearly. More than the Israelis have liked, however, the US has come to see the need for a significant Palestinian role in any peace settlement. But it has not gone so far as to support Arab demands for Palestinian self-determination or statehood.

On the formalistic level of peace proposals, the United States has been comparatively steady since Resolution 242 was adopted in 1967. On the level of tactics, there has been much more vacillation. Underlying these tactical shifts is a changing sense of urgency with respect to Arab-Israeli peace as the memories of the most recent war fade and administrations become less worried about the dangers of a new explosion. In addition, each administration has attached its own priority to the Middle East within its broader foreign-policy concerns.

The Carter Presidency

If we look at the last two American administrations, we will see quite significant differences in terms of how the presidents saw the Arab-Israeli conflict within their broader worldview. For President Jimmy Carter, the Arab-Israeli conflict came to be one of the most important issues of his presidency. In part, this was no doubt a reflection of deep personal values, some stemming from his own religious beliefs, and some derived from his commitment to human rights. In addition, there was a strategic concern growing out of the memory of the October 1973 Arab-Israeli war. That conflict had been extraordinarily dangerous and costly. More than any crisis since the Cuban missile affair of 1962, the 1973 war had risked direct US-Soviet confrontation. In addition, it had triggered Arab actions that resulted in disruptions of oil markets and led to a significant increase in the price of oil, with damaging consequences for the industrialized world, as well as the Third World. Any president would have been obliged to pay some attention to the Arab-Israeli conflict as a result of those recent memories, but Carter brought to the task a personal commitment that was unique. In the end he played a major role in bringing about the Camp David Accords between Egypt and Israel, and the signature of an Egyptian-Israeli peace treaty in March 1979. Let us look now at each of those agreements.

At Camp David two separate frameworks were agreed upon by Egyptian President Anwar Sadat and Israeli Prime Minister Menachem Begin. One was a general framework setting forth principles for an overall Middle East peace settlement. Included in that framework were details of how to address the Palestinian question. The second document signed at Camp David was an outline of an Egyptian-Israeli peace treaty. It contained many details, and was based explicitly on the 'land for peace' formula of Resolution 242. In this document Israel agreed to return to the international border with Egypt — the 1967 line — and in return the Egyptians agreed to establish normal diplomatic relations, to exchange ambassadors, and to limit military deployments in Sinai. This second agreement can be seen as a classical interpretation of what Resolution 242 called for. It was fully consistent with the interpretation of the elements of peace between Israel and her Arab neighbours held by every American president since Lyndon Johnson.

If the Arab-Israeli agreement reached at Camp David was very much within the mainstream of American proposals ever since 1967, the same cannot be said for the broader framework and its particular interpretation of the Palestinian question. At Camp David, for the first time, the West Bank and Gaza were treated as substantially different from other occupied Arab territories. Instead of trying to model an agreement concerning the West Bank and Gaza on the Egyptian-Israeli formula for Sinai, the negotiators instead developed a concept for a transitional period. In large measure this was due to the fact that Egypt and Israel fundamentally disagreed on how the West Bank and Gaza should ultimately be governed, but they could both agree on the need for some transitional steps.

The change of focus with respect to the West Bank and Gaza was a direct reflection of the views of Israeli Prime Minister Menachem Begin. Elected in 1977 to head the Israeli government, Begin brought with him a fundamentally different concept of how to address the question of peace with his Arab neighbours to the east, that is Jordan and the Palestinians. In previous Israeli governments there had been no significant difference in the way Sinai, the West Bank and Golan were treated. The 'land for peace' formula applied on all fronts, although Israel always held out the possibility of significant changes in borders. Now, however, with Menachem Begin in power, Israel fundamentally reinterpreted the meaning of Resolution 242 so that it no longer called for peace based on a return of territory on each front. Instead, it would be enough, according to Begin, if Israel agreed to withdraw on only one front, such as Sinai. Once that was accomplished, Israel was under no further obligation to withdraw anywhere, even in return for peace, recognition and security.

The reason for Begin's change in interpretation of Resolution 242 was quite simple. As part of his ideology and his deepest political beliefs, Begin felt that Israel must retain control over the West Bank and Gaza, which he always referred to by their biblical names of Judea and Samaria. He rejected Jordan's claim to sovereignty over these areas, and argued that Jordan had been an interloper, annexing the territories against the will of the international community.

Begin's own concept for dealing with these areas was clearly set forth. Israel should retain complete authority over the disposition of the land and its water resources, and should retain a security presence indefinitely. Israeli settlers should be allowed to acquire land and build settlements, and should be able to live under Israeli jurisdiction and protection. The Palestinian Arabs residing in these territories would be allowed a measure of cultural autonomy, and might be able to manage some of their own internal affairs. But Begin was adamant in rejecting the return of any of these territories to Arab political control, whether it be by Jordan or by the Palestinians.

When the Americans were first exposed to Begin's thinking in the summer of 1977, there was a tendency to say 'Begin doesn't really mean it'. Some believed that his was simply a tough bargaining position, and once negotiations got underway, some thought, Begin would return to the more familiar offer of 'land for peace'. It took some time to realize that Begin was completely serious. In endless discussions with Secretary of State Cyrus Vance and President Jimmy Carter, Begin reiterated his position that he would never relinquish control over one square inch of the West Bank. He would only consider some changes in the way the region was administered, and he would agree to refrain from claiming Israeli sovereignty for at least a five-year period.

Camp David and the Palestinian Question

In time, the Carter Administration came to accept the necessity of treating the West Bank and Gaza differently from Sinai and Golan. The idea of a transitional period was accepted, at first reluctantly, and then with more enthusiasm. Those who were most optimistic saw that during the transitional period the Palestinians might be able to build institutions and develop leadership of their own, so that eventually the West Bank and Gaza could be governed effectively in association with Jordan, while developing peaceful relations with Israel. In addition, some believed that the idea of a regime offering autonomy to the Palestinians in the West Bank and Gaza would help to preserve the territorial dimension of these occupied areas, and would lay the groundwork at a later date for a settlement based on the principles of Resolution 242, including withdrawal. In any case, some degree of staged implementation of any agreement was necessary, and thus an interim agreement seemed reasonable. To have insisted on resolving the questions of sovereignty and final borders would have, in any case, been a formula for failure.

It was not only Menachem Begin who contributed to the shift of American thinking concerning the West Bank and Gaza. There was also an Arab contribution. From October 1974 onward, the official Arab position was that only the PLO was authorized to negotiate with Israel concerning the future of the West Bank and Gaza. But Israel was adamantly opposed to dealing with the PLO, as was the United States. In part this was due to the PLO's continued adherence to a policy of 'armed struggle' and its reluctance to accept Resolution 242.

Jordan, which had controlled the West Bank until 1967, seemed to be on the sidelines, although King Hussein repeatedly said that he would play some role in future peace negotiations if he could be assured of Israeli withdrawal from all of the occupied territory. This created considerable confusion in the minds of American officials about who, if anyone, was really prepared to negotiate on behalf of the Palestinians.

Since neither Jordan nor the PLO seemed to be acceptable negotiating partners for Israel, the Egyptians moved into that role almost by default. From the time that Anwar Sadat travelled to Jerusalem in November 1977, he had presented himself as a spokesman not only for Egyptian interests but also for those of the Palestinians. But since the Palestinians, and other Arabs, refused to follow his lead, increasingly he found that he was speaking alone on behalf of the Palestinians. At Camp David it seemed likely that neither Jordan nor the Palestinians would join the peace process, and therefore President Sadat made it clear in writing that Egypt would assume their role in negotiations for an interim regime if they did not come forward to speak for themselves. This was a controversial decision even within the Egyptian delegation, and it carried with it both promise and peril. Egypt, as the strongest Arab state, could afford to ignore the criticism of other Arabs. It was not shackled by the requirement of consensus. At the same time, it was never clear whom, if anyone, Sadat could really speak for among the Palestinians.

By the time the Camp David negotiations had been completed, Egypt and Israel were committed to two tracks of negotiations: one dealing with their bilateral problems, which would lead to an Egyptian-Israeli peace treaty; and the other involving negotiations to establish a self-governing authority for the West Bank and Gaza for an interim period of five years.

The Camp David Accords invited Jordan and the Palestinians to join this second track of negotiations, and held out the possibility that elections for a Palestinian self-governing body would be held at an indeterminate date in the future. If all went well, within three years of the establishment of the self-governing authority, a new round of negotiations would begin which would include Palestinian and Jordanian representatives, along with the Egyptians and Israelis. These negotiations would address the question of the so-called 'final status' of the West Bank and Gaza, in brief, the question of sovereignty and borders. But the basis on which those latter negotiations would take place was not explicitly spelled out, except for a vague reference to the principles of Resolution 242. Begin quickly interpreted this as being consistent with Israel's claim to ultimate sovereignty over all of the occupied territories. In short, Begin continued to reject the idea of withdrawal as part of the formula for peace with Jordan and the Palestinians.

The negotiators at Camp David were well aware that the framework concerning the West Bank and Gaza contained many loopholes. Had it been possible to obtain greater precision, greater precision would have been desirable. But no one saw a realistic way to bridge the enormous gap that separated the Egyptians and Israelis with respect to the ultimate future of the West Bank and Gaza. Nor did anyone see how the Camp David Accords could be modified to ensure that Jordan and the Palestinians would enter the negotiations alongside Egypt. In the end, of course, the Egyptian-Israeli framework was successfully carried out and the peace treaty was signed in March 1979. The other framework concerning the Palestinians led to lengthy and inconclusive negotiations between Egypt and Israel in 1979 and 1980, but no successful conclusion was reached. Finally, in 1982 the Egyptians made it clear that they had no further interest in negotiating with the Israelis on autonomy, and that if the peace process were to be resumed it would be only with Jordanian and Palestinian participation.

One of the reasons that the Palestinians and Jordanians were unwilling to give the Camp David Accords the benefit of the doubt had to do with an immediate dispute between Carter and Begin over the question of Israeli settlements in the West Bank and Gaza. On the next to the last day at Camp David, Carter tried to get Begin to agree that there would be no new Israeli settlements in the occupied territories during the negotiations to establish self-government for the Palestinians. Begin resisted, seeing that this could lead to an indefinite freeze on Israeli settlement activity, since the negotiations could go on for a very long time. In a late-night meeting on 16 September 1977, Carter believed that Begin had made the concession he sought concerning settlements. The next day, however, Begin sent a letter to Carter promising a freeze on Israeli settlements in the West Bank and Gaza for only the three-month period of negotiations with Egypt. Carter thought that a mistake had been made and sent the letter back, asking for a corrected copy.

That night the Camp David Accords were signed without the new draft of the letter having been received. It was only the day after the Camp David Accords were signed that Begin's letter reached Carter, reiterating his commitment to a three-month freeze on settlement activity and no more.

In this first test of strength between the Camp David participants, Begin won. It was a strong signal to the Palestinians and Jordanians who were watching to see what in reality the Camp David Accords meant for them. In short, the one tangible gain that Carter thought he had achieved at Camp David for the Palestinians was immediately lost, and with it much of the credibility of the agreement in the eyes of the Jordanians and Palestinians.

The Reagan Presidency

Let us now turn to the policies of the Reagan Administration. Ronald Reagan did not come to the office of the presidency with a deep concern for the Arab-Israeli conflict. Instead, when he looked at the Middle East he worried most about threats of Soviet expansion, and his policies were initially designed to check that threat rather than to promote Arab-Israeli peace. Perhaps understandably, Reagan was also unwilling to identify enthusiastically with Jimmy Carter's most significant foreign-policy achievement, the Camp David Accords. As a result, there was very little interest in 1981 and the first part of 1982 in trying to promote an Arab-Israeli peace settlement. There was, however, continued dedication to the smooth implementation of the Egyptian-Israeli agreement. On that front considerable progress was made, resulting in the final withdrawal of all Israeli troops from Egyptian territory in April 1982.

Shortly after the Israeli withdrawal from Sinai, Israeli forces crossed the Lebanese border in a war aimed at destroying the Palestine Liberation Organization. The American attitude toward the Israeli decision for war had been, to say the least, tolerant and understanding. But within a short period Israeli's war goals exceeded those that had been explained to the Americans, and Washington was coming under pressure from various Arab capitals to do something to restrain the scope of the Israeli action. In addition, Ronald Reagan's first secretary of state, Alexander Haig, was replaced in summer 1982 by George Schultz, a man who brought with him a somewhat different perspective on issues in the Middle East.

As the war in Lebanon came to an end in late summer 1982, Secretary Schultz and a small group of advisers persuaded President Reagan to go on record with a clear American statement concerning the Arab-Israeli conflict. On 1 September 1982 Ronald Reagan moved American Middle East policy back into the mainstream by anchoring his vision of Arab-Israeli peace clearly in Resolution 242, the 'land for peace' formulation. In doing so, President Reagan also sought to modify several of the key elements of the Camp David approach to the West Bank and Gaza.

One of the issues that had most troubled the Arab parties with respect to the Camp David Accords was the ambiguity concerning the final status of the West Bank and Gaza territories. Reagan sought to dispel this concern by putting the United States clearly on record as favouring Israeli withdrawal and the association of the West Bank and Gaza with Jordan. Reagan said the United States would not support Israeli annexation of these territories, nor would it support a fully independent Palestinian state. In addition, Reagan made it clear that the primary role on the Arab side in resolving these questions should go to Jordan and representatives of the Palestinians, not Egypt.

The image evoked by Reagan's statements was of a Jordanian-Palestinian confederation, consisting of the East Bank and most of the West Bank and Gaza. Little was said about the future of Jerusalem, other than to repeat the well-known American position that it should remain a united city, but that its political status was subject to negotiations. The president also spelled out an interpretation of the 'land for peace' formula of Resolution 242, in which he stated that the greater the peace offered to Israel, the greater Israeli withdrawal from occupied territories should be. In brief, if the Arabs were unwilling to go all the way toward a full and open peace with Israel, Israel would not be expected to withdraw completely. By the same token, if the Arabs were prepared for full peace, Israel should be ready for virtually full withdrawal.

Toward the end of 1982 President Reagan met with King Hussein of Jordan to explore how the negotiating process might be resumed. Several promises were made to the King during those meetings. First, if the King would agree to negotiate with Israel, Reagan would try to get the Israelis to stop further settlements in the West Bank and Gaza. In short, he would seek to remedy the error made by Carter at Camp David when he failed to pin Begin down on the question of settlement activity. In addition, Reagan implied to King Hussein that negotiations on the final status of these territories could begin almost immediately. The interim period could be shortened and need not last the full three to five years envisaged in the Camp David Accords. All of this was designed to entice King Hussein into the negotiations by addressing some of his main worries about the Camp David formulations.

As soon as the Reagan plan had been unveiled, it elicited very strong support within the American body politic. Former President Jimmy Carter, among others, was open in his support of the Reagan formulations, declaring that they were fully consistent with the Camp David Accords. But despite this broad base of support within the United States, the Reagan Plan evoked only modest interest in the Middle East itself. King Hussein was clearly tempted, but in April 1983 he was unable to persuade the PLO to join him in a positive response to President Reagan, and for a period of time the prospects for negotiation seemed quite dim. In addition, the Likud-led government in Israel immediately rejected the Reagan proposals because of their insistence on ultimate Israeli withdrawal from the West Bank and Gaza.

The fate of the Reagan Plan was not only sealed by the reactions of Jordan and Israel. It also fell victim to the deteriorating circumstances in Lebanon. The Reagan Administration devoted much time and effort in 1982 and 1983 to brokering a Lebanese-Israeli peace, resulting in an agreement on 17 May 1983. But this agreement had failed to take into account Syrian opposition, and during the remainder of 1983 the Syrians demonstrated that they could unravel the best laid of American plans.

This was a reminder, if one were needed, that neither the Camp David Accords nor the Reagan peace proposal had taken Syria's interests into account. Nor had either administration successfully designed a strategy for checking Syria's opposition to its policies. Instead, it seemed as if the regime in Damascus was simply ignored or taken for granted. No positive incentives were offered to draw the Syrians into the process, nor were disincentives articulated that would make it costly for the Syrians to stand in the way of the American policy.

Conclusions

From this examination of the peace policies of recent American administrations, it seems clear that there has been an essential continuity in the way American officials have seen the outline of Arab-Israeli peace. Resolution 242 captured the essence of the trade-off that Americans have supported in negotiations, namely 'land for peace'. In addition, some role for the Palestinians has come to be part of the American package.

But even a cursory examination of American peace proposals suggests that the formulation of a peace plan is considerably easier than its implementation. Where American policy has often fallen short has been in carrying out a diplomatic strategy designed to promote a genuine Arab-Israeli peace settlement. President Carter, through a remarkable act of will, was able to help move the Egyptians and the Israelis to a formal peace settlement, but even his efforts bogged down on the Palestinian question.

President Reagan, who articulated as clearly as any American president ever has the essential ingredients of an Israeli-Palestinian-Jordanian peace, was almost totally uninterested and uninvolved in the follow-up to his stated policy. Not surprisingly, it soon joined the category of other well-intentioned peace proposals that left little mark on the history of the Middle East.

By the mid-1980s it was not so much a peace plan, whether American or of some other origin, that was lacking in the Arab-Israeli arena. What was most needed was the will to make peace on the part of the parties to the conflict. That will was manifested when President Sadat travelled to Jerusalem, and he and Prime Minister Begin were able to take a step toward peace as a result. But the leadership in all of the countries of the Middle East in the mid-1980s seemed weak and uncertain, and the issue of peace had only a feeble constituency where it was most needed.

The American view in Reagan's second term seemed to be that if the parties themselves were not ready for peace, there was little that Washington could do to promote the process of accommodation. This stand-offish attitude was somewhat new to American diplomacy in the Middle East. In the past it was generally believed that purposeful action by the United States could in fact influence attitudes in Israel and in the Arab world, and that prospects of a fair diplomatic solution would strengthen moderate forces in both camps.

More recently, Americans seem to be saying that their interests are not vitally at stake in the Arab-Israeli conflict. There is little real chance of war. The oil weapon has lost its credibility. The Soviet menace in the region no longer seems critically tied to the Arab-Israeli conflict. In short, the United States has learned to live without Arab-Israeli peace, and therefore it has relegated the diplomacy of Arab-Israeli peace-making to a lower priority than in the past.

The plans still exist. They reflect a deep consensus on the shape of a peace settlement, but there is no longer consensus in the United States over the stakes involved in promoting an Arab-Israeli peace. Proponents of 'benign neglect' are taken seriously, and those who urge an activist diplomacy which seeks to translate peace proposals into the diplomacy of peace are treated as naïve, or worse.

In the end one must conclude that the easy part of American diplomacy toward the Middle East has been the formulation of peace plans. The difficult part, and the part that will remain as a challenge to American presidents in the future, is to translate those plans into an effective strategy to use American power and influence on behalf of Middle East peace.

5 SOVIET PEACE PLANS FOR THE MIDDLE EAST

Vladimir N. Sakharov

Planned mischief and a grandiose design to control Arab oil? Paranoid xenophobia bordering on schizophrenic concern about border security? Fear of a Moslem fundamentalist spillover into Soviet Asian territory? Or a sincere desire for lasting peace with the affirmation of sovereign territorial rights for all Middle Eastern countries including Israel? Often discussed by American scholars and analysts, these questions cannot help but accentuate the diversity of possible motives and concerns that influence Soviet behaviour in the Middle East.

In the broader context of Soviet-American rivalry and East-West confrontation, the prospects for peace in the Middle East depend on how the Soviets perceive real and imagined dangers to their national security, emanating from what they term 'American imperialism', the 'Zionist conspiracy', and 'the dark forces of Western monopolies'. These labels have become part of Soviet political jargon describing the sources of instability in the Middle East.

The struggle between the two opposing ideological and political systems — the East and the West — contributes to the present shape of Soviet policy-planning for the Middle East. According to Soviet perceptions, peace in the Middle East has become not an imminent end in itself, but a process of struggle led by 'international democratic forces and socialist countries headed by the Soviet Union in solidarity with the struggle of the Arab countries against imperialism, Zionism, and reaction'.[1] Within this context there is little room for compromise, and the chances for peace in the Middle East are remote, unless the USSR and its allies or the United States and its allies make concessions for the sake of greater stability in the Middle East.

Another important but overlooked factor that will determine future prospects for peace in the Middle East is the current trend towards anti-Semitism in the USSR and its influence on Soviet policy-planning and conduct.

Moslems and Jews: The Soviet View

During the first months after the Great October Socialist Revolution in 1917, peace with the Moslems of the Arab World was an immediate item on the Bolsheviks' agenda. Anticipating a brutal, prolonged civil war against internal enemies of the revolution, aided by Western powers through the Entente Alliance, the Soviet government was eager to secure, at least marginally, the oil-rich regions of the Caspian Sea. Securing this vital economic and energy centre meant a political and ideological compromise with its Moslem population. Lenin's vision of Middle Eastern stability was also founded on a broad concept of Soviet tolerance not only of local Moslem undercurrents but of Moslem states bordering on Soviet territory.

The key to understanding Soviet peace efforts in the Middle East lies in the 'Appeal to All Moslem Workers of Russia and the East', authored by V. Lenin and J. Stalin. The appeal was intended to win the Moslems to the Soviet side by denouncing the expansionist Middle Eastern policy of the Tsars: 'Constantinople must remain in the hands of Moslems . . . Moslems of the East! We anticipate your sympathy and support'.[2] The appeal put an end to the 1907 treaty with Great Britain on the division of Persia and set the initial framework for Soviet Middle Eastern policy.

Early Soviet Middle Eastern policy had two basic objectives: to create a Middle Eastern rim of Moslem countries friendly to the USSR, and to make sure they could not serve as a launching pad for Western military, political and economic aggression against the USSR. A peaceful alliance with Russia's anti-Western Middle East was an essential component of the success of the Soviet Bolshevik Revolution. In the period 1919–24 Lenin, known for his keen interest in the Moslem world, implemented a series of practical measures designed to establish close ties with the then key Middle Eastern states. The format for those ties was bilateral peace treaties. The essence of these measures was a pragmatic ideological compromise based on Lenin's official recognition that to be a Moslem and a Communist at the same time was quite acceptable. In 1921 Lenin sanctioned a permanent ban on anti-religious propaganda in the areas predominantly populated by Moslem populations. This coincided with the official terror against the Russian Orthodox Church and the destruction of church buildings. Since that time the term Moslem-Communist has assumed standard positive connotations in the Soviet political lexicon. What is remarkable about this is that no one has heard about Baptist-Communists or Catholic-Communists in the USSR.

Lenin's flexibility in accommodating local Soviet Moslems under the protection of the Communist Party, and his drive to gain the support of and sympathy for Moslems outside the USSR, was followed by a series of peace-and-friendship treaties with Afghanistan, Iran, Turkey, Yemen and Saudi Arabia. The Red Thread that tied all of them to Soviet Middle Eastern policy was a commonality of interests; for example, 'mutual aid against wild and carnivorous foreign animals grabbing for our property and freedom'.[3] Mutual interests — liberation from the yoke of Western imperialism and aggression, geographic proximity, a common fear of foreigners, and the pressing need to have peace in order to rebuild deteriorating economies — contributed to a climate of brotherhood that has existed between the USSR and the Middle East ever since.

In order to understand current Soviet decision-making in the Middle East, one must review the origins of Soviet perceptions of Zionism and Islam. Islam was not new to either the Soviet government nor the Communist Party. By 1929 pan-Islamism and Islam in the USSR were officially sanctioned by the Communist Party. Although an accurate census of the Soviet Moslem population at that time does not exist, it numbered somewhere between 7 million and 10 million, representing a sizeable socio-economic force. The majority of them were Sunni, with Shi'ites clustered in Azerbaijan. There is a certain Byzantine commonality in the development of both the Russian Orthodox Church and Islam. Historically, both religions have never been warring factions, unlike Russian Orthodoxy's battles with the West European religious sects. Russians viewed Moslems as traders, craftsmen, and mysterious offspring of folkloric figures like Ali Baba and the Forty Thieves, Sinbad the Sailor, and characters from the Thousand and One Nights.

Contrary to the positive perceptions of Islam and Middle Eastern people, the Russian view of the Jews and Zionism was rooted in hatred. Before the 1917 Revolution the Russian Orthodox Church supported an anti-Jewish mood among the Russian population, which believed that the Jews were responsible for Christ's killing. 'Pogroms', or mob-beatings of Jews, and the looting of Jewish homes and stores were semi-official outlets for this hatred. The Tsarist regime perceived the Jews as intellectual trouble makers, a lower race incapable of loyalty to Russia.

After the revolution and the Jewish exodus to Europe and America, less than three million Jews were left in Russia. In addition to a traditional animosity towards the Jews, the Soviet government began to fear the impact international Zionism might have on the Jews still in Russia. According to Dr Ivo J. Lederer,

> in the 1930s Stalin's purges began to assume, among other things, the form of official anti-Semitism. Leading Jewish communists perished in the political cannibalism of the day. The party and police made strenuous efforts to sever all contacts between the Jews of Russia and those in Palestine and elsewhere. It became commonplace to charge prominent or nameless Jews with foreign Zionist connections, and thereby with treasonous activities in the service of capitalism.[4]

Those were the two opposing Russian perceptions of the Moslems and the Jews. They were to play a decisive role in the Soviet view of the future Middle Eastern conflicts and Soviet political and military planning to address them.

Evolution of the Soviet Approach, 1948–67

The Soviets made several attempts to solve their Jewish problem before World War II. The Jews were encouraged to change their children's nationality at age 16, that is, at the time they were issued internal passports. Some of those who did not, perished in Siberian labour camps or were killed. In 1934 Stalin attempted to create a special Jewish Autonomous Oblast (district) with Birobijan as its capital. The experiment did not work. Except for several thousand forcibly relocated families, the barren, inhospitable, desolate district of Birobijan was never to become an attraction for Soviet Jews. They had neither roots nor a reason to have residence there. Regardless of worldwide feelings of sympathy towards European Jews put to death in Nazi concentration camps, the Soviets did not and could not prevent the continuous internal animosity of Russians towards Jews after World War II. On the contrary, popular belief among the Russian population was that the Russians suffered most during the war, losing 20 million on the battlefield and winning a victory against the Germans. In the meantime, according to the same popular belief, Soviet Jews used every opportunity to escape the front and to obtain jobs associated with food and supplies.

By 1948 this antagonistic perception of the Jews influenced Stalin's and Molotov's decision to support the creation of the independent state of Israel and to be first to recognize it *de jure*. The Soviets calculated that they would solve their internal Jewish problem: all Soviet Jews would run away to Israel. Except for a limited number of Jews from satellite countries and a trickle from the USSR, the experiment was hardly successful. It led, however, to consequences for future Soviet Middle Eastern policy which would become the centre of world attention. One might say that by endorsing the formation of Israel, the Soviets turned its local Jewish problem into an international issue with gigantic proportions which would haunt them in the years to come. According to some post-Stalin Soviet Middle Eastern experts, Stalin rushed in to force the British departure from Palestine by pressing for the creation of Israel. However, the Soviet government had no plan for the relationship it would have with the newly formed state.

The next decade in Soviet Middle Eastern policy was influenced by the grim post-war realities within Russia itself, and by an internal political volatility preceding and following Stalin's death in 1953. By the time of the Suez crisis in 1956, the USSR had no clear vision of the future of the Middle East. It had no expertise in sophisticated peace-making diplomacy in the Arab World and Israel. By then most Soviet Middle Eastern experts were too old, or had been exterminated during Stalin's purges in the 1930s and 1940s. Until Moscow formulated its doctrine of peaceful coexistence and support for national liberation in the early 1960s, all Soviet efforts in the Middle East — including military aid to Egypt and Iraq after the Suez crisis — were reactive. American policy responded in kind:

> In the rising competition over the Arab area, reactive diplomacy made the United States a consequential polarizer. The United States prodded the so-called conservative Arab regimes . . . But most of their leadership seemed to be losing ground steadily in the Arab World at large.[5]

While American prestige and leverage in the Arab World declined, the USSR opened the Patrice Lumumba University in

Moscow, modelled after Lenin's University of the Toilers of the East in the early 1920s. Numerous scholarships were provided at Lumumba University, Moscow State University and various institutions throughout the USSR to students from Arab countries. The Ministry of Foreign Affairs initiated intensive comprehensive programmes for training professional Arabists to represent Soviet interests in Arab countries on a broad scale.

The Soviets did not waste time taking advantage of opportunities abandoned by the US. In this sense, the 1967 war between Israel and the Arabs is not significant from the standpoint of how it began and whether the Egyptians were warned or not. What is most important is that the Six-Day War clearly delineated the alignment of the two superpowers in the Middle East. The USSR and its allied 'progressive' bloc consisted of Egypt, Syria, Algeria, North Yemen and Iraq; the US and its 'reactionary' allies included Israel, Saudi Arabia, Morocco, the Emirates, Iran and Turkey. The Soviet Union's renewed commitment to the Arabs' cause echoed Lenin's early call to win the 'sympathy and support' of the Middle East. For the Soviets the question of peace in the Middle East after 1967 became less of an issue of peace between the Jews and the Arabs than one of a Middle East friendly to the USSR and intolerant of the US presence.

Championing the Arab Cause

To the Arabs, the words *crises*, *peace* and *settlement* mean little by now. The Arab world has become entangled in inter-Arab conflicts, many of which concern the growing influence of the PLO. The Palestinian settlement became part of the larger, barely reconcilable Arab-Jewish conflict, while approaches to the solution of this conflict ranged from Arab radicalism to various shades of Arab conservative and middle-of-the-road attitudes. Among the Arabs, the only unifying force has been their intolerance of Zionism, led (according to their perceptions) by the forces of international imperialism.

Afraid of losing prestige in the Arab World in 1967 — caused by what some Arabs saw as its apparent hesitation to commit fully all its resources to the defeat of Israel — the Soviet government had to find new ways to maintain its position in the Middle East:

Under such circumstances, one can only conclude that diplomacy alone no longer is able to cope with the overpowering problems . . . it must seek new means to execute foreign policy. It needs a 'new arm' . . . enormously powerful and influential. The new arm is propaganda.[6]

This reference to propaganda as a means to conduct foreign policy describes the direction in which the Soviet peace plan has evolved since 1967. The Soviet Union reverted to propaganda on a bilateral basis with the Egyptians, Syrians, North Yemeni, Iraqis, Algerians, Sudanese and Palestinians in order to reassure them of Soviet support. This bilateral propaganda emphasized the mutual Soviet and Arab hope of defeating Israel and retrieving the occupied territories without having to negotiate peace with the Zionists. Consequently, the Soviets found willing, sympathetic listeners. Worldwide, the USSR proclaimed itself the champion of the Arab cause and called for a free sovereign state of Palestine, to be established after the withdrawal of Israel from occupied Arab lands.

Soviet representatives at the United Nations pioneered harsh, anti-Israeli rhetoric supporting all General Assembly resolutions demanding Israeli withdrawal — examples include the 4 July 1967 Resolution on Jerusalem, Yugoslav Resolution 522, Latin American Resolution 523 — which the UN tried to devise for a Middle Eastern settlement. The Soviets reaped a bonanza of Third World Support for what was perceived as their peace-making efforts in the Middle East. The Soviet peace plan for a broader Jewish-Arab-Palestinian settlement should be called a 'thematic peace campaign' rather than a specific plan. It has served the basic campaign purposes of bringing the Arabs closer to the USSR with few specifics on exactly how peace in the Middle East should be achieved. At the same time, the Soviet government assigned the Middle East a position of strategic importance for Soviet national security. The Soviet naval presence in the Mediterranean became a source of permanent conflict, and 'Gromyko maintained that the area was within the Soviet security sphere . . . by right'.[7]

'The guidelines of the Soviet peace plan — Israeli withdrawal from the occupied lands followed by the creation of an independent, self-governed Palestine and consequent determination of the status of Jerusalem — established then still hold true today'.[8] This is obviously in conflict with American policy which had also developed in the meantime and has remained, with some variations, the American peace plan in its present form.

The polarization is clear. The Soviets want Israeli withdrawal first from all occupied lands and an independently governed Palestine. According to all Soviet official communiqués, the PLO must be the government of Palestine. Of course, neither America nor Israel will accept this. The Soviet peace plan since 1967 — through the escalation of the Israeli-Arab conflict in 1973, 1975, and the current Lebanese crisis — has related to Israeli occupation.

American decision-makers discount the Soviet position on its own merits. To them it is strictly a propaganda ploy directed against the United States. The Soviets, in turn, have labelled American support of Israel as a threat to their own national security and to any prospects for peace in the Middle East. In the context of superpower rivalry, both superpower peace plans are on a collision course. At the same time, both seem to have done their best to avoid direct confrontation.

The Machinery of Peace

The Soviets have developed a multifaceted machinery to implement their version of peace in the Middle East guided by national security interests. This machinery consists of the International Department of the Soviet Communist Party's (CPSU) Central Committee, which has groups of skilled information officers working under diplomatic cover in all Soviet embassies. The machinery also includes highly trained cadres of Arabists working for the Ministry of Foreign Affairs, the Ministry of Foreign Trade, TASS, and APN news agencies, supported by endless hours of propaganda in Arabic on Moscow Radio.

In addition, the intelligence corps consisting of the State Security Committee (KGB) and the Main Intelligence (Military) Directorate (GRU) are part of this machinery. A new breed of highly educated, linguistically fluent Middle Eastern specialists form an elite group. Many are graduates of Middle Eastern studies programmes which have been given the highest priority in the Soviet Union since 1967. Only the best students academically and intellectually are selected for admission into the Middle Eastern programmes at the Institute of International Relations and at Moscow State University. Since then, these students have formed a lobby within the Soviet foreign-policy structure, commanding a higher standard of living, faster promotion, and generally greater power.

Western analysts elaborated on the ousting of the Soviets from Egypt in 1971–3, noting the incompatibility of Communism and Islam as well as the supposedly deep-rooted differences between the Russians and the Arabs. However, it must be noted that the real strength of the Soviet position in the Arab World is only in part derived from the common Soviet-Arab position of anti-Zionism. The real strength of their position lies in Soviet foreign-policy executives who communicate on a daily basis with the Arabs. Unlike the US State Department or the Central Intelligence Agency, both of which tend to transfer their officers from country to country, the Soviets emphasize maximum area specialization, and keep their foreign affairs officers in areas where their previous expertise and established contacts can be utilized to the fullest. This is especially true of the Soviet Middle Eastern foreign-policy structure, given the strong demand for fluency in Arabic.

The majority of Soviet ambassadorial assignments to Arab countries correspond with past Middle Eastern specialization. The following men serve as examples:

(1) *Victor Minin*, ambassador to Iraq as of January 1982, headed the Near Eastern Department at the Ministry of Foreign Affairs (MFA) between 1972 and 1978.[9]

(2) *Pogos Akopov*, ambassador to Kuwait, started his career as third secretary at the embassy in Cairo in 1960; moved through the ranks to minister-counsellor by 1977; and from 1978 to 1983 worked as first deputy chief of the MFA's Near Eastern Department.[10] He is considered by many one of the top Soviet Arabists.

(3) *Oleg Peresypkin*, the newly appointed ambassador to Libya, replacing Ambassador Anatolii Anisimov,[11] is a career Middle Eastern diplomat with a track record in Iran, Jordan and Moscow. He started as an Arabic translator in Baghdad in 1965, working his way up to counsellor in Aden (1971–6) and eventually to ambassador to the Yemen Arab Republic (North) in Sanaa (1980–September 1984).

(4) *Evgenii Nersesov*[12] worked as a counsellor in Damascus from 1965 to 1969 and then as ambassador to Chad 1969–74.

(5) *Vladimir Iukhin*, a former minister-counsellor in Algeria and ambassador to Mali, is currently the ambassador to Syria.

(6) *Vladimir Zhukov*,[13] ambassador to the People's Democratic Republic of Yemen (South), is one of the most prominent experts,

in Arab affairs. His career assignments have included first secretary in Baghdad (1963–4), counsellor in Beirut (1966–71), and ambassador to Sudan (1978–82).

While Soviet ambassadors to the Middle East participate directly in and influence Soviet decision-making through annual consultative meetings at the Central Committee, the MFA's Near Eastern Department provides operational support for policy. The department is one of the largest in the MFA. It is also one of the youngest: the median officer age is 36–38. The relatively young age of these officers indicates that they were educated at the time when the USSR reconfirmed its commitment to the Arab cause. All speak Arabic in addition to one or two Western languages. Their primary Middle Eastern specialization is enhanced by background training in the behaviour of the United States and other capitalist countries in the Arab World. Many officers have strong ties with key officials in the countries where they have served. Examples are Sergei Arakelian[14] at the Egyptian desk, formerly Nasser's personal translator; Vasilii Kolotusha,[15] chief of the section covering Syria, Lebanon and Jordan; Counsellor Viktor Posuvaliuk,[16] chief translator for key Politburo members and many others of similar calibre.

New Russianism: Its Influence on Soviet Intentions

While Western analysts ponder the strategic and security goals influencing Soviet peace plans for the Middle East, they overlook one seemingly obscure but powerful peculiarity that preconditions Soviet behaviour. This is the distinct imprint made by the domestic post-1967 environment on the clannish elite of Soviet Middle Eastern experts.

It is easy to understand, of course, how the new post-1967 Soviet international objectives have shaped the thinking of the new policy-making elite cadre of Middle Eastern experts. However, the domestic environment also has imposed on this Arabist elite what David Shipler remarkably describes as 'Russianism',[17] a linking of Russian Slavic chauvinism and anti-Semitism relative to the Middle East.

Bolstered by the Soviet official press since 1967, this process was accelerated by the Jewish exodus during the period of US-Soviet detente in the early 1970s. The Jewish exodus to Israel and the US left the Russians bitter. For them it was more proof that the Jews were traitors, never loyal to Russia but always loyal to international Zionism and supported by US imperialism. Moreover, Russians could never dream of leaving their country, not even for a short while. By now, anti-Semitism in the USSR has reached such mass proportions that to be a Russian means being an anti-Semite and an anti-Zionist. This is the environment that shapes the decisions and the conduct of the present generation of the Soviet political establishment carrying out Soviet affairs in the Arab world. Of course, there are no Jews in the Ministry of Foreign Affairs, the KGB or the Central Committee's International Department.

In the West it is generally believed that the public consensus in the Soviet Union means nothing and that the government does whatever it wishes without asking the people's opinion. In some cases, like the invasion of Hungary or Czechoslovakia, it might be true. But if, for some inexplicable, improbable reason, the Soviets had decided to side with Israel in the Middle East settlement, domestic unrest would have been possible. In fact, this is the only scenario that could lead to quiet outrage in the USSR. Russianism, therefore, is a unifying factor that further strengthens sincere public support of all Soviet Middle Eastern planning and operations supportive of the Arabs.

The Thematic Campaign and 'Side' Conflicts

Since its inception in 1967, the thematic peace campaign has changed very little. Its original purpose of championing the Arabs on the Soviet side, according to Soviet observers, has been fulfilled. Now, the Middle East has entered a stage that the Soviets call 'side conflicts', which, according to their perceptions, are used by the Reagan administration for counter-propaganda purposes; that is, blaming the origins of these 'side conflicts' on the Soviets.

Last October, an official Soviet commentary noted that 'President Reagan, his Secretary of State, and Secretary of Defense stated that the isolation of the USSR from the Arab World is one of the main goals of American Near Eastern policy'[18] in view of the continuous US-Israeli dictatorial language and 'stubborn unwillingness to let the people of the Middle East return to a normal life'.[19] This reconfirms the official Soviet 'thematic peace plan':

All lands occupied by Israel since 1967 must be returned to the Arabs. It is imperative to ensure by practical means the undivided right of the Palestinian people, lawfully and solely represented by the Palestinian Liberation Front, to self-determination and the establishment of its own state in the lands that will be liberated from the Israeli occupation. The Soviet thematic plan is beginning to win some marginal support from countries that, until now, have been labeled pro-American. Even strongly pro-Western governments such as Jordan and Saudi Arabia talk with increasing seriousness of involving the Soviets in the peace process. 'The Soviets have influence in the Middle East, so some role for the Soviets would seem unavoidable', says Saudi Foreign Minister Saud Al Faisal.[20]

The Soviet thematic plan, aimed at appealing to the Arab mainstream, has never denied Israel the right to exist, which has resulted in various Soviet-PLO quarrels over the past 18 years. However, these arguments have had more tactical significance rather than being a continuous detriment to the Soviet-PLO relationship. As in the case of the Arab World at large, the political differences between the Soviets and the PLO have been overpowered by their mutual disdain for Israel. Many PLO members who spent several years studying in the USSR unquestionably feel the climate of anti-Zionism there, which further solidifies the Soviet-Palestinian bond.

Soviet handling of the switch in 1984 from Yasser Arafat to the PLO-splitters headed by Salah Khalaf is remarkable from the standpoint that it did not jeopardize the Soviet position to the extent Western observers perceived it. At a particular point Arafat became a liability within the Soviet 'thematic peace campaign'. The Soviet government felt that his seeming willingness to talk to the Americans would allow the United States to infringe on the Soviet thematic peace-making monopoly. They legitimized the switch by inviting Habash and Kubba of the Popular Front for the Liberation of Palestine (PFLP), Hawatmeh and Abd Rabbo of the Democratic Front for the Liberation of Palestine (DFLP), Nadjab of the Palestinian Communist Party, and Ya'kub of the Palestinian Liberation Front (PLF) to Moscow from 19 to 23 November 1984. The International Department of the CPSU explained the ousting of Arafat to Palestinian liberation leaders and an agreement was achieved. The participants at the meeting would support the new PLO 'based on the democratic bloc and

Fatah's Central Committee . . . while overcoming difficulties with the Palestinian liberation in order to remain an active force of the Arab anti-imperialist movement'.[21]

While the delegation was in Moscow, it was invited to observe the plenary session of the Anti-Zionist Committee of the Soviet People, an official Soviet anti-Zionist agency formed in 1983. The Palestinian leaders witnessed, first-hand, the commitment of the Soviet government and the Soviet people to fighting Zionism at home and abroad. The goal of the committee is 'to unmask the crimes of Zionism, the mortal influence of its ideology for the cause of peace, progress, and humanity; to uncover the racist policy of Israel's Zionist leadership'.[22] In its declaration, 'Zionism: Threat to Peace and Security of People', the committee called for all people in the world to 'join the fight against international Zionism and the aggressive expansionist policy of Israel in the Middle East'.[23] It could be argued that the highly sloganistic tone of such an official Soviet statement was aimed at a particular audience; namely, the Palestinian liberation leadership visiting Moscow at the time. The fact that it appeared in official Soviet newspapers and radio broadcasts, however, confirms its broader significance. The new twist, therefore, in the Soviet 'thematic peace campaign' for an Arab-Jewish settlement is its more hostile attitude towards Israel and its official open anti-Zionist militancy. Considering this radical approach, the prospects for an Arab-Jewish peace are more remote now than ever.

Side Conflicts

The past several years of continuous splits in Arab unity have somewhat overshadowed the larger Arab-Israeli peace issue. The Soviet thematic campaign has taken second place to immediate Soviet concerns in several hot and potentially hot spots on the Middle Eastern map. The USSR can no longer handle the Middle East as a whole, but tries to approach each side conflict on a case-by-case, country-by-country basis. The conflicts that concern the Soviets are similar to the world's concerns. However, their importance is determined by the degree that they represent a threat to the Soviet national security sphere. For example, the Iran-Iraq war has an immediate impact on Soviet border security, making it a priority for Soviet diplomatic and political management. The PLO conflict and the Lebanese crisis are of the same importance because the USSR is tied to a peace and friendship treaty with Syria, committing the USSR to act in support of Syria with arms supplies, economic aid and other means. The unsettled situation in Lebanon is also a source of worry for the Kremlin leadership. It continuously puts Soviet security interests, along with thousands of Soviet military advisors in Syria, under a constant peril.

Other side conflicts of lesser national security concern also demand of Soviet policy-makers and diplomats the utmost in ingenuity, skill and public-relations expertise. Among these conflicts are the Polisario issue in sub-Saharan Africa, Egyptian-Libyan problems, Libyan escapades in Chad, Algeria versus Tunisia, the Moroccan-Libyan and Moroccan-Mauritanian conflicts, and potential problems between South Yemen and Saudi Arabia. In the spring of 1983, President Mubarak of Egypt resumed relations with King Hussein and re-entered the Arab mainstream, thus closing the chapter on the Camp David Accords. The Egyptian-Jordanian bloc is supported by Iraq and Saudi Arabia but scolded by the Syrians. Soviet advisors are moving back to Egypt while the Kremlin keeps the Syrians happy, trying not to antagonize Iraq and to pacify Libya's Moammar al-Qaddafi. As for the long-term issues between Kuwait and Iraq, the Soviets are walking a thin line, selling both countries military wares and continuously re-emphasizing their commitment to both sides.

The general approach to all side conflicts does not necessarily become a peace-making proposition but a maintenance of good relations on a bilateral basis and conflict monitoring, while simultaneously winning political ground for escalating anti-American and anti-Zionist propaganda. With the exception of the Iraq-Iran war, the Soviets attribute the rest of the problems in the Arab World to Western machinations. With regard to Egypt, for instance, *Pravda* would publish an *exposé* on the activities of the Central Intelligence Agency (CIA) in Egypt in order to undermine the American presence:

American organizations connected with the CIA . . . gather secret economic, political, and military information in Egypt . . . Among them are the USIA, the Ford Fund, AID, the International Research Center of Harvard, MIT, and others . . . This suspicious 'research' conducted by CIA helpers . . . is used by Washington to block processes that may be contrary to its strategy in the region.[24]

Lebanon is a clear case of a side conflict being used to the

USSR's advantage as the sole peace-maker:

> The fiery hurricane of Israeli aggression rolled through [Lebanon] . . . And the bloody finale is the American intervention . . . and the destruction inflicted by the guns of the Sixth Fleet . . . There is no justification for the committed crimes, barbaric annihilation of Lebanon's peaceful civilians and the U.S. and Israeli actions directed against the sovereign rights of this Arab country.[25]

Translated and skilfully presented in Arabic by the new breed of Soviet diplomats, intelligence officers and information experts from the Central Committee's International Department, this type of propaganda helps the Soviets maintain a friendly footing in most of the area.

Anti-Western propaganda, however, may be inadequate. Khomeini's involvement in Lebanese hostilities has generated a new impetus to the wave of Islamic fundamentalism sweeping the Middle East. Many Arabs, particularly the young, recognize that conventional war and attrition have not produced victory over Israel or freedom from Western domination of their minds. Therefore, Islamic fundamentalism represents an untried alternative. 'Islamic fundamentalism is rising', says a Jordanian official. 'It has already spread to Lebanon and is on the rise in Algeria, Morocco and Tunisia. The countries of the Persian Gulf, particularly Saudi Arabia, are next'.[26] However, Islamic fundamentalism is particularly worrisome to the Soviets because nationalistic and religious extremism not only threaten Communism but the Soviet Union itself. Nevertheless, it is questionable that the USSR has a definite plan to deal with this growing problem, as indicated by its tentative position *vis-à-vis* the war between Iran and Iraq.

Soviet Stance on the Iran-Iraq War

Since sixteen of their diplomats were expelled from Tehran for espionage by the Khomeini government in May 1983, the Soviets have found it difficult to hide their bitter feelings toward the Iranians. Nevertheless, the Soviet press has not gone beyond very mild criticism of Iran, an indication of how extremely sensitive the Soviet position is on the Iran-Iraq war.

The Soviets are concerned about the export of Khomeini's fundamentalist revolution to Arab countries allied with the USSR.

They are afraid that it will undermine the self-proclaimed role in the peace and liberation processes which the Soviets have worked long and hard to achieve in the Arab World. They are not about to give it up by default, especially under pressure from a non-Arab dictatorship.

Soviet internal demography reveals another major factor contributing to Soviet sensitivity about the Iran-Iraq war. The following excerpts from official statistics indicate where in the USSR Khomeini fundamentalism could have impact. In essence, the Iran-Iraq war is an important Soviet national-security concern.

Table 5.1: National Composition of the Population of the USSR

Census data for 1926 and 1979, thousands		
Total population	1926	1979
Russians	77,791	137,397
Uzbeks	3,989	12,456
Azerbaijanis	1,713	5,477
Tajiks	981	2,898
Turkmenis	764	2,028
Kirghiz	763	1,906
Turks	9.8	93

Source: Central Statistical Board of the USSR, *Peoples of the USSR: Facts and Figures* (Moscow: Novosti, 1982), pp. 16–18.

Table 5.1 shows that, while the Russian population has not doubled since 1926, the population of the Soviet republics and regions inhabited by Moslems and situated close to the outside Islamic world has at least tripled, and in the case of the Soviet Turks has increased ten-fold. This trend — high birth-rates among the Soviet Moslems and very low Russian birth-rates — will soon put the USSR in an unprecedented position. The Russians will be in the minority but in charge of domestic and foreign policies. Sooner or later, the Soviet Moslems, probably within the next 20 years, will reach a majority status. Since there is a compulsory military draft in the Soviet armed forces, the minoritization and Islamization of the armed forces must be expected. The Islamic revival is already evident in the Soviet Islamic republics. Mosques operate quite openly; children at schools are encouraged by their parents to study their native language. The Islamic families of the southern portion of the USSR have stronger unity and mutual support while the Russians are experiencing high divorce-rates, extreme alcoholism problems and poor labour discipline. Soviet Moslems enjoy better living standards than do their Russian counterparts in the north due to entrepreneurship based on climate and children's help to their parents on small family agricultural plots.

Immediately a series of questions comes to mind. How would predominantly Russian commanders communicate their commands to soldiers who cannot speak Russian well? Would the soldier be loyal to Islam first and Moscow second? Moreover, the fear of a fundamentalist spillover onto Soviet territory, however officially unexpressed, is on the mind of decision-makers in the Politburo and the Ministry of Foreign Affairs. Should the spillover occur, Soviet Moslems — especially the 6 million Shi'ites in Azerbaijan — could represent a potentially destabilizing force for the whole Soviet system. It is from this standpoint that the Soviet plan (or lack of one) to end the war between Iran and Iraq must be evaluated.

Except for a short outburst of criticism toward the Khomeini regime after the expulsion of Soviet personnel and the jailing of Tudeh leaders in 1983, the Soviets have maintained a tactful stance on the war. The Soviet press has neither criticized the war nor questioned Iran's and Iraq's intentions. The Soviets treat the war as if it just happened because hostilities may occur from time to time between neighbours. In fact, both sides are occasionally praised for correct conduct in the war. *Pravda* writes: 'Artillery exchange continues on the Iran-Iraqi front. However, both sides behave in accordance with the mutually recognized commitment to refrain from attacking civilian targets and populated city and village districts'.[27] This is typical coverage of the war by the Soviet press. When the Soviets report losses on each side, the attitude is 'war is war and people get killed'. While the Soviet-Iranian relationship is far from smooth, the Soviets continue to maintain a façade of friendship by maintaining the so-called 'working visits' to Tehran by Soviet officials. In 1984 Tehran was visited by two Soviet cultural delegations, the Ministry of Foreign Trade and the State Committee for Foreign Economic Aid.

Unquestionably, the Soviet annexation of Afghanistan has had a negative effect on Soviet-Iranian relations. However, as the Soviets maintain good relationships with the Arabs in the Arab-Israeli conflict through mutual identification of a common enemy — that is, Israel and Zionism, supported by the United States — they identify the same common enemy in Iran's conflicts, i.e. Israel, Zionism and the United States. Accordingly, the Soviets offered a helping hand to Afghanistan against the machinations of the CIA, the common enemy. Whether the Iranians buy this story or not, the rhetoric sounds good at least to the Soviets.

The Soviets have been equally cautious in handling relations with the Iraqis. Contrary to the opinion of some American experts, Iraq is not a Soviet satellite. To be sure, Soviet military advisors have been present in Iraq since 1968. The Soviets have provided Iraq with many items in its military arsenal, including tanks, air-to-ground missiles and combat arms. However, the present government of Saddam Hussein is also keeping its door open to Western and American business, technology and military wares. He is using the West's deep animosity towards Khomeini's revolution to his own ends.

The Soviets are clearly concerned by the increasing Western presence in Iraq, but they are powerless to stop it. The Soviets are aware that one of Khomeini's objectives in the war against Iraq is to liberate the Iraqi Shi'ites. The population of Iraq is predominantly Shi'ite. Saddam Hussein is Sunni. If the Soviets tried to undermine Hussein's position there is, they fear, the possibility that it might provoke a fundamenalist Shi'ite uprising to the benefit of Iran. Iraq could lose the war. Fundamentalism would make a giant leap. The net effect would not be in the interests of the Soviet Union.

Therefore, the Soviets relate to the Iraqis on the basis of bilateralism. Both countries have an established framework of bilateral treaties on peace, friendship and economic and technical co-operation. Within this framework an example of bilateralism is the visit to Baghdad by Soviet Deputy Prime Minister Ia. P. Riabov from 1 to 3 October 1984, to discuss bilateral co-operation in various spheres. 'Both sides stressed their mutual thrust to further strengthen friendly relations between the USSR and Iraq . . . in the development of Soviet-Iraqi economic and technical cooperation', reports *Pravda*.[28]

While there is no evidence that the USSR is planning to influence Iran and Iraq to end the war, there is evidence that the Soviets are using the war issue to gain respectability in the Persian Gulf area. Their goal is to paint the United States as an interventionist in the Iran-Iraq war:

Washington had an interest in draining the natural and human resources of both countries [Iran and Iraq], as well as of the whole region which has since undergone certain changes. The White House does not like it. Currently the Pentagon is using the escalation of military activities to impose its military presence in the Persian Gulf and to turn it into a launching pad for achieving the global strategic designs of American imperialism.[29]

Pravda also adds:

American intelligence planes constantly fly over the airspace of the countries of this region [the Persian Gulf]. By acting in this manner, Washington is attempting to re-establish its position, which has deteriorated following the shameful failure of its neocolonialist plot in Lebanon.[30]

Obviously, the USSR is using the war between Iraq and Iran as well as the unsettled climate in the Persian Gulf to rally the Gulf states against the United States and against any peace proposals it may make. At the same time the Soviets, who have not been able to come up with an Iran-Iraq peace plan on their own, hope to use this anti-American paranoia as a counterbalance to the growing threat of Islamic fundamentalism.

In the Middle East, however, propaganda, proclamations, stances, alliances and general posturing rarely reflect reality. The weakness of Arab regimes, the upcoming power struggle after Khomeini's death, and a possible reduction in Soviet anti-American rhetoric are all factors to be considered. Additionally, if a new Soviet-American detente is somehow achieved, the Soviet Union might tone down its anti-American propaganda campaign. Given the possibility of any number of such changes taking place in the region, therefore, it is worthwhile to examine what hard gains the Soviets have achieved in the Middle East beyond mere anti-American agitation.

They have definitely managed to hang on in Iraq and Iran without relinquishing much of their interest in either. However, even more importantly the war has given them an opportunity to patch up some problems in the area from before the war. On 10 October 1984 the USSR signed a comprehensive treaty of friendship and cooperation with the Yemen Arab Republic (North). It is stronger by far than the treaties signed in 1928 and 1964. One should expect that the Soviet Union and North Yemen are back on the road toward an intimate friendship. The treaty signing ceremony was an elaborate event chaired by Chernenko and attended by most Politburo members.

In South Yemen the USSR has attained the role of the older brother to whom the Yemenis look up. During the festivities in Aden on 25 October 1984, commemorating the fifth anniversary of the treaty of peace, friendship and co-operation between the Soviet Union and South Yemen, Abdel Gani Abdel Kader, member of the Politburo of the Yemeni Socialist Party, expressed the Yemeni people's 'deep thanks to the Soviet Union for its comprehensive aid to Yemen to gain important socio-economic achievements'.[31]

Two observations are important regarding Soviet tactics and strategy. First, the Soviets handle complex issues on a bilateral basis. Secondly, Americans look at the world in a fashion similar to that in which they watch a Hollywood movie that has a happy ending. American foreign-policy makers look for solutions and happy endings where there may be none. The Soviets view the world as a continuous crisis. Therefore, local conflicts like the war between Iraq and Iran need not have a happy resolution with the actors riding off into the sunset. What counts is whether the interests of Soviet national security can be furthered or jeopardized in this Soviet 'national security sphere'.

War in Lebanon: Towards a Peace Conference

The Soviet position in the Lebanese conflict is not as complex as it is in the Iran-Iraq war. Nevertheless, the USSR must be very careful not to antagonize its Syrian and Libyan allies. While the Soviet position in the Persian Gulf is to maintain neutrality and reap the benefits of anti-American propaganda on a bilateral basis, the USSR is clearly committed to the Syrian side in the Lebanese war. According to Soviet publications, the enemy side is clearly defined: Israel, the United States, and their puppets.

Until the Camp David Accords, Lebanon did not figure prominently in Soviet Middle Eastern politics. Although Lebanon was the best location for diplomatic, trade and intelligence assignments, it was not in the main line of the Soviet thematic peace campaign in the Middle East. Soviet liaison with the PLO and PLO factions in Beirut was severely complicated by the presence of many other foreign intelligence organizations in the country, and fears that the PLO in Beirut was infiltrated by the Americans and the British. Contrary to the opinions of certain Western analysts, the Soviets were not controlling the PLO or Palestinian factions in Beirut, including Yasser Arafat.

Of course, this does not mean there was no close relationship; the relationship was friendly, supportive and broad. However, since 1970 the Soviets have put much emphasis on working with the PLO based in Damascus, a safe area relatively free from foreign intelligence operatives. With thousands of Palestinians routed to the Soviet Union and the bloc countries for training, the Damascus connection grew stronger. Nevertheless, the non-Kremlin-controlled PLO based in Beirut continued in the meantime to branch out.

The family feud between PLO factions and various religious, ethnic and terrorist groups has made it impossible for the Soviets to maintain a definitive political course in Lebanon. On the one hand, the Soviets have always been committed to supporting the PLO; on the other hand, they have been careful not to be identified with extremist Palestinian terrorist groups, many of which used Beirut for their operational headquarters.

The Camp David Accords helped the Soviets to crystallize their positions on the PLO generally and in Beirut in particular. To the Soviets, the peace agreement between Israel and Egypt meant the radicalization of the Arab World. First, it radicalized the Arab states that identified the agreement as an American-Israeli plot that denied forever the establishment of a Palestinian state. Secondly, it radicalized the PLO itself, especially in Beirut. Therefore, the Soviets decided to commit themselves completely to political, ideological and military support of the well-organized and highly controlled Damascus organization. The choice was clear: the Damascus-based PLO enjoyed the blessings of the USSR's main Arab ally, Syria. Yasser Arafat was sacrificed well before the Israeli invasion and occupation of southern Lebanon for what the Kremlin leadership felt was a far more stable relationship with the Damascus-based PLO dissidents.

The Israeli occupation, the Syrian response, the struggle between the Salah-Jibril group and the Arafat followers for control of the PLO, the proliferation of the Islamic Jihad movement, the Sabra and Shatilla massacres, the bombings of the US marines and the embassy — these were all tragic results of US plans to retain its foothold in the Middle East. According to the Soviets:

[Butchery] and the crimes against the civilian population of

Lebanon during the barbaric Israeli invasion can only be compared to the practices of the Nazis during the Second World War. The Reagan Administration, which backed and coordinated the barbaric Israeli invasion and which is still supporting the aggressive and expansionist policy of Israel, has recently exercised its right of veto in the Security council on the situation in southwest Lebanon and the Bekaa Valley.[32]

Such denunciations are a trademark of the official Soviet press:

Powers connected with Israel and the U.S. have tried to realize their goals in Lebanon, prevent its democratic development, split it from the Arab World, tie it to the chariot of imperialism and Zionism, and turn it into a base for achieving their aggressive designs for the region.[33]

The Soviets see the Lebanese crisis, like the Camp David Accords, as an attempt by the United States and Israel to further split the Arab World. Therefore, they applauded the Lebanese government when it annulled the Lebanese-Israeli agreement of 17 May 1983. The Soviets took the initiative toward the government of National Unity. The first step was a recognition of Rashid Karame's joining forces with the Amal movement and the Progressive Socialist Party in the early autumn of 1984. Several Soviet delegations visited Beirut and expressed their support to Karame. Simultaneously, the Soviets won Arab sympathy by pressing on a bilateral basis and via mass communications in the United Nations for an Israeli withdrawal.

The second step was the Soviet-Syrian communiqué signed in Moscow on 18 October 1984 by Hafez al-As'ad and Konstantin Chernenko. It sealed the significance of the previously signed friendship treaty between the USSR and Syria. Its content, however, dealt with border problems of a Middle East peace and especially the war in Lebanon. Special attention was devoted to the split in the Arab World and to the prospects for Arab unity:

The sides once again confirmed their firm condemnation of the Camp David agreements and the policy of all separate deals which might activate them . . . The USSR and Syria are identical in their belief that the real interests of the Arab people demand the unity of anti-imperialist, patriotic forces of all Arab countries to fight imperialism and Zionism and to achieve a just and lasting peace in the Middle East.[34]

Obviously, for the Soviets Camp David was evil; Arab unity is the key to peace in the Middle East. This is also true regarding Lebanon, where the Soviets endorsed the government of National Unity for peace. None of this was possible, according to this communiqué, so long as Israel remained in the occupied territories, East Jerusalem and southern Lebanon.

Having achieved progress in its relationship with the Karame government and solid footing with the PLO in Damascus, the USSR came up with a 'showpiece' peace plan for Lebanon. Counting on broad Arab support and US bickering, the Soviets called for an international peace conference. Although not necessarily new — the USSR called for an international conference in 1967 in support of Security Council Resolution 242, which never passed — this initiative addresses broader subjects, i.e. not only the Arab-Israeli conflict but also the Iran-Iraq war, which the Soviets call 'senseless', and the Lebanese crisis. However, the Soviets estimated that this time an international peace conference had a better chance despite a US-Israeli boycott: King Hussein of Jordan and the Egyptians initially supported the idea and the Syrians, the new PLO and Karame's government all were eager to participate. This would legitimize their positions in the Arab world, of course, and ensure Soviet guarantees of their support.

As for the Lebanese crisis, the Soviets saw the conference as the only way out. They trusted neither the consequences of an Israeli withdrawal nor a Syrian pull-out after the Israeli withdrawal. The Soviets appeared to be moving toward open diplomacy without hiding their economic, political and military support for Syria.

The Case of a Distant Side Conflict

The Soviets did not include the Western Saharan conflict between the Polisario and Morocco and Mauritania in the agenda of their proposed international conference.[36] The Polisario fits the Soviet category of a national liberation movement, i.e. oppressed people struggling for independence. The Polisario rejected the division of the Western Sahara between Morocco and Mauritania and announced the creation of the Saharan Arab Democratic Republic (SADR) in 1976. Both Libya and Algeria recognized it immediately and supported it with arms and money.

Two problems arose instantly for Soviet policy-makers: (i) how to end the Polisario's military operations without antagonizing its allies Libya and Algeria; and (ii) how not to break a long-standing relationship with Morocco without compromising Soviet prestige as the leader of the national liberation movement. The Soviet handling of the Western Sahara conflict reflects the larger pattern of shift in Soviet global and regional (Middle Eastern) diplomacy to bilateralism with strong anti-Western, especially anti-American, propaganda undertones. Continuously emphasizing that the war is far too expensive for Morocco and Mauritania, the Kremlin singled out Morocco in the 'Arab World' category. Mauritania remained on the periphery of the issues important to Soviet policy until 1979, when it relinquished its claims to the southwestern Sahara under pressure from Libya and Algeria. Whether the pressure was orchestrated by the USSR remains a guessing game. However, so far as the Soviet position in the area was concerned, half the problem was solved.

The Moroccan-Polisario conflict, which has remained unresolved, took a lot more than pressure or substantial economic incentives given to Mauritania. In its physical manifestations this conflict is small. It is not as bloody as the war between Iran and Iraq. It is not a family war like the one in Beirut. It is the farthest Near Eastern conflict from the Soviet border. Nevertheless, its significance for the Soviets in the Arab World is not necessarily of lower ranking. It may influence Soviet relations with Libya, Algeria and Morocco. It is also crucial to its prestige with member countries of the Organization of African Unity; a continuous flow of convertible currency from Libya; and a strong naval presence in the Mediterranean.

Considering all the above aspects, the Soviets have been careful in formulating any definitive plan to solve the conflict. Except for cease-fire calls and warnings to the Moroccans and the Polisario to exercise caution and to look for a common ground, the USSR has avoided any involvement. Instead, the Soviets have followed the proven path of anti-American propaganda, i.e. 'revealing' US plans to give arms to Morocco to fight the Polisario, send American military advisors, and so on, which would lead to a bloody war. Most Arabs, especially the Libyans and Algerians, are appeased by the rhetoric which apparently has taken the edge off the Soviet's lack of commitment to the Polisario.

From 1979 to the present, the Soviets have concentrated their efforts on strengthening bilateral relations with Libya, which has entered a network of agreements with the USSR, with Algeria — which recently signed a protocol between the Front of National Liberation and the CPSU on mutual co-operation — and particularly with Morocco. According to the Soviets, bilateralism is better than a relationship with desperadoes; moreover, two-way deals with Arab countries are more favourable for the Soviets in the Arab World at large. The Soviet Press avoids mentioning the Saharawi Arab Democratic Republic (SADR) of the Polisario. Emphasis is given to the development of bilateral relations, including Soviet-Moroccan co-operation.

Recently, *Pravda* published a lengthy article about Soviet-Moroccan relations, entitled 'On Mutual Ground: USSR-Morocco, Horizons of Cooperation'. The article, published under the official editorial rubric, went into considerable detail describing various facets of Soviet-Moroccan economic, scientific and agricultural co-operation. It noted that the USSR is the main supplier of petroleum to Morocco and is willing to move from convertible currency-payment receipts to barter.

This is a remarkable statement since the USSR has a severe shortage of convertible currency. Obviously, it must have been a top political priority for the Kremlin to forgo the demand for hard currency. It is a valid indicator of the Soviets' interest in keeping Morocco on its side. *Pravda* quotes King Hassan II as saying that 'Morocco and the USSR wish to establish exemplary relations which will ensure the reduction of international tension and will achieve a real peace'.[36]

Given the present state of affairs, it is unlikely that the USSR will offer any kind of peace plan for the Western Sahara. So far as Soviet objectives in the area are concerned, it is clearly not a priority nor a vital necessity. The Soviet ability to maintain excellent relations with countries in conflict with one another is truly remarkable.

The Future: Is There a Way Out?

In an article on Soviet plans for a comprehensive Middle Eastern settlement, a noted Soviet Arabist, Piotr Demchenko, states that the

   prolonged character of the Near Eastern crisis had led some

foreign circles to believe that it is impossible to establish lasting peace in this part of the planet. The occurrence and continuation of side conflicts along with the Arab-Israel conflict, like the Iran-Iraq war and internal Lebanese conflicts, seem to lend credence to such thinking.[37]

While placing the blame for the Middle East crises as usual on Tel Aviv and Washington, the article expresses concern that the new 'strategic alliance' between Israel and the United States will further escalate an already explosive situation.

The Soviets apparently desire peace. In any case, they want to sound optimistic. On the one hand, they indicate that a peaceful Middle Eastern settlement is impossible given the current American posture, particularly the American-Israeli strategic alliance and its huge aid package for Israel. On the other hand, the new Soviet bilateralism that characterizes its approach to Middle Eastern issues allows the Soviets a certain pragmatism. Unlike the ideological constraints of Marxism, the new approach allows for flexibility.

There is also a growing realization inside the USSR that the demographic trends, especially the growing Moslem population, must be taken seriously. In January 1984 the Central Statistical Department of the USSR made a brief announcement of an immediate partial census. Unlike most projects of this sort in the Soviet system, this apparently was not planned well in advance. It appeared to be something of an emergency, an indication of Moscow's anxiety about Soviet minorities. Moreover, the results of the partial census have yet to be made public.

Translated into the terms of Soviet Near Eastern planning, this concern will further pragmatize Soviet relations with the Arabs. The Soviet Press is beginning to acknowledge the phenomenon of Islamic fundamentalism and to indicate official concern. It is definitely opposed to the 'extremist Moslem organization Al-Jihad Al-Islami'[38] and its actions against American personnel. In opposing Moslem fundamentalism, the USSR is likely to find understanding partners among moderate Arab governments — such as those in Jordan, Saudi Arabia, Kuwait, Qatar, the Emirates and Bahrain — which fear the spread of fundamentalism and a more severe split in Arab unity. The Soviets consider fundamentalism a three-headed hydra that may pose a threat to their national security, a challenge to their hard-earned preponderance in the Arab World, and a threat to the peace process on which the Soviets feel they have a patent.

The Soviets are also worried about the growing military capabilities of Israel, evident when Israeli troops marched through southern Lebanon and when the Soviet ground-to-air rockets could not shoot down Israeli planes and themselves became 'sitting ducks' on the ground. The Soviet military was undoubtedly and unpleasantly surprised by Israeli technological sophistication. The military role and potential of Israel have grown tenfold in the eyes of Soviet military experts as well as policy-makers. The propaganda campaign against the Israeli military was pursued both on a bilateral Soviet-Arab basis and at the UN level, where the Soviet Deputy Representative, P. S. Ovinnikov, stated:

> The U.S. systematically shares the responsibility for the Israeli crimes. Israel's refusal to join the Treaty on Non-Proliferation of Nuclear Arms and to put its nuclear installations under the control of the International Agency for Nuclear Energy proves its desire to possess nuclear weapons for the establishment of its rule in the Near East. According to a report published last week by the Carnegie Endowment for International Peace, Israel already has twenty nuclear bombs.[39]

The active measures undertaken by the Soviet government against what they perceive as a dangerous Israeli military edge over the Arabs will add more heated rhetoric to the campaign conducted by the USSR both in the Arab World and on a larger global scale. Besides being sharply anti-Israeli, the campaign is assuming a new dimension, namely, to widen the differences between the United States and its Western European allies on the search for peace in the Middle East. The Soviets are beginning to distinguish between Western Europe and the United States. If their propaganda in the 1960s and 1970s was aimed at undermining all Western influence in the area — including that of Great Britain, France, West Germany, Italy — now it depicts only the United States in a negative light to the Arabs. Other European countries are hailed for their 'constructive attitudes' regarding Middle Eastern problems. For example, the Soviets welcomed an Italian initiative to assert a stronger Western European, as opposed to American, role 'in the plan to create conditions favorable to the solution of the Near Eastern problem'.[40] Commenting on the newly concluded economic agreement between Italy and Egypt on 21 November 1984, the Soviet press went so far as to say in a positive tone that 'the Cairo visit by the Italian leadership resulted in the further development of Italian-Egyptian cooperation in the military area'.[41]

Soviet military advisors in Iraq work side-by-side with French military specialists. The latest arms sales by Greece to Libya, supposedly a monopoly of Soviet military procurement, also show that the USSR is trying to avoid any adversarial relations with Western Europe while at the same time escalating its active political stance against the United States. The historical experience of the Soviet presence in the Middle East clearly shows that a priority has always been given to avoiding direct superpower confrontation that may be caused by local Middle Eastern conflicts. The USSR abstained from direct military involvement in the Suez crisis, the US marine landings in Lebanon, the 1967 war, the 'hot' conflicts of 1973 and 1975, and more recently, Syrian actions in Lebanon, as well as the Iran-Iraq war. Quite often the USSR has abstained even at the expense of possibly losing face *vis-à-vis* its allies, as happened immediately after the 1967 war when the Middle East experienced a short anti-Soviet backlash, and recently when the USSR kept hesitating on support for the PLO as it was removed from Beirut.

Since the avoidance of a larger Soviet-American conflict seems to be one of the main motivating forces of Soviet Middle Eastern policy, the USSR will continue to be extremely cautious in formulating peace plans and making obligations and firm commitments in local wars or peripheral conflicts. For example, this direction is evident in Soviet policy *vis-à-vis* the Iran-Iraq war, the Lebanese crisis and the Polisario issue. This is the main direction in which Soviet policy will develop in the future.

The other direction depends on what the Soviet government perceives as a process of mutual, worldwide weariness with war. After the Geneva talks Soviet Foreign Minister Andrei Gromyko described this process as follows:

> In general, I must say, during the past several years the majority of the countries in the world, even those that have no heart-warming relations with us, are instinctively, I repeat, instinctively driven to support those proposals that help prevent war and strengthen peace.[42]

Based on this perception, there is no doubt that the Soviet Union intends to broaden its peace campaign for the Middle East in order to reach a wide international consensus in support of a larger Soviet peace plan:

Complete and just Middle Eastern settlement based on the full and unconditional Israeli withdrawal from all occupied Arab territories after 1967, including East Jerusalem, on the fulfillment of undivided national rights of the Palestinian people, including its rights to create its own independent state, and the return to their home in accordance with U.N. resolutions.[43]

The USSR will continue to present this platform at every international forum on the Middle East. It would be the keynote of the international conference on the Middle East, which the USSR proposed and intends to lead. So far the Soviets claim that up to 120 countries have agreed to participate, making it one of the largest international forums. Therefore, if the United States refused to attend it would generate considerable international feeling against the American position on the Middle East.

The third direction in Soviet planning for the Middle East is the new bilateralism. This trend will continue quite strongly into the next century. Some Middle East experts might argue that one cannot be a friend to everybody. Moreover, it is often said that the Arabs do not trust the Soviets. In effect, these two factors will indeed cause a rift between the USSR and the Arabs, accelerated by the proliferation of Islamic fundamentalism.

To be sure, there is some truth to this observation. Nevertheless, there is one important aspect of Soviet policy which may counter this negative development, i.e. the Soviet-Arab mutual perception and identification of a common enemy: Israel and international Zionism. This mutuality of interests is complemented by the Soviets' unsurpassed capability in developing skilful and knowledgeable Middle Eastern, particularly Arabic, expertise. When any situation worsens, human contacts play a most important role. By now the Soviets have established significant ties in the Middle East.

Notes

1. *Pravda*, 9 November 1984.
2. Ministerstvo Inostrannykh Del, *Dokumenty vneshnei politiki SSSR*, vol. 1

(Moscow, 1957), pp. 43–4.

3. Ibid., p. 175.

4. Ivo J. Lederer and Wayne S. Vucinich (eds), *The Soviet Union and the Middle East* (Stanford, Calif.: Hoover Institution Press, 1974), p. 9.

5. J. C. Hurewitz (ed.), *Soviet-American Rivalry in the Middle East* (New York: Praeger, 1971), p. 2.

6. Kurt London, *Permanent Crisis* (Toronto: Xerox College Publishing, 1968), p. 198.

7. Willard A. Beling (ed.), *The Middle East: Quest for an American Policy* (Albany: State University of New York Press, 1973), p. 212.

8. Ibid., p. 271.

9. Central Intelligence Agency, Directorate of Intelligence, *Directory of the USSR Ministry of Foreign Affairs*, CR 83-12416 (1983), p. 36.

10. Ibid., p. 37.

11. Ibid., p. 38.

12. Ibid., p. 39.

13. Ibid., p. 45.

14. Ibid., p. 14.

15. Ibid.

16. Ibid.

17. David Shipler, *Russia: Broken Idols, Solemn Dreams* (New York: Penguin Books, 1984), p. 344.

18. *Pravda*, 27 October 1984, 4.

19. Ibid.

20. *The Wall Street Journal*, 11 December 1984.

21. *Pravda*, 24 November 1984, 5.

22. Ibid.

23. Ibid.

24. Ibid., 31 August 1984.

25. Ibid., 15 October 1984.

26. *The Wall Street Journal*, 11 December 1984.

27. *Pravda*, 16 June 1984.

28. Ibid., 5 October 1984.

29. Ibid., 16 June 1984.

30. Ibid., 20 June 1984.

31. Ibid., 26 October 1984.

32. *Flashes*, 39, Prague, 28 September 1984.

33. *Pravda*, 12 November 1984.

34. Ibid., 19 October 1984.

35. The Arab Meghreb falls within the definition of the Middle East.

36. *Pravda*, 27 August 1984.

37. Ibid., 27 October 1984.

38. Ibid., 23 September 1984.

39. Ibid., 11 November 1984.

40. Ibid., 22 November 1984.

41. Ibid.

42. Ibid., 14 January 1985.

43. Ibid., 19 October 1984.

6 WEST EUROPEAN PEACE DIPLOMACY IN THE LEVANT: BUT WILL THEY COME?

Adam M. Garfinkle

Introduction

It is a truism that the Arab-Israeli dispute is an international problem, involving dozens of nations directly and indirectly. Military manifestations of the dispute have had and may again have global economic repercussions. Diplomacy and war in the Middle East pit the United States and the Soviet Union against each other, and these interactions in turn affect US-Soviet relations more broadly conceived. Through the United Nations, nearly the entire 'community of nations' has taken sides on the dispute, colouring the articulation of the issues and affecting the functioning of the UN itself. As a collision of competing nationalisms — Jewish and Palestinian Arab — that involves as well important 'non-state actors', some observers inclined toward abstractions profess to see patterns of evolution in global society at work. Finally, of course, the Arab-Israeli dispute is international in the sense that proposals for its solution or amelioration have come from many quarters, including Western Europe. That is the special interest of this chapter.

The beginning of wisdom in approaching this subject is to recognize that the political statements of individual West European countries, and the European Economic Community (EEC) as a whole, differ in their very nature from those of the local protagonists and those of the superpowers. Peace proposals put forward by the Arab states, by Palestinian groups, by Israel, by the United States and, to a lesser extent, by the Soviet Union can have, at least potentially, a direct bearing on the outcome of intersecting diplomatic, political and military strategies. This is because, for the local actors, very vital interests are very directly engaged. It is so for the superpowers because of their potential to help or hurt in concrete fashion the interests of the local protagonists. But Western Europe lacks the power to help or hurt the local parties in any decisive way. Just as important, European interests in the political core of the Arab-Israeli dispute are subsidiary to more parochial European

115

economic and strategic interests. West European countries can be hurt by the disputes of the Middle East, but there is little they can do directly to reduce their vulnerabilities.

Any analyst who seeks to grapple with the whys and wherefores of West European peace diplomacy toward the Middle East in recent years — most especially toward Arab-Israeli problems — must therefore confront the troublesome reality that there is both more and less to this diplomacy than first meets the eye. Unless a writer begins with his conclusions already embedded in his premises — and this is, regrettably, not an uncommon phenomenon in this neck of the woods[1] — the honest author ought to commence by alerting the honest reader as to just what is really at issue. This chapter endeavours to do just that.

In a presentation of this length, the assumption of any further analytical ambitions would likely result in an erosion of coherence. In particular, this chapter does not aspire to review the chronicle of events over the past decade and a-half, this having been done already both by this writer and by others,[2] but instead to stand back from the details and offer a synoptic interpretation of what has transpired. The narrative may at times seem to take the subject a bit far from the central issues, but that is undoubtedly because some readers may have a faulty impression of what is and is not central. By way of illustration, the chapter will discuss briefly two fairly recent clusters of events: the first having to do with the ill-fated Multinational Force that shared the tragedy and frustrations of the Lebanese crucible; and the second concerning the less dramatic, but no less illustrative, adventures of the Italian government during the winter of 1984–5.

The Emperor Has No Clothes

In what sense is Western Europe's Middle Eastern peace diplomacy less than meets the eye? Since the states of Western Europe are not themselves located in the Middle East and are not direct parties to the conflict between Israel and its Arab neighbours, we are presumably speaking of West European diplomacy as the diplomacy of a mediator. Mediators can be of two sorts: those whose good offices are invited by parties on both sides in the hope that a judicious, but prodding, neutrality might move reluctant and emotionally estranged parties toward one another; and those who for their own vested interests insinuate themselves into the affairs of others for purposes predicated not so much on fairness or peace for its own sake as on removing obstacles to the pursuit of their own objectives. If Western Europe's diplomacy in the Middle East is mediatory, as many assume, of which variety is it?

It is most certainly not that judicious, prodding neutrality, though West European politicians and bureaucrats often have insisted that it is. At no time since the June 1967 War has Israel considered Western Europe, as constituted collectively in the EEC or individual West European countries, as an acceptable mediator. As early as the ill-fated Four Powers Talk of 1969,[3] Israel harboured strong suspicions that West European mediation was likely to be detrimental to its interests as well as likely to prove a nuisance to the only promising mediation available — that of the United States. Following the 'oil shock' of 1973–4, Israelis viewed West European mediation with a disdain and a hostility roughly proportional to — in their view — Western Europe's fawning at the feet of the Arab oil parvenus.[4] So there has not been, since 1967, an Israeli 'invitation' to the EEC.

Nor for that matter have the Arab parties taken a unanimously positive attitude toward EEC or individual member-state mediation. Certain Arab states, notably Saudi Arabia, Egypt, and especially Hashemite Jordan, have at times used European statements and activities to further their own local, inter-Arab agendas.[5] The PLO has been deeply concerned and hopeful about European efforts, but in general very disappointed with European results despite the protestation of European policrats[6] that what they really want to do most is to help the PLO best promote the rights of the Palestinians. Syrian commentary on West European efforts has been for the most part abusively unpleasant.

Have the West Europeans then been self-serving mediators? Here too there are two types. The first is not typically described as diplomatic mediation but as diplomatic pressure, the most extreme form of which is intervention. US diplomacy in the latter stages of the October 1973 war is a good example. The United States virtually forced Israel to stop the fighting, thereby saving the entrapped Egyptian Third Army, although neither Egypt nor Israel directly asked Washington to do so. Subsequent negotiations, leading first to 'kilometre 101', later to two Israeli-Egyptian disengagement agreements, and ultimately a treaty of peace, involved numerous examples of somewhat milder pressure. The very liberal use of US pressure against Israel is today heartily recommended by a host of Third World pundits and their European and American sympathizers.[7] Yet if the United States were to undertake such actions to separate not Arabs and Israelis, but Indians and Pakistanis, Somalis and Ethiopians, or Iraqis and Iranians, then no doubt these same pundits would decry such action as neo-imperialist gunboat diplomacy. They would be correct. That they nevertheless persist in recommending such a policy when it is to be aimed at Israel reminds us of La Rochefoucauld's witticism: we all have the strength to endure the misfortunes of others.[8]

It is clear that, right or wrong, the use of such pressure requires complementary powers to harm and to help in sufficient amount and proportion to promise success. In the Middle East only the United States has demonstrated such an ability. Western Europe has not and cannot. First, it lacks military power in the region. When West European troops *have* been deployed in the area — in the Sinai and in Beirut — they have come in tandem with American forces in the context of a diplomacy guided by the United States. Indeed, even the success or failure of these deployments has corresponded directly to the vicissitudes of US policy. US policy is succeeding in the Sinai and the West Europeans are succeeding with it; US policy failed in Beirut and the Europeans failed with it.[9] Secondly, Europe lacks not only sticks, but also carrots. Whereas American wealth can and has played a positive role in undergirding peace, as in the US-sponsored Egyptian-Israeli relationship, Western Europe's financial weakness has tended to erode the balance and independence of its diplomacy, and therefore its general credibility. When the weak deign to advertise rewards, the strong prepare their tables.

The second variety of self-helping mediation is also not typically called mediation, but appeasement. Some believe that West European diplomacy fits this mould quite well; disagreement centres over whether it is an ignoble diplomacy or a pragmatic adaptation to new realities. Appeasement describes a diplomacy that endeavours to barter asymmetrical values. One side agrees to sacrifice a subsidiary value in order to enhance a more central value. The second side agrees, because what is subsidiary to the first party is central to it, and what is central to the other side is subsidiary to it. To be explicit, economic considerations have been, and remain, foremost in Western Europe's Middle East diplomacy. This has been the case at least since 1973, if not also before. Political considerations have generally been more important for most of the Arab actors. Therefore, West European states, and the EEC as a whole, have been increasingly willing over time to promote certain Arab desiderata, especially with regard to the PLO. Since 1980 the EEC has declared the PLO to be a legitimate interlocutor in Middle East diplomacy, and has urged that it be 'associated' with existing and future negotiating fora notwithstanding its refusal to accept United Nations Security Council Resolutions 242 and 338. Moreover, some European states have urged mutual and simultaneous recognition by Israel and the Palestinians of each other's rights, which in practice entails a demand that Israel accept the PLO's self-proclaimed domination of Palestinian politics. Most European states also overwhelmingly interpret Resolution 242 as implying *total* Israeli withdrawal from territories occupied in 1967, presumably including East Jerusalem. Finally, although most official proclamations have been deliberately ambiguous, most favour an independent Palestinian state to be established in the West Bank and Gaza when Israel leaves.

In return for all of this, the Arab states have declined to go out of their way to injure European economic interests in the region. This is about as charitably as one can put it. West European states have received no special favours from Arab oil-producers with respect to the price or supply of petroleum. Ironically, the state-to-state oil-for-arms deals that proliferated during the middle 1970s actually functioned to dilute the protective role played by the international oil companies.[10] It is true that West European exports to the Middle East have increased considerably, and that some West European states have even borrowed money from Saudi Arabia. But given the economic balance-of-interests, it is hard to understand any of this as entailing sacrifice. The Arab states positively desire European goods and require European markets. As for lending money, that is often good business too, or banking would not be such a remunerative career. There is no clear evidence that the Arab states would have balked at mutually beneficial economic arrangements with Western Europe even in the absence of Europe's willingness to take the Arab side on some selected issues.[11]

Thus, the tilt of European diplomacy in the Middle East, as it developed in the 1970s, may be characterized as an insurance policy against unlikely, but not impossible disaster. If one believes that the premiums on this policy have been actively solicited by the very source of potential catastrophe, then one might instead characterize the relationship as paying for protection — the 'deal you can't refuse'. Needless to say, observers disagree about which metaphor is most appropriate. The evidence suggests that West European governments generally have elected to assume the worst and, erring on the side of safety, have engaged in a form of anticipatory deference to Arab oil producers in a manner characteristic of a 'soft sphere of influence'.[12] In either case, few would deny — including West Europeans and Arabs — that economic considerations have played a very significant role in Western Europe's Middle East diplomacy of recent years.

West European Middle East diplomacy is thus less than meets the eye because it has never had the base of power, either military or economic, from which to wage an active, suasive diplomacy. Wisely or gratuitously, Western Europe inserted itself into the political affairs of the Levant in the 1970s as supplicant before the supposedly awesome political shadow of Arab oil riches and financial clout, not as great power *demandeur* or honest broker. In this sense, progress toward a just solution to the Arab-Israeli dispute — and most central, to the problem of accommodating Palestinian nationalism — has never really been anything more than the *rhetorical* focus of West European efforts. The true focus in practice has been to establish the governments of Western Europe as mediators not between Israel and the Arabs, but between their own beleaguered economies and expectant citizenry on the one hand, and Arab markets and petroleum supplies on the other.

There are other ways in which EEC Middle East diplomacy is less than meets the eye. Clearly, the European Community, with its 'unified' foreign policy, does not even exist as a discrete actor in international relations. Notwithstanding the 'social construction of reality',[13] actors in international politics do not come into being merely by speaking as though they existed. EEC policy has frequently been a supplement to the policies of individual West European countries or a group of countries. This would be uncomplicated if all the major West European governments had arrived at a specific consensus on Middle Eastern affairs. But they have not, and attempts by individual governments, most notably but not exclusively that of France, to attach the EEC as a helpful adjunct to their own particularist interests have led on occasion to considerable acrimony. This is not surprising, since economic competition in the Middle East has involved not only the West Europeans on the one hand and the United States on the other, but competition among European states themselves. Particularly in the aftermath of the spate of state-to-state barter deals of the mid-1970s, some West European governments strove to co-ordinate their views with their most significant Middle Eastern trading partners more than with their allies in Europe. For example, French investment in the Middle East includes substantial economic dealings with Iraq, Libya and Algeria. These being among the more radical Arab states, the French found themselves 'out in front' of, say, the West Germans, whose economic efforts concentrated more on Saudi Arabia and non-Arab Iran. These differences were imported into the intra-EEC discussion, the result being that EEC declarations on the Middle East often reflected what other analysts have called a sort of lowest common denominator. A better description, perhaps, is that they reflected Janus — a unitary god facing two ways simultaneously. Janus is intriguing and colourful. He is also mythological.

Since the EEC is not a unitary actor and has no integral power of its own, it follows that its 'policy' has amounted to little more than a series of verbal exhortations. Now, words are not insignificant in international politics; in many respects words are acts. But the reason that words are not insignificant is that diplomats and statesmen have learned to assess them as indices of intentions, as harbingers of deeds to come.[14] Where there is no power, no capacity to act with force or consistency, the power of words decays. Only those who would convince others that their words do indeed presage action, and those who become convinced, take a serious interest in them. As far as the Israeli government and the governments of the Arab states are concerned, the EEC can, as did Shakespeare's Glendower, 'call spirits from the vasty deep'. The rub is, however, as Hotspur put it in reply, 'But will they come?'[15]

The juxtaposition of the EEC's political ghostliness with the self-assumed seriousness of some European policrats has been almost amusing. As an offshoot of the Euro-Arab dialogue — more precisely, the EEC-Arab League dialogue — a 'parliamentary' delegation from the Council of Europe agreed to meet with a 'parliamentary' delegation of the Palestine National Council (PNC). If the EEC may be described fairly as the ghost of West European foreign policies, the Council of Europe might be aptly characterized as this ghost's 'domestic' shadow. The PNC too is at best a 'parliament' in exile that empowers no government, rules no territory, and has no internationally recognized citizenry. It too is a sort of ghost.

Council of Europe and PNC delegations have met together on a few occasions, starting in 1980 in Strasbourg. Many words have been spoken, much breast-beating and ego-stroking has taken place, all of it resulting in absolutely nothing of practical consequences — as should have been obvious to all clear-headed observers from the start.

The Diplomacy of Economic Vulnerability

If Western Europe's Middle East diplomacy is in some respects less than first meets the eye, in other ways it is more. EEC diplomacy, as a collective expression of West European governments, has aspired to mediate in order to narrow the distance between its economic dependency on the Arabs and its military/security dependency on the United States, dependencies that in practice if not in theory tend to pull European policy in opposite directions. Thus, a subsidiary but actual mediation, flowing from Western Europe's multiple dependencies, has been to set up the EEC and individual West European governments as mediators, again, not between Israel and the Arabs, but between the Arabs and the United States.

The Arabs have had a definite interest in a higher profile West European diplomatic role — at least those Arab states for whom good relations with the West are important. It should have been clear in Riyadh, Amman, Cairo and elsewhere — and it almost certainly *was* clear — that by themselves, the Europeans could achieve nothing of political significance with respect to the Palestinian issue, and certainly nothing on matters concerning Israeli territorial withdrawal from the Sinai, the West Bank, Gaza and the Golan Heights. Yet West European diplomacy has had three, modestly useful, aspects for the Arabs. First of all, the Europeans have insisted — to their credit — on not formally recognizing the PLO as the sole legitimate representative of the Palestinian people until the PLO showed genuine movement toward moderation, epitomized by acceptance of Resolution 242 of 1967. Whatever the Arab states — especially Jordan and Egypt — have said in public, such West European pressure against PLO rejectionism actually supplemented and strengthened their own local diplomacies, which also have striven to remove the PLO's veto on their own policies. West European diplomats have not often been aware of this Arab motive. They should have heeded President Carter's indiscreet but at least partly accurate statement that no Arab leader privately favoured an independent Palestinian state, though all said they did in public.[16]

Secondly, the Arabs hoped (aloud) that West European arguments might prove persuasive or at least useful in Washington where, in certain bureaucratic crannies and in certain administrations, there had already been movement away from long-standing US positions on the Palestine issue that the Arabs had long opposed.[17] During the Carter Administration some believed that the United States wished Western Europe to pursue its own independent line in the Middle East in order to make it easier for Washington to follow suit. The perception was quite widespread in Europe, and in Washington too the remark was often heard that the Europeans were doing the Americans a favour by bringing pressure to bear. Many Americans were said to secretly appreciate the gesture. Initially, this assessment was close to being accurate, but things changed in Washington during the next few years, and some West European diplomats began to take this scenario a bit too seriously. Joseph Sisco put it well in 1981 when he wrote: 'Western European leaders are wrong if they really believe that the United States secretly welcomes such pressure'.[18]

Finally, it was of modest use to let as many Europeans as possible believe that their taking to the hustings on behalf of the Arab cause *did* lubricate the wheels of commerce. Apart from the mutually beneficial economic relationship, future issues might arise on which European advocacy could be useful, if it could be chided into existence. Why waste a valuable psychological precedent? If the Europeans insisted on selling their services to the Arabs at a bargain rate, was this not *their* problem?

The West European states believed that they had a good deal to gain by interposing themselves as interlocutors between the Arabs and the Americans. This function had many aspects, the most important being the desire to maximize their economic interests. The United States would not or could not trade with certain countries, and would not trade in certain commodities — notably arms — with many countries for explicitly political reasons. It was not enough for West European countries to seize these opportunities whilst American hands were tied. There had to be a reason, or better, a justification. So West European policy became more 'even-handed' than that of the United States, allowing the sale of weapons to countries such as Libya and Iraq. The West European willingness to peddle sophisticated military and nuclear technology against the backdrop of American refusals was often portrayed benignly as an effort to keep some of the local recipients from 'rushing headlong' into the arms of the Soviet Union.[19] West European governments thus proffered political judgments, transferred technology, arms and wealth, and engaged in oratorical political acts deviating appreciably from the basic themes of US regional diplomacy, but conforming perfectly to the commercial policies of West European countries. This was not a coincidence.

There were also rather stark differences in perceptions that arose, at least in part, from the European disinclination to contradict their Middle Eastern trading partners. Sensing European, and to a lesser extent the US vulnerabilities on economic issues, the Arab statesmen sought to establish a political linkage between the supply of oil from the Persian Gulf on the one hand and the political troubles of the oil-less Levant on the other hand. The Arab line was not hard to discern: if you in the West do not press Israel into concessions on Arab-Israeli questions, then we in the Gulf will punish you by manipulating the supply and price of oil. Though never more than a bluff after the 1973–4 embargo ended, taken seriously only by the fainthearted or the unprincipled, this threat nevertheless spawned an axiom in many West European foreign-policy establishments in the 1970s: the Arab-Israeli conflict was the most important threat to continued oil supplies. Once formed, axioms are hard to dislodge; so much so in this case that neither the Iranian revolution and the Gulf War, nor the Soviet invasion of Afghanistan — events that involved Israelis and Palestinians not one whit — could change this bizarre conviction.

Successive US administrations, from Nixon to Reagan, have been disturbed by both West European policies and by West European rationales for them. But they should not have been surprised. The basic policy motivation of most West European governments, at least since 1973 and perhaps before, has been the same with respect to the Soviet Union. West European states have at times fallen over one another to bribe goods into export to the Soviet Union and Eastern Europe.[20] Credits and technology-transfers facilitated by West European states to the Soviet Union for their own short-term economic benefit allow the Soviets to bail out their stagnant economy and those of their satellites without having to make hard choices about structural economic reform or the reallocation of resources away from the military sector. West

European assistance to the Soviet economy thus amounts to an indirect subsidy to Soviet arms programmes which are directed against Third World sources of supply for West European industry and ultimately against Western Europe itself.[21] Who pays to offset and deter this military power? The United States foots the bill disproportionately in Europe. In the Middle East the United States foots the bill nearly in its entirety.

West European arguments with respect to policy *vis-à-vis* the Soviet Union and security issues outside of NATO's formal domain echo those made about the political troubles of the Levant. In the former instance the argument is made that squeezing the Soviet Union economically and isolating it politically will only make Moscow more belligerent and hostile.[22] Besides, the United States, it is said, does not experience concretely the benefits of detente as do the Germans, and these benefits are too much to sacrifice lightly. With respect to the Persian Gulf, some Europeans are fond of explaining to Washington that the real threats to the region are not external but internal, and their easement does not depend primarily on a Rapid Deployment Force or on the existence of land-based air power, but on (inevitably amorphous) programmes of political reform. Indeed, some Europeans now view US military preparations for a Persian Gulf contingency rather than US-abetted Israeli recalcitrance to be the main threat to the oil supply.[23] Thus do many Europeans endeavour to grease the wheels of commerce, take care not to irritate their Persian Gulf, Soviet and East European trading partners, all the while criticizing (and not paying for) the military undergirding of US diplomacy which remains the bedrock of their own security, and which allows such myopic statements to be made without fear of palpable damage.

There is yet another set of reasons not to be surprised about the distance between the rhetoric and the reality of West European Middle East diplomacy. When, in this century, have West European words accurately reflected West European motives? During World War I, in both the Balfour Declaration and the Hussein-McMahon correspondence, the British government promised political freedom to those repressed under the Ottoman yoke. At the same time, the British were plotting secretly with their wartime allies to carve up the region in the infamous Sykes-Picot Agreement. Soon thereafter, due in part to the pressures of the Wilsonian crusade to make the world safe for democracy by better aligning nation with state, the British and the French undertook

League of Nations' mandates in the Middle East — ostensible half-way houses to national independence. But historians have been hard pressed to find evidence that either London or Paris intended such a political destination for these 'mandates'. After World War II, even the weakened British and French empires clung tenaciously to their Middle Eastern preserves. There is some evidence that by turning the Palestine question into a United Nations issues in 1946–7, the British hoped to gain the sanction of the international community and the pocketbook of the United States to insure a continued British presence there.[24] The French left Syria and Lebanon only when American and local pressure forced them out. In 1956 Britain and France invoked the Tripartite Declaration of 25 May 1950 to protect Egypt and the Suez Canal from the invading Israelis, yet in truth they sought to overthrow the Egyptian regime and had colluded secretly with the Israelis in the first place. In 1967 French policy turned suddenly against Israel, ostensibly because of Israel's resort to war. In retrospect it seems clear that a combination of cold-blooded geopolitical and economic calculations, buttressed perhaps by General de Gaulle's eccentric attitude toward Jews, was behind Paris's *volte face*.

In 1971–2, in the face of a well-orchestrated terror campaign in Western Europe, which reached its hideous apex at the Munich Olympic games, we were told that the sudden willingness of scores of West European countries to allow PLO missions and offices on their territories was not a consequence of intimidation, but the result of mature reflection and reconsideration of the basic issues in the Middle East. The legacy of this diplomatic legerdemain is with us still. An Italian magistrate, Carlo Mastelloni, was presented in 1984 with evidence linking the PLO to the notorious Italian Red Brigades, the same group that had 'taken credit' for, among other things, the murder of Aldo Moro. He issued arrest warrants for those who were, in effect, accomplices of the Red Brigades — Yasser Arafat and his deputy, Salah Khalaf. But Italy's prime minister, Bettino Craxi, and Foreign Minister Giulio Andreotti visited Mr Arafat in Tunis in December 1984, *after* the magistrate's warrants had been issued. How does one explain such a thing? Part of the explanation lies in the fact that evidently no one had told Mr Mastelloni, who is but 34 years of age, that Italy and the PLO had made a deal. Judicial sources in Rome and in Venice believe that since a PLO terrorist attack on a Pan-American airliner in Rome in 1973, there has been an unwritten agreement between Italy and the

PLO to allow the PLO a political office in Rome in return for a promise to ban PLO terrorist actions on Italian soil.[25]

Finally, it is not difficult to recall the behaviour of Western Europe in the aftermath of the oil embargo of 1973–4. The period between the Copenhagen Conference of December 1973 and the eventual founding of the International Energy Agency in June 1974 is an especially noteworthy illustration of raging unilateralism among West European states. Stunned by OPEC price hikes, and taunted by Nixonian testaments of global multipolarity, European rhetorical pretensions to a unified foreign policy buckled under the pressure of possible Arab retribution. The atmosphere of *sauve qui peut* that seized the governments of Western Europe at the time amounted to sheer panic. The Europeans, led by France and Britain, resisted American leadership only to fall over one another competing for Arab favours. Paris and London were even willing to employ arcane legalistic arguments to avoid implementing emergency oil-sharing plans with the Dutch, who had been singled out by the Arabs for specially harsh treatment because of their pro-Israeli stand.[26]

If this were not enough, the EEC summit at Copenhagen in December 1973 was 'attended' by five Arab ministers, thus opening the *sanctum sanctorum* of EEC summitry into which no foreigners, not even Americans, had previously been invited. The ministers addressed the gathering on behalf of the Arab League, mixing vague threats with still vaguer promises. One outcome of this encounter was the Euro-Arab dialogue — a semi-institutionalized EEC-Arab League forum designed to deal with issues that, as of early 1974, were not well defined. For the Europeans the dialogue was to be another avenue of approach toward stabilizing the price of oil and ensuring its supply, by placing EEC-Arab economic relations on a long-term footing. The Arab states considered the dialogue more a political instrument than an economic institution and, newly full of themselves after the successes of 1973–4, never hid their intentions. Under such conditions it was unavoidable that the birth of the Euro-Arab dialogue would be seen by many as a European concession to the Arabs.[27]

The stream of solemn pro-Arab statements and declarations that gushed forth from EEC councils in 1973 and 1974 were pleasing to the Arab states, not for their actual impact on US or Israeli policies, for there was none, but for the sheer gratification of bringing their former colonial masters to their knees. After four centuries of humiliation, the Europeans were again paying a form of the *Türkenverehrung* — 'the Turkish tribute'.[28] The true balance of civilization had finally been set aright. West European portrayal of its policies to the United States mentioned not a Turkish tribute, but verged publicly on blaming Washington for allowing its one-sided support of Israel to bring Western Europe — an innocent hostage of US policy — to such dire times.[29]

With a historical record like this, it is a wonder that anyone possessed of a memory or an education takes West European declamations about the Middle East at face value.

A Deeper Stake

The point is that West European diplomacy with respect to the Arab-Israeli dispute fits a broader pattern than is evident in the history of West European policies toward the Middle East and, in a different way, in its contemporary policies toward the Soviet bloc, the Persian Gulf, and the Third World generally (witness the Lomé Accords of 1975).[30] This pattern describes a diplomacy of relatively wealthy and proud but economically fragile states pursuing their national interests; to do so without advertising their vulnerabilities, the public diplomacy of West European states has been sometimes evasive, sometimes dissimulative, sometimes confused. That is why many observers find it difficult to take seriously the proposition that West European views on Arab-Israeli and Palestinian questions are anything other than derivative of more parochial concerns. But those who share this view of the true sources of European Middle East diplomacy — and its diplomacy in general — do not agree on what to do about it.

One school of thought holds that Western Europe could be brought into line with a steadfast US Middle East strategy if only the United States were itself steadfast and if only it had a real strategy.[31] To corroborate this view, some cite the ability of the Atlantic partners to manage and adjust their economic relations tolerably well over the last four and a-half decades. More specifically with respect to the Middle East, it is noted that when the United States *insists* on reining-in wayward European tendencies, as for example in the set-to over the Multinational Observer Force (MNO) in the Sinai during the spring of 1982, the United States prevails. When it does, the locals benefit, the United States benefits, and the West

Europeans benefit. When the United States fails to lead, or when it leads in the wrong direction — as with the Beirut Multinational Force (MNF) — everyone loses. According to this view, it is no longer a question of whether key NATO partners can find ways to function effectively outside of NATO's formal domain, the realities of European security concerns having long since spilled over the boundaries of NATO 'at the creation'.[32] The Beirut MNF episode suggests that, indeed, where there is an American will, there is an alliance way. The real question is not whether the allies can work together, but whether they can succeed.[33]

Clear-headed US leadership is the main thing, in this view. When US policy narrows the distance between itself and Western Europe by aligning itself more closely with wrong-headed European attitudes on the Middle East — as was initially the case in the Carter Administration — it removes the restraints on West European policy ordinarily in place due to the US role, thereby undermining both US and West European policies. The most dramatic example of this was the embarrassing Andrew Young affair of August 1980, the outgrowth of an especially maladroit US-West German scheme to attract PLO 'moderation' by way of amending United Nations resolutions.[34] But, in its own way, the US-West European showdown over the Venice Declaration of June 1980 was a better example. US policy since 1977 had by deeds of commission and omission encouraged the Europeans on their quest for an 'independent policy' that seemed to many to presage parallel changes in US policy. But after the invasion of Afghanistan, the fall of the Shah, the stake in peace accumulated in the Camp David process, and the aforementioned Andrew Young fiasco, the Carter Administration had second thoughts about the European agenda in Venice. But what it earlier had helped set in motion, it now found that it could not stop — hence, no doubt, the acerbity of US-West European exchanges over Venice, following as they did the bitter and frustrating attempts by the United States to erect Atlantic-wide economic sanctions against Iran and the Soviet Union.[35]

According to the other view, the Europeans are hopeless. Atlantic relations are utterly fouled and, in the long run, irreparably damaged. Fruitless disagreements — over Venice, over sanctions against Moscow and Tehran, over who pays for NATO military modernization, and over the sale of gas pipelines and computers to the Soviet Union — are said to be the rule, not the exception, in US-European relations. What the West Europeans do and say about the Middle East only confirms this impression. For this school, European participation in the Beirut MNF, however helpful at the time, was nevertheless predicated on a general view of the problem and on specific tactics that diverged sharply from US policies. More to the point, they argue, is the still impossible task of getting many NATO members to consider the Soviet military threat in global terms. In this, Washington has some friends in London and Paris, but few elsewhere. As NATO planned for Persian Gulf contingencies in 1983, even while the MNF was in Beirut, one British officer said that the West Germans, the Dutch, the Belgians and others simply 'refuse to see the realities of the situation', that a Middle East contingency might divert forces from NATO-Europe.[36] Another NATO planner noted that in the event of a Persian Gulf contingency that would draw down US forces normally committed to Europe, 'we would expect the European allies to try to compensate' for the diversion. But, he went on, they 'won't look' at the problem, suggesting the toddler tactic of covering one's eyes and announcing: 'You can't see me'.[37]

The conviction that US and European interests are increasingly incompatible makes for strange bedfellows, from neo-conservatives (like Irving Kristol) and rightist unilateralists (like Sam Cohen and Lawrence Beilenson), to neo-Marxian structuralists (like Immanuel Wallerstein) and both libertarian and leftist isolationists (like Earl Ravenal and Mike Davis).[38] Those, like Wallerstein, who insist on the growing structural economic chasm between the United States and Western Europe, make a challenging point. The real question is, if this is true, can economic disharmony ultimately be reined in by transcendent political/security values held in common? The jury is out.

It is in this sense, then, that West European diplomacy toward the Arab-Israeli conflict is *more* than meets the eye. It is no exaggeration to say that West European policies on Middle Eastern issues are more important in the long run for their impact on the possibility of designing and implementing a coherent Western security policy than for any impact they may have on the many troubles of the Middle East. At issue here, not just in Western Europe's Middle East diplomacy but in its diplomacy more broadly viewed, is whether the United States and Western Europe are doomed by supposedly inexorable laws of economic interest to work at cross purposes, or whether what is euphemistically called the West can muddle through — screaming and seething with suspicion, no doubt — in the interest of higher values.

The Dialectic of Justifying the Necessary

It would be both petulant and inaccurate to leave matters here, having thus far characterized post-1970 West European Middle East diplomacy as — to put the worst face on it — an exercise in self-serving hypocrisy rooted in economic dependency and military impotence. It may indeed have *begun* as an exercise in self-serving hypocrisy, but it is no longer, at least not in any simple way. Nor is it generally so seen in Europe either by practising policrats or by publics at large. To see why, one must turn one's gaze for a moment to European society itself.

At the very worst, some Europeans will admit not to a predilection for the hypocritical, but only to the habits of survival. Contemporary West European countries are overwhelmingly welfare-state polities; hierarchies of public values are such that material comfort and cradle-to-grave security rank very high.[39] Many Europeans are proud of this sobriety. To them it is neither cultural narcissism nor crass materialism, but a rational response to a vanished world of national chauvinisms and pretentious ideologies that led Europe twice in this century to world war. In their most private honesty, many Europeans seem deeply suspicious of appeals for public sacrifice in the name of any political abstraction. How else is it that the Oxford Student Union in 1984 — of all years — could even think to debate the question that the United States and the Soviet Union are morally equivalent?[40]

Moreover, given the demands of modern technology for capital-intensive economies-of-scale, the small size of West European economies has of necessity made them export-oriented to an extraordinary degree. Most Europeans — statesmen and citizens — believe that their high standards of living are inextricably bound up with very high levels of international commerce. Because of the compelling domestic political significance of this commerce, West European foreign policies writ large have tended to become servants of West European commercial policies. If it was true during the colonial era that trade followed the flag, it seems to be true nowadays that the flag follows the trade.

But there is more to US-West European disagreements about the Middle East than economic differences. There is a question, too, of what is perhaps best termed 'style'. There are many people, in Europe and in the United States, who believe that US foreign policy is excessively ideological, and needs to become more mature, i.e. more pragmatic. To many Europeans, the American refusal, for example, to recognize officially the PLO is counterproductive, as is the 'unrealistic' American attitude toward terrorism. Both of these US attitudes are sometimes criticized by Europeans for their being rigidly idealistic, to the disservice of the possible. Yet, as is often the case in human affairs, some people like to have it both ways at once if they can. Thus, is it not so unusual to hear European complaints about the impracticality of US diplomacy by reason of ideological dementia coupled with both assertion of the *moral* superiority of West European promotion of Palestinian causes and utterly impractical alarums about how next to proceed.[41] The point is that, notwithstanding its origins and innermost motivations, West European policrats and publics for the most part have come to earnestly believe in the *correctness* of their views on the Middle East, whether on ostensibly pragmatic grounds, moral grounds, or both. This in turn girds up the propriety and sense of European-Arab commercial relations. This is the dialectic of justifying the necessary.

This is not the place to debate the substantive issues of who is right and who is wrong about a Palestinian state, about Camp David, or about the PLO and a 'comprehensive' settlement. Middle Eastern problems are sufficiently complex that honest men (as well as others) can disagree about how to deal with them. That this writer happens not to agree with what often passes for common knowledge about the Middle East in Western Europe today is not to say that this paradigm is utterly wild-eyed or craven, only that it is mistaken.[42] The United States government and those of Western Europe will continue to disagree over the Middle East. Nevertheless, it would be useful on every side if disagreements did not lead to accusations of calumny. US politicians, journalists and diplomats should stop dismissing European efforts as fatuous, self-aware appeasement, because they are not; and West European politicians should stop imagining a US policy that is locked in the conspiratorial clutches of the 'Zionist lobby' — which it is not — or a policy otherwise cynically disposed against fairness — which it also is not.

Aside from differences in style, there are some differences in psychology. Part of Western Europe's confident espousal of positions differing from those of the United States is a function of striving to differentiate itself from the paternalistic legacy of US protection. For a group of formerly prestigious states still adjusting psychologically after World War II, it is sometimes cathartic to oppose the United States. Sometimes the mere fact of noticeable difference seems to add weight to convictions whose source lies elsewhere.[43] Some American observers — and even some West Europeans — have argued that European dependence on the United States as its protector of last resort in its own homeland ought to discipline European governments not to oppose American policies in other areas. The European tends to see it rather diferently. It is precisely *because* of American protection in the most central of Europe's security problems that West European governments feel free to express their differences on more marginal matters.[44] This may defy geopolitical logic, but not the logic of human relations.

Some observers have suggested that one motive for the degree of Western Europe's positive sentiment toward the Palestinians rests in a subtle combination of guilt and empathy for the underdog. There may be something to this. Ironically, the same conditions are also said — rightly I think — to account for Western Europe's sympathetic attitude toward Israel between the late 1940s and the mid-1960s. There was guilt about the Holocaust, and empathy with a small nation surrounded by implacably hostile neighbours. It helped that some of those hostile neighbours were then keeping themselves busy by assaulting what remained of the European position in the region at a time when empire was something in which one could still take a measured amount of pride. Things changed. The Israeli image shifted from that of a David to that of a Goliath — alas, the price of success is high. The Palestinian issue arose, somewhat ironically, out of an Arab débâcle, for the PLO guerrilla movement grew directly from the defeat of Arab armies in 1967. For those disposed emotionally to side with the underdog, nothing is so poetically evocative as apparent paradox.

In the late 1960s and the 1970s, moreover, the 'plight' of the Third World became international news; the UN New International Economic Order grew to be a popular hobbyhorse in democratic socialist circles in Western Europe. That it was by and large an anti-Western programme was blunted in Western Europe by the fact that it was above all anti-American. And this all happened at a time when the image of the United States in Europe was at a nadir over Vietnam, America's racial unrest, and the debilities of Watergate.

Simultaneous with the plummeting images of both Israel and the United States in European eyes, Israel and the United States developed ever closer ties with each other. 'Decadent', violence-prone Americans and 'abrasive, domineering' Israelis locked in each other's embrace made for suggestive, sinister images in Western Europe's generally left-of-centre mass-circulation media.

Such images intensified in the late 1960s and early 1970s. They grew faster still after 1977, with the ascendancy in Israel of the Likud under Menachem Begin, and the increasingly successful attempts by the PLO to present itself in Europe as now above and beyond terrorism. A new generation of Europeans has all but forgotten the Holocaust, Leon Uris's *Exodus*, and the hateful rantings of the Mufti. They remember Begin and Sharon, Sabra and Shatilla, and the hateful rantings of Meir Kahane. The fact that Israel is a democracy struggling with the improbable problem of an extended occupation is not often mentioned in Western Europe, leading some observers to wonder whether Europeans still value their own hard-won democratic institutions.[45] Europeans have instead focused on 'human rights' abuses, thus lumping Israel together willy nilly with the autocracies and military juntas of the Third World at its worst. Even the Israeli evacuation of the Sinai and the peace treaty with Egypt were greeted sceptically, as devious tactics to divide the Arabs and to gobble up the more critical West Bank.

It will be objected by some that such common images are 'soft' variables — irrelevant to the actual functioning of a foreign policy. This is not so. The foreign policy of democratic societies cannot be explained as a kind of mechanical *Machtpolitik*. Images, sentiments and emotions, no matter how irrational, nevertheless influence public policy, not only by setting outer boundaries on the permissible, but also by affecting the articulation of the issues. He who manages to seize the vocabulary of a political debate has a much easier time seizing victory in that debate. Thirty-five years ago, Europeans saw in Zionism the indomitable human will — evidence that Hitler had been defeated not only militarily, but spiritually. Nowadays, Zionism has all but become a dirty word in Western Europe. That matters. In addition, many hard images start out as soft ones, and the distance that we assume exists between the images of the street and the considered views of foreign policy professionals is often less than we would hope.

There is one final consideration, bearing on the relative weakness of West European states as seen against both their former grandeur and their need for good relations with the Arabs. At one time, not so very long ago, West European foreign ministries and common-wealth offices not only influenced what happened in the Middle East, they controlled it more or less directly as imperial overlords. Today, West European power in the region has nearly disappeared, but the traditions and ambitions in Whitehall and the Quai d'Orsay have not. There is a bureaucratic momentum arising from hoary-headed veteran diplomats and eager young graduates that, when combined with the rather obvious inclinations of West European business communities, makes for a potent intra-governmental force. This is not to posit anything like a foreign-service-business conspiracy, and certainly not to parrot vulgar Marxists who insist against all evidence that the foreign policy of a capitalist country is in practice indistinguishable from the interests of its oligopolistic class. But those prominent in business and those prominent in politics and diplomacy tend to know one another socially, and they share many of the same cultural orientations. These days, these urban, well-educated men and women tend toward a view that generally discounts Israeli security concerns and elevates the humanitarian and political grievances of the Palestinians.

Innocents Abroad

The weakness of West European Middle East diplomacy is evident too in the failure of West European 'policies' to move from the abstract level of the good and fair to the specific level of hard and specific choices. West European pronouncements on the Middle East have remained at a high level of generality not only because intra-EEC disputes relegate its diplomacy to a lowest common denominator, and not only because actually mediating between the Arabs and Israelis has never been, as noted above, the most proximate aim of EEC diplomacy. EEC policy has remained vague and general because the solemnity of European pronouncements is not matched by any real responsibility to bring them into being. The great divide between West European and American views of the Middle East (and the Persian Gulf) stems ultimately from the differing interests, power and responsibilities among the allies. The United States must *think* strategically about the area because it has the power to *act* strategically, while the Europeans, though more dependent on the region's oil than the United States, do not. The

United States has a duty to address the issues between the parties because it is the only acceptable mediator with the power to provide incentives to agreement and credible guarantees of compliance. The EEC, on the other hand, is not engined by any such potential responsibility to transform its general declarations and catch-all study documents into anything more specific.

The absence of real West European responsibility in the region has also led European governments to persist with exclusively exhortatory diplomatic tactics, even though those tactics have failed repeatedly to accomplish even modest goals. This repetition is no doubt a consequence of the lack of other alternatives; diplomacies that have little prospect of success easily learn to be patient. Thus it was, throughout the late 1970s and into 1980, that PLO emissaries in Western Europe suggested that if only the EEC would take one *more* small step toward the PLO, the PLO would reciprocate by moving toward more moderate positions. EEC diplomats repeatedly accepted this 'challenge'. But after teasing and taunting West European policrats for years, the PLO, hamstrung partly by its own internal divisions and partly by genuine ideological extremism, moved not at all. There is only so much that even well-intentioned and sympathetic diplomats can take before they recognize a stratagem of diplomacy by attrition for what it is. In EEC-PLO relations that point was reached for many in the aftermath of the Venice Declaration.

The only time that the EEC, by itself, attempted to translate its exhortatory generalities into actual policy, the experience was truly sobering. After the June 1980 Venice Declaration, the EEC dispatched Gaston Thorn, then President of the EEC (and Luxembourg's foreign minister) to the Middle East on a fact-finding mission. He pursued his mission for some weeks, reporting his findings to the EEC foreign ministers gathered at Brussels in mid-September. European and Middle Eastern interest in Thorn's trip and in the potential for West European diplomacy increased steadily after the Venice meeting in direct proportion to the ill fortunes of the US-sponsored autonomy negotiations, which were many. The governments of the major West European states, believing their considerable economic interests in the area to be jeopardized by stalemate, responded to invitations tendered by some local parties to the conflict — especially Jordan[46] — for heightened EEC participation in regional diplomacy.

Armed with the prod of self-interest and invitations putatively refused only at their peril, the Europeans declared themselves up to the task and set to work to fill the vacuum created, in their view, by the American electoral session of 1980. EEC staffers worked to transform Thorn's September report into a more systematic document — ostensibly secret, but leaked lavishly on three continents — in preparation for the December summit of EEC heads of government in Luxembourg.[47]

Before they could finish the job, however, Ronald Reagan's unexpected victory over Jimmy Carter in the American presidential election deterred the EEC states from taking their next step.[48] Though concerned about the new administration's attitude toward the Middle East, the Europeans were nevertheless mindful of private pleas during and after the transition period, not to force Washington's hand with a pre-emptive initiative. The EEC statement on the Middle East issued at Luxembourg reflected this caution; it was somewhat more deferential to the US-sponsored peace process, as well. The Reagan Administration was being awarded a grace period in which to demonstrate the redemption of American foreign policy. In the meantime, since the EEC chairmanship would be split in 1981 between the Netherlands and Great Britain, the expectation developed that the Dutch, having better relations with Israel than other EEC members, would begin talking quietly to Israelis (of both major political groupings) during the first half of the year, and that the British Conservative government, having closer political affinities with the Republicans, would work with the Americans once Washington had put its house in order.

Europe's deference to the new US administration was in large part motivated by a rather embarrassing fact: the European Community *had no initiative to propose*. It seemed that the more the Europeans learned about the misanthropic realities of the problem, the less sanguine they became about finding a comprehensive solution. It even occurred to some that perhaps the pro-Israeli lobby in the United States was not the only thing preventing Washington from finding the right formula for curing the region's ailments. The issues really *were* complex, too complex to be solved by facile but high-sounding EEC Summit declarations. And as Mr Thorn and his successor, Christopher Van der Klaauw (the Dutch foreign minister) discovered, it was not only the Israelis who were recalcitrant; so were many Arabs. Thorn and Van der Klaauw, as well as their colleagues back home, were genuinely surprised by the negative PLO reaction to Venice, and by the frigid reception they received from many Arabs during their tours of the region.[49]

The 'secret' EEC Luxembourg document was ample testimony to the new sobriety in Europe. Contrary to early expectations, it was less an initiative or a position than a study document outlining obstacles and alternatives in four areas: Israeli withdrawal from occupied territories, self-determination for the Palestinians, security guarantees, and the status of Jerusalem. For the most part, the study favoured options unacceptable to Israel. For example, it called for full Israeli withdrawal within two years. But it was also reported to have suggested that Israel might maintain limited military forces in the West Bank after withdrawal, and that demilitarized zones might play a role in long-term security arrangements — propositions sure to disturb the Arabs. On the most intractable issues, like Jerusalem, the EEC study was expansive but noncommittal.[50] Like the Venice Declaration, the Luxembourg study, if made public, would likely have asked too much of most Israelis and promised too little for most of the Arabs.

That the rather clumsy EEC-Arab diplomatic minuet went on for so long is testimony to another, somewhat curious factor that seemed to be at work in shaping the general approach of many West European diplomats to the problems of the Middle East. Notwithstanding the frequent self-assured assertions about the intellectual maturity and long experience of Western Europe in the Middle East — as compared to the supposed reckless idealism, militarism and naïvete of the United States[51] — European diplomats who should have known better often acted as though their Arab counterparts could be dealt with as though they had been colleagues at Eton or the Sorbonne. Some seemed utterly oblivious to the very real cultural differences between Europeans and Arabs (and between Europeans and Israelis). This occasionally led them to take Arab declarations at face value when they conformed to their own intellectual paradigm, and to discount others when they did not so conform. So, the British Foreign Office once accepted an Arab-inspired typification of certain PLO organizations, such as Nayef Hawatimeh's Popular Democratic Front for the Liberation of Palestine (PDFLP), as 'moderate', when in fact such moderation was illusory or at best misinterpreted.[52] When it was brought to the attention of West European policrats that PLO spokesmen often phrased their political objectives in starkly different terms when speaking to Western rather than to Arab audiences, many West Europeans discounted the PLO's Arab-to-Arab declamations as rhetorical flourishes designed only to appease the supposedly few remaining radicals among the Palestinians. The more reasonable interpretation, that PLO doublespeak was directed toward Europe rather than toward its own people, seems never to have occurred to many.

The combination of European empathy for the Palestinians, and the European failure to appreciate properly the diplomatic tactics of the PLO and its Arab supporters, had interesting and unintended consequences. As a form of indeliberate condescension, the European assessment of the 'Palestinian revolution' as essentially a nationalist/bourgeois phenomenon that could be contained by a 'civilized' Western diplomacy, no doubt disturbed a number of Arab intellectuals. It is one thing for one's arguments to be rejected, but quite another not to be taken seriously. Little wonder, then, that episodic tours by West European emissaries to the region often evoked more hostility than gratitude from 'the natives'. The same can be said, in a way, for the European assessment of Israeli concern about the security-relevance of the West Bank as an example of irrational paranoia. Without denying that some Israelis are as paranoid about security as some Palestinians are unflinching in their determination to annihilate Israel, Israel's security concerns are not groundless. Too few West European policrats have stood on the Golan Heights and on the crest of the mountain ridge running through the West Bank and looked around.

Two Tales of the Levant

Notwithstanding all this, EEC Middle East diplomacy has lately displayed a creditable tendency to learn from the mistakes of the past. Starting in late 1980 with the denouement of Venice, and continuing through the sobering experience of the MNF in Lebanon in 1982–3, a new realism seems to have crept into European thinking, if not about Israel, then certainly about the PLO. What is the reason for this?

Some have suggested that the shift in European demeanour away from the obsequious and toward the hardheaded has had less to do with the frustrations attendant on repeated failed attempts by the EEC to move PLO policy, and more to do with the greatly diminished power of the Organization of Petroleum Exporting Countries (OPEC), and especially its Arabs members. The formula is simple: there have been dramatic changes in the international petroleum market over the last few years leading to serious divisions within the cartel, and diminished Arab oil leverage equals a less compliant West European attitude. There may be a gram of truth to this, but as a synoptic explanation for the recent movement of European policy, it leaves a great deal to be desired. In the first place, it is unrealistically cynical. If it were true that the only current reason for Western Europe's sympathy for the 'moderate' Arab view was the intimidating power of Arab oil, then such an explanation might carry more weight. But, as the foregoing analysis has implied, it is not that simple a matter. Moreover, the easing of the upward pressure on the price of oil has not been felt as much as one might think. Oil prices are tied to the US dollar, and the increasing strength of the dollar owing to high US interest-rates has resulted in offsetting financial costs to Western Europe and Japan. The International Energy Agency has estimated that in 1984 alone, the strength of the dollar resulted in effect in an 8 to 9 per cent *increase* in Japan's and Western Europe's oil bill.[53]

Changes in the oil market are perhaps a third-echelon factor in explaining the new sobriety of EEC policy since Venice. Most important, West European diplomats have clearly reassessed the likelihood that the PLO will soon be able or inclined to do what the EEC has wanted it to do: declare its recognition of Israel's right to exist with sufficient clarity and authority to allow the creation of a Palestinian political voice capable of negotiating seriously with Israel. The paralysis of the PLO after Camp David, the PLO civil war around Tripoli in the spring of 1983, and the failure of the Arafat-Hussein negotiations of April 1983 and February 1985 to produce anything of real substance, have driven home a message to West European diplomats that they could have seen, but did not see, long before. Many have finally begun to appreciate that in the face of the dominant fractious pattern of Palestinian nationalism and the constraints of inter-Arab politics, EEC verbal exhortations can have little impact, if any.

Secondly, for reasons having nothing at all to do with the Middle East, there are now governments in the major states of Western Europe that are more Atlanticist in orientation and less adamant about putting distance between European and American policies for its own sake. The British Conservative government of Margaret Thatcher, the CDU government of Chancellor Helmut Kohl in Bonn, the Mitterand presidency in France, and the Craxi government in Rome, all attest to this trend. As a consequence, internal EEC deliberations today have a decidedly different tone when it comes to policies that would lead to confrontation with the United States over the Middle East. The EEC will not cease its efforts, but as long as this political constellation endures it will be less inclined toward the vigilante diplomacy of years past. There will not be another Venice. The discussion below of recent Italian adventures bears this out.

Last of all is the relaxation of the pressure of the oil market. In this regard it is interesting to note that the continuing economic troubles of some West European states are not related exclusively or even directly to the oil bill, as was once widely believed. Of the major European states, Great Britain is best off in regard to oil by virtue of its North Sea operations, yet its economy is in as serious a slump as any in Western Europe.

The new realism and sobriety of recent West European approaches to the Middle East have been reflected both in the unpleasant experience of Beirut and in the recent activities of the EEC, led by Italian president, Bettino Craxi, and his foreign minister, Guilio Andreotti. Let us address these two matters in turn.

This is not the place to review in full the chronicle of exactly how the Multinational Force of US, French, Italian and British soldiers came to be in Beirut. But it is noteworthy that West European willingness to participate with the United States in Beirut represented a sort of split decision between the defiant independence of Venice — which ended in an inconsequential whimper — and their clearly dependent, but successful, role in the MNO for the Sinai. It seemed that the Europeans had debated the Miltonian adage — 'Tis better to reign in hell than to serve in heav'n' — and settled on a compromise. The Beirut MNF proposition was an American project at centre, but through it the European participants sought to 'smuggle' the Palestinian issue — as *they* saw it — into the proceedings.[54]

West European accession to the Beirut MNF took place against a background of expected dramatic change in US-Israeli relations.[55] This was epitomized by the exit of Alexander M. Haig, Jr, from the State Department and his replacement by George Shultz, a man who in his confirmation hearings had been tantalizingly forthcoming about US concern for the problems of the Palestinian people. Nevertheless, US and West European motivations regarding the MNF did not coincide. US policy sought first to speed the exit of the PLO from Lebanon — a goal it thoroughly shared with Israeli policy — and secondly to prevent protracted combat in a heavily populated area. But for the Europeans the most immediate mission of the MNF as it entered Beirut for the first time in August 1982, was to save the PLO from an Israeli onslaught. (This was reminiscent of one motivation for Dutch, Irish and French participation in the UNIFIL force in southern Lebanon in the spring of 1978, namely, that it would make it more costly politically for Israel to act militarily in Lebanon because Israel would risk confrontation with European troops to get at the targets of its military missions.[56]) Some European analysts even purported to know what they were saving the PLO for: its transformation from a 'military' force into a 'political' force that would be willing, at last, to pick its way between the Reagan initiative of 1 September 1982 and the Fez Plan of the same month. Indeed, some Europeans saw in their own Venice Declaration the most benign mixture of the two. The attempt to use the crisis of the moment in Beirut to advance the Palestinian issue along lines pleasing to the West European states was illustrated well by a Franco-Egyptian discussion that had as its ostensible goal just such a transformation of the PLO.[57]

Initially, the MNF's prospective mission had been defined rather expansively as contributing to the restoration of Lebanese sovereignty by overseeing the evacuation of all foreign forces from Lebanon. But the Israeli siege of Beirut had made the more immediate mission of overseeing the exit of PLO forces really the only goal of the MNF that remained above the line of sight. Thus, when the PLO evacuation was completed ahead of schedule, none of the members of the MNF elected to stay around in anticipation of more ambitious tasks. So they left: the Americans on 10 September 1982 and the Europeans very shortly thereafter.

But only four days later, Lebanese President-elect Bashir Gemayel was assassinated, Israeli troops entered West Beirut to 'mop up' and, under Israel's nose, Maronite Christian militia massacred hundreds of Palestinians at Sabra and Shatilla refugee camps. The MNF returned forthwith, but this time the reasons for its deployment were even less well defined and thought out. Officially, the US mission at least, was described as designed 'to establish an environment which will permit the Lebanese Armed Forces to carry out their responsibilities in the Beirut area'.

Unofficially, US diplomats later admitted that little thought was given to the redeployment; it was described as a knee-jerk reaction to Sabra and Shatilla based more on diffuse guilt than on any notion of a diplomatic or military mission.[58]

A rationale for the MNF was soon devised; not surprisingly, it was similar to the original conception. The MNF was there to help President Amin Gemayel assert Lebanese sovereignty over Lebanon, the better to facilitate the exit of all foreign troops, the better to get on with the central issues of the Reagan initiative — the future of the West Bank and Gaza and the resolution of the Palestinian problem. The West European governments certainly did not object to this basic agenda. Indeed, their help in Lebanon, it seemed to some, would newly 'entitle' the Europeans to a more prominent role in Israeli-Arab negotiations once they commenced.

Regrettably, things did not work out. Washington mis-estimated the willingness of Syria to leave Lebanon under any conceivable condition short of military expulsion. Washington mis-estimated too the extent to which President Gemayel could piece Lebanon back together, the result being that the MNF came to be seen by internal Lebanese factions as partisan external support for the Maronite Christians. The Syrians were quick to seize on this development; Damascus was determined that the 'foreign' forces that would leave Lebanon would be those of Israel and the MNF, not those of Syria. And thirdly, Washington mis-estimated the incentive that the Reagan initiative had given the Syrians, the PLO and the Israeli Likud government to tarry in Lebanon lest the initiative — which all three opposed for different reasons — come to the fore of the diplomatic agenda.

The European MNF contingents generally acquiesced in American judgments, including the judgment to pursue a separate Israeli-Lebanese accord. When Syrian-backed violence came to be directed against the MNF, Washington first temporized, then after a long delay, responded with force on behalf of the Lebanese government — such as it was. The Europeans protested against US policy, but they admitted to having no alternative proposal. French action epitomized this dilemma: Paris enlarged its force in Beirut but refused to allow it to be used offensively. None wished to bug out, lest they be accused of cowardice and disloyalty to the other MNF members.

After the 23 October 1983 bombings of the US and French military compounds, the die was cast. By 1 April 1984 the MNF was gone. Not only had the MNF failed in its proclaimed mission, but the Europeans never had the opportunity to influence the Palestinian issue through association with a US initiative, because that initiative failed of its own poor timing. We will never know if European ambitions could have been realized had things not gone awry in Beirut. But the EEC 'initiative' of 1984–5 suggests that the answer is no.

The Craxi-Andreotti 'initiative' of the winter of 1984–5 contains elements of both the tragicomic and farcical. The story begins with a glimpse of Italian politics.

For well over a dozen years the currents of Italian politics have been resistant to producing a strong government. As a rule, coalitions have been weak, internally fractious, and not particularly long lasting. Many non-expert American observers might well have wondered how Italy survived at all under such difficult circumstances. It did so by dint of two factors: a tradition of local and regional autonomy, and a relatively depoliticized civil service whose bureaucracy functions without regard to national politics even when there *is* a strong government. The Craxi government, formed in August 1983, has been Italy's longest-lasting, stable and economically successful government for some time. It too is a coalition of five parties, the main two being Bettino Craxi's smallish Socialist Party and Foreign Minister Guilio Andreotti's Christian Democratic Party. Despite endless internal jockeying between the Socialists, the Christian Democrats and the Italian Communist Party, and more than a few Mafia-related scandals, the government has endured and has even become a mild source of pride for weary Italian patriots.[59]

As a six-month Italian tenure (January-June 1985) as head of the EEC approached, Prime Minister Craxi's good fortune crested. His own confidence merged with three other factors to produce a pulse of intense diplomatic activity in the Middle East in anticipation of the Italian EEC Presidency. The first of these factors was the desire to take an activist role on behalf of the EEC in the Middle East of no *less* serious mien than that of previous British, Dutch and Irish chairmanships. Italian politicians frequently feel as though others do not consider Italy to be equal in political status with Great Britain, West Germany and France. They resent this. The second factor is that Italian politicians generally, and the Italian Foreign Ministry, in particular, believe themselves to be specially suited to understand the Middle East because Italy is a Mediterranean country. This is not the place to discuss the validity of that belief, only to note that *because* of it the Middle East is a natural focus for Italian foreign-policy activism. The third factor is Bettino Craxi's personal belief in the integrity of Yasser Arafat and the legitimacy of the PLO, a belief that he has expressed many times, including before the Italian parliament. Craxi is out in front of his own foreign ministry and his own foreign minister on this issue; the reverse tends to be the case elsewhere in Western Europe.

Craxi adheres firmly to the general West European foreign-ministry consensus on the Middle East, accepting the thesis that the continuation of the Arab-Israeli problem is the main threat to the oil supply. He believes not only that the Palestinian issue is at the heart of the problem, but that it really is the only problem, and that were it solved, Israel and its other Arab neighbours could rather easily come to terms with one another. The solution to the problem must involve virtually total Israeli withdrawal from the Gaza Strip and the West Bank and the establishment there of an independent Palestinian state with fewer, rather than more, organic political connections to Hashemite Jordan.[60] Craxi has also voiced support for some Soviet role in an eventual settlement, and he has been critical of US step-by-step diplomacy, and diplomacy resembling the step-by-step though called by other names.

Girded with such views, and seated firmly on the chariot of Italian confidence in its special grasp of the Middle East, the Craxi government set out in late 1984 to revive the failed effort to transform the Venice Declaration into an operative policy. Craxi and Andreotti visited Riyadh, Cairo, Algiers, and most important, Tunis, where they held a secret meeting with Yasser Arafat. From the Italian point of view, the proximate aim of these travels was clear: to move the PLO toward acceptance of Resolution 242, thereby to establish the *sine qua non* for a negotiated settlement. Another aim, not surprisingly, was to sell Italian weapons. With a Labour prime minister in Israel and a PLO militarily weakened by defeat in Lebanon at the hands of both Israel and Syrian-backed rebels within the PLO, the Italians thought such a change to be on the cusp of realization.

In any case, Craxi and Andreotti left Tunis convinced that Arafat had finally broken with extremist PLO factions and was ready to negotiate in tandem with Jordan on the implicit, if not explicit, basis of Resolution 242 and the American Reagan initiative.[61] Evidently, Arafat voiced support for a European initiative which would support such a stratagem. Hearing this from Arafat in December, Andreotti decided that it was now time to visit King Hussein in Amman. This meeting took place in early January 1985; it was an odd affair. The Italians had begun their odyssey thinking Jordan to be a somewhat marginal actor. But they had discovered in Tunis that they had in mind a more independent 'Filastin' than Arafat himself could realistically seek from the king and this was reconfirmed in Amman.[62] So much for Rome's special insight into the Middle East.

Why did Arafat encourage the Italians in December? The best guess is that amid (unfounded) rumours in the Middle East that the United States planned a dramatic post-inaugural Middle East initiative, Arafat turned to the old tactic of trying to influence Washington through the Europeans. Arafat has long hoped — so far in vain — for American recognition and support in the long run, and he well knows that there are many in the US foreign-policy establishment who would like to move the United States openly toward him if only they could manage it. Clearly, the highly publicized meeting of the minds between Arafat and King Hussein on 11 February 1985 had as its main target not Israel but the United States — Arafat because he craves US recognition, Hussein (and the Egyptians and the Saudis to the extent that they facilitated the 'deal') because he needs Palestinian 'cover' to enter any negotiations, and because he wants US weapons.

It appears that the flurry of diplomatic activity in the Middle East in January and February struck the Italians rather differently. Craxi and Andreotti evidently thought the 'motion' was real 'movement', or could be turned into real movement, and they determined to redouble their efforts. Then a strange thing occurred. In different degrees, it then struck the Israelis, the US, the British, the French, the Egyptian, and even the Jordanian governments and the PLO that, indeed, something of modest but real importance could come of all this. In other words, the atmosphere turned serious.[63] And when it did, the advice tendered by one and all to the Italians was the same; do not interfere, lest you cloud and confuse the channels of communication. Thus, at the very moment when it appeared (to some) that a central desideratum of EEC policy over the past half-dozen years might be within reach, all of the major local actors as well as the United States preferred overwhelmingly a very modest, controllable, supportive and essentially reactive EEC role — a far cry from an independent policy.

The State Department had been aware of Italian activity from the start. But since there had been nothing in the offing that could be spoiled by EEC activity, it was viewed as a minor but inconsequential irritant. What was not so minor was that the Italians did not inform the United States in advance about the meeting with Arafat in Tunis, and the Department's view was that such a politically sensitive matter ought not to be handled with such cavalier looseness. When the air turned serious, Washington pressed Rome for restraint. This dovetailed with similar British, French and West German remonstrations sharing the US view that the EEC could not change Israel's mind about talking with Arafat or his men, and would most likely contribute only delay and confusion.[64]

It is not known precisely what was communicated to Rome by Arafat and King Hussein in early February as yet another Arafat-Hussein summit approached. But it is clear that the Italians rather abruptly changed their tune on 18 February 1985 during a visit to Italy by Israeli Premier Shimon Peres. In a joint statement, Craxi and Peres stated: 'There are not yet enough conditions for a new [EEC] peace initiative.'[65] After the meeting Peres told reporters that Craxi had rejected the idea of an international conference on the Middle East — a position vigorously supported by Israel. Peres added that he and Prime Minister Craxi 'saw eye to eye on most matters'.[66] The next day, Peres ridiculed the idea of an international conference as a 'show', not a dialogue, and announced that he was ready to go to Amman in search for peace. The Italian government praised his offer, hoped for progress, and that was all. A few days later, Andreotti downplayed the significance of the Jordanian-PLO 'deal', and reaffirmed obliquely that there would be no Italian-led EEC initiative.[67] Thus, what had begun in late autumn as an enthusiastic effort to rebuild an independent European role in the diplomacy of the Middle East, ended meekly in February with recent pilgrims to Yasser Arafat seeing eye to eye with the prime minister of Israel. Let the reader judge the seriousness of a diplomacy that can produce such a peculiar spectre.

Time and Tide Change Everything

There is a phenomenon in linguistics called metathesis, whereby (usually) the consonant sounds in a word are accidentally and spontaneously reversed, the new product gradually coming to assume a lexical signification of its own, dictated by the needs of those who would use it.[68] All analogies limp, but in a sense the evolution of West European Middle East diplomacy fits such a pattern.

The pro-Palestinian shift in European thinking about the Middle East — and the deeds that followed that thinking — did have its proximate origins in the panic-ridden, economically propelled diplomacy of the early 1970s. Nevertheless, the creedal anchors of West European policy have since changed. Nowadays, it is somewhat less the fear of crushing economic penalty imposed by the Arab states that accounts for Western Europe's generally pro-Palestinian and anti-Israeli attitudes, and somewhat more a sincere, 'principled' belief in the justice of the moderate Arab case. In other words, a shifting confluence of factors over time best accounts for Western Europe attitudes — a sort of sliding calculus of interacting motivations. So on the one hand, the pro-Arab attitudes of the post-1973 period did not fall from the sky; clearly, such attitudes heavily populated West European foreign ministries throughout much of the postwar era, and this had little to do with the economics of oil. But they did not become the dominant European view until economic strictures, the psychological loosening of the US-European security relationship, and the amorphous but crucial shift in popular images of the Middle East came together after 1973. But on the other hand, narrow economic arguments pertaining to Western Europe's recent acquisition of a somewhat more realistic diplomacy miss the point. The receding or the easement of one or more of the original sources of change will not now reverse West European policy inclinations, their having since acquired a different *raison d'être* — whatever one may think of it. What one tide washes ashore, the next tide does not necessarily recapture.

This is not to say that there are no unrepentant cynics today in Western Europe; there are a few. But the relationship between chronic self-preservative fears and the evolution of the new European consensus on Arab-Israeli problems is a subtle one. For most people it is more uncomfortable to appear selfish than to be selfish. On more than one occasion hypocrisy bred by rationalizations for selfish acts has been the advance wave of a new truth. The stronger the need to believe, the easier the arrival of conviction. And having arrived to soothe the conscience, the easier it is to sever the connection to first causes. Thus, one can assert *both* that the contemporary European consensus on the Middle East would

probably not exist were it not for Europe's weaknesses and vulnerabilities before the Arabs, and that it is nevertheless self-consciously
honest.

The most determined critics of Western Europe's Middle East
gambits will not be troubled greatly by such an interpretation. If
one is decidedly critical of declared West European attitudes, their
sources are of little consequence. What is worse, they might ask:
craven, self-aware appeasement, the intellectual vacuity of post-
imperial senility, or the malign mingling of the two? It is not hard
to understand why many Israelis and Israel's staunchest sympathizers see things in this light, and why the Europeans do not. It
is one of the perpetual pranks of international diplomacy that one's
own perspective is at the same time partly illuminating, partly
blinding. The United States thus finds itself in a unique position to
mediate not only between Arabs and Israelis, but also between
Europeans and Israelis. In its own interest, owing to the importance of both Israel and Western Europe to the United States,
Washington is wise to do so. And it is fair to say that in recent years
— partly because of US efforts — Israelis and West Europeans no
longer think the worst of each other.

Precisely because EEC policy is no longer a wholly fatuous one
born of panic and fear, it is capable of a degree of level-headedness
and realism that it sorely lacked even five years ago — though it
does not always rise to its own potential. US and West European
views of the Middle East problem remain divergent, but the
potential for alliance-splitting independent EEC initiatives is much
less. Indeed, disagreement over the Middle East may be the least of
NATO's problems. From the US perspective the problem has
changed: on the attitudinal level, the chasm has widened in some
respects because European attitudes cannot accurately be dismissed
any longer as shallow and insincere, sustained solely by economic
duress, but on a tactical level, the problem has eased considerably.
Indeed, the potential for the United States and the West European
states to work together in co-ordinated fashion could grow appreciably if tenacity of purpose can contain the tempers of the
moment.[69]

Notes

1. See, for example, Saadallah Hallaba, 'The Euro-Arab Dialogue', *American-*

Arab Affairs, no. 10 (Fall 1984), 44–59. At one point, Hallaba writes that the 'United States has continually obstructed the progress made by the EAD [Euro-Arab Dialogue] by refusing to take a balanced view of the conflict . . . There is still hope, however. According to well-informed sources,' never identified by Hallaba, 'the EEC countries are inclined now, more than ever, to recognize the PLO.' But for this to occur, the PLO must demonstrate its 'independence of any form of outside pressure' — patently impossible — and

> the Arab states, which provide the largest consumer market for a Europe suffering from economic strains, must be willing to use their market as a means of persuading Europe that it is in its interest to recognize the PLO and the legitimate rights [sic] of the people of Palestine.

Clearly, this is not scholarly analysis but a partisan plea for the use of economic leverage against European governments dressed up for an academic occasion. Thus, we see that both the original aim and the original tactics, from the Arab point of view, of the Euro-Arab dialogue have not changed. In this regard, see Ahmad Sidqi al-Dajani, 'The PLO and the Euro-Arab Dialog', *Journal of Palestine Studies*, vol. 9, no. 10 (Spring 1980), 97. For a slightly more serious, yet similarly inclined, analysis, see Saleh al-Mani and Salah al-Shaikhly, *The Euro-Arab Dialogue* (New York: St Martin's Press, 1983). Finally, I owe it to the reader to explain my use of 'sic' following the phrase 'legitimate rights' above. I do not mean to imply that the Palestinians have no rights; my point concerns English usage. If something is a right, it is by definition legitimate. This is proved by the lexical nonsense of its formal opposite for what, after all, could possibly be meant by an 'illegitimate right?' The phrase is more than redundant, however. It reflects the Arab obsession with 'moralist' propaganda aimed at the West: it is verbal overkill.

2. I refer to Adam M. Garfinkle, *Western Europe's Middle East Diplomacy and the United States* (Philadelphia: Foreign Policy Research Institute, 1983); the articles by Janice Gross Stein, Joan Garratt and Dominique Moisi in Steven L. Spiegel (ed.), *The Middle East and the Western Alliance* (London: George Allen & Unwin, 1982), pp. 49–81; Harvey Sicherman, 'Politics of Dependence: Western Europe and the Arab-Israeli Conflict', *Orbis*, vol. 23, no. 4 (Winter 1980); and Hans Maull, 'The Strategy of Avoidance: Europe's Middle East Policies After the October War', in J. C. Hurewitz (ed.), *Oil, the Arab-Israeli Dispute and the Industrial World* (Boulder, Colo.: Westview Press, 1976).

3. For background here, see William B. Quandt, *Decade of Decision* (Berkeley: University of California Press, 1977), pp. 83–5.

4. In this regard, see the remarks of Shlomo Argov, quoted in Alun Chalfont, 'Israel, the Palestinians, and the West,' *Encounter*, vol. 56, no. 5 (May 1981), 67; and Werner J. Feld, 'West European Foreign Policies: The Impact of the Oil Crisis', *Orbis*, vol. 22, no. 1 (Spring 1978), 69.

5. See Garfinkle, *Western Europe's Middle East Diplomacy*, Chapter 3, for details.

6. By 'policrat' I mean mainly career foreign-ministry officials who seem, in Europe, to be more prominent, more permanent and more influential than their counterparts in the United States. 'Policrat' strikes me as a more convenient word than 'politically-minded bureaucrat' — an awkward phrase.

7. Regrettably, examples of this bad advice are not hard to find. For one suitably insipid example, see Sardar Muhammad, 'Restoration of Human Rights of the Palestinian People: The Role of the United Nations and the Super Powers', *Pakistan Horizon*, vol. 35, no. 1 (1982), 31–50.

8. I speak here of François, duc de la Rochefoucauld, (1613–80). For this maxim and a great many others, see *Réflexions ou sentences et maxims morales: réflexions*

diverses (Paris: Larousse, 1967).

9. This is a basic thesis of Harvey Sicherman's essay, 'Europe's Role in the Middle East: Illusions and Realities', *Orbis*, vol. 28, no. 4 (Winter 1985).

10. See here, for details, Robert J. Leiber, 'Energy and the Western Alliance' in Spiegel (ed.), *The Middle East and the Western Alliance*, p. 110.

11. See the somewhat polemical but still sound essay by Douglas J. Feith, 'The Oil Weapon De-Mystified', *Policy Review*, no. 15 (Winter 1981), 19–39.

12. The term 'anticipatory deference' is mine; it is explained in my *'Finlandization': A Map to a Metaphor* (Philadelphia: Foreign Policy Research Institute, 1978), pp. 22–4. For a description of the 'soft sphere', see John P. Vloyantes, *Silk Glove Hegemony: Finnish-Soviet Relations, 1944–1974* (Kent, Ohio: Kent State University Press, 1975).

13. The general reference here is to phenomenological epistemology in the cultural sciences; the specific reference is to Peter Berger and Thomas Luckmann, *The Social Construction of Reality* (Garden City, New York: Doubleday-Anchor, 1966).

14. On words as indices in international politics, see Robert Jervis, *The Logic of Images in International Relations* (Princeton: Princeton University Press, 1969).

15. The reference is to Shakespeare's *Henry IV*.

16. Carter's remark is recorded in the *New York Times*, 31 August 1979.

17. Others later argued that, given division and strife between Western Europe and the United States, the

> . . . Arab states should shift the emphasis of their foreign policy to exploit US European differences rather than counting on Europe's dwindling ability to influence Washington . . . Europe should be encouraged to develop a distinct economic, political and military entity capable of making serious inroads into US interests. In this way Washington will be forced to take Arab wishes into account or to risk losing lucrative economic and military links in the region.

> In short, a Europe which is strong, independent and sympathetic to the Arabs will force Washington to review its overall Middle East policy.

Judith Perera, 'Not Seeing Eye to Eye', *The Middle East*, no. 89 (March 1982), 15. By movement in US position, I speak primarily of the Saunder's Memo of 1975. For a brief discussion, see Harvey Sicherman, *Broker or Advocate? The U.S. Role in the Arab-Israeli Dispute, 1973–1978* (Philadelphia: Foreign Policy Research Institute, 1978), pp. 8–9. The document itself is to be found in 'Prepared Statement of Harold H. Saunders', *The Palestinian Issue in the Middle East Peace Efforts*, Hearings before the Special Subcommittee on Investigations of the Committee on International Relations, House of Representatives, 30 September, 1, 8 October and 12 November 1975, pp. 178–80.

18. Joseph J. Sisco, 'Selective Engagement', *Foreign Policy*, no. 42 (Spring 1981), 41.

19. See, for example, the remarks of President Mitterrand in a BBC interview taped in London, in *Foreign Broadcast Information Service* (*FBIS*), Western Europe, Daily Report, 8 September 1981, p. K1.

20. The phrase 'bribe goods into export' refers to the policy of stimulating demand by tying generous credit terms to foreign purchases, usually of industrial goods. See David Curry, 'Export Finance', *Financial Times* (London), 18 February 1975, 1.

21. This argument has been put recently by Richard Pipes in *Survival is Not Enough* (New York: Simon and Schuster, 1984), especially pages 102–9, and 248–59. See also the remarks of Albert Wohlstetter, 'Meeting the Threat in the

Persian Gulf', *Survey*, vol. 25, no. 2 (111), (Spring 1981), 133.

22. For a moderate expression of this view, see Giovanni Agnelli, 'East-West Trade: A European View', *Foreign Affairs*, vol. 58, no. 5 (Summer 1980), 1016–33.

23. The United States has not, by the way, denied the salience of internal threats, only that the existence of internal threats is not a reason to ignore external threats, even remote ones. And the *reason* that external threats are as remote as they are — *if* they are — is due to countervailing US power in the region. See the comments of Melvin A. Conant, 'The Allies as Petro-Partners', *Washington Quarterly*, vol. 4, no. 4 (Autumn 1981), 101–6. See also David D. Newsome, 'America Engulfed', *Foreign Policy*, no. 43 (Summer 1981), especially 26–7.

24. See the brief discussion in Evan M. Wilson, *Decision on Palestine: How the U.S. Came to Recognize Israel* (Stanford, Ca.: Hoover Institution Press, 1979), pp. 105–6. Some may object to this supposition about the motives of British policy on the grounds that it would have been ludicrously at variance with the realities of British weakness at the time — and not only in Palestine. I would not argue with this assessment, but it is beside the point. Most of British policy toward the Middle East at the time was ludicrously at variance with the realities of British weakness. See William Roger Louis, *The British Empire in the Middle East, 1945–1951: Arab Nationalism, the United States, and Postwar Imperialism* (London: Oxford University Press, 1985). More casual observers — those who may fear a book 800 pages long — can get the flavour of Louis's work by consulting Conor Cruise O'Brien's review, 'Wishful Thinking', *New York Review of Books*, vol. 32, no. 3 (28 February 1985), pp. 9–12. Alan Bullock, for one, disputes the supposition; see *Ernest Bevin, Foreign Secretary 1945–1951* (New York: W. W. Norton & Company, 1983), p. 367.

25. See Sari Gilbert, 'Dispute in Italy Over Arafat, PLO', *Washington Post*, 2 January 1985, A17–18.

26. For a review of this period, see Romano Prodi and Alberto Clo, 'Europe', *Daedelus*, vol. 104, no. 4 (Fall 1975), 98–100.

27. See the discussion in Garfinkle, *Western Europe's Middle East Diplomacy*, pp. 4–7.

28. It is often forgotten, but at the height of the Ottoman penetration into Europe in the 14th and 15th centuries, fear of further Moslem encroachments prompted many German princelings to offer tribute to the Turks. For one fascinating angle on this, having to do with clocks, see David S. Landes, *Revolution in Time* (Cambridge, Mass.: Harvard University Press, 1983), pp. 99–100.

29. See the comments of an anonymous West European diplomat in 'Worldwide Oil Politics', *National Journal Reports*, 13 October 1973, 1540, cited in Joan Garratt, 'Euro-American Energy Diplomacy in the Middle East, 1970–1980: The Pervasive Crisis' in Spiegel, *The Western Alliance and the Middle East*, p. 90; and Garratt's own analysis, p. 90.

30. See the discussion by Simon H. Serfaty, 'The Atlantic Settings: Enduring Balance But Fading Partnership' in *United States-Western European Relations in 1980*, Hearings before the Subcommittee on Europe and the Middle East of the Committee on Foreign Affairs, House of Representatives, 25 June; 27 July; 9, 15 and 22 September 1980, pp. 6–25.

31. This view is at least implicit in Pipes, *Survival Is Not Enough*, as it is in Sicherman, 'Europe's Role in the Middle East', *Broker or Advocate?*

32. The reference is to Dean Acheson's well-hewn phrase, and the title of his memoirs on these subjects, *Present at the Creation* (New York: W. W. Norton, 1977).

33. This basic question is raised by Sicherman, 'Europe's Role in the Middle East', and by Luigi Caligaris, *Western Peace-Keeping in Lebanon: Lessons of the MNF*, *Survival*, vol. 26, no. 6 (November/December 1984), 262–8. See also

Richard W. Nelson, 'Multinational Peace-Keeping in the Middle East and the United Nations Model', *International Affairs*, vol. 61, no. 1 (Winter 1984–5), and Naomi Joy Weinberger, 'Peacekeeping Options in Lebanon', *Middle East Journal*, vol. 37, no. 3 (Summer 1983), 341–69.

34. For details, see both Carl Gershman, 'The Socialists and the PLO', *Commentary*, 68; 4 (October 1979), and Harvey Sicherman, 'American Policy in the Middle East, 1978–79' in *Middle East Contemporary Survey*, vol. III, 1978–9, edited by Colin Legum, Haim Shaked and Daniel Dishon (New York: Holmes & Meier, 1980), pp. 23–5.

35. There are details in *Western Europe's Middle East Diplomacy and the United States*, pp. 31–4.

36. Quoted in Drew Middleton, 'On Big Picture, Allies Aren't in Step', *New York Times*, 15 June 1983.

37. Ibid.

38. The relevant literature includes Irving Kristol, 'Does NATO Exist?' *Washington Quarterly*, vol. 2, no. 4 (Autumn 1979); Samuel T. Cohen, 'Should America Defend the Persian Gulf?' *Policy Review*, no. 26 (Fall 1983), 88–92; Lawrence W. Beilenson, *Security and Peace in the Nuclear Age* (Chicago: Regnery-Gateway, 1980); Immanuel Wallerstein, 'Friends as Foes', *Foreign Policy*, no. 40 (Fall 1980), 119–31; Earl Ravenal, 'Counterforce and Alliance: The Ultimate Connection', *International Security*, vol. 6, no. 4 (Spring 1982); and Mike Davis, 'Nuclear Imperialism and Extended Deterrence' in *Exterminism and Cold War* (London: Verso, 1982), pp. 35–64.

39. See Ronald Inglehart, *The Silent Revolution* (Princeton: Princeton University Press, 1977). But some claim to see changes ahead. See Alan Wolfe, 'The Death of Social Democracy', *The New Republic*, vol. 192, no. 9 (3,659) (25 February 1985), 21–3.

40. See the piece by Leon Wiseltier, 'A Neutral Europe?' *The New Republic*, vol. 185, no. 19 (3,487) (11 November 1981), 22–3.

41. For an example almost embarrassing because of its lack of realism and its august author, see Lord Caradon, 'Looking Back and Ahead on U.N. 242', *American-Arab Affairs*, no. 10 (Fall 1984), 28–32. Among other sins, Caradon manages in this article to place blame for the non-imposition of Resolution 242 exclusively on Israel (and the United States), ignoring entirely the Khartoum Summit and the general tenor of Arab attitudes at the time.

42. See Adam M. Garfinkle, 'The Politics of a Palestinian State', *Orbis*, vol. 27, no. 1 (Spring 1983), 207–20; and '"Common Sense" About Middle East Diplomacy; Implications for U.S. Policy in the Near Term', *Middle East Review*, vol. 17. no. 2 (Winter 1984–5), 24–32.

43. This is a phenomenon that cognitive psychologists have tried to explain. One article that throws some light on the general problem of cognitive-affective balance is Milton Rosenberg, 'Cognitive Structure and Attitudinal Affect', *Journal of Abnormal and Social Psychology*, vol. 53 (1956), 367–72.

44. See here the remarks of the former British ambassador to the United States Peter Jay, 'Europe's Ostrich and America's Eagle', *The Economist*, vol. 274 (7123) (8 March 1980), 19–29.

45. See Wiseltier, 'A Neutral Europe?'.

46. See the discussion in Adam M. Garfinkle, 'Europe and America in the Middle East: A New Coordination?' *Orbis*, vol. 25, no. 3 (Fall 1981), 638–43.

47. See Raphael Calis, 'The Europeans: Can They Piece It Together?' *The Middle East*, no. 75 (January 1981).

48. Quoted in Ibid., 8. And see also the remarks of Karl Kaiser before the US House Subcommittee on Europe and the Middle East, *United States-Western European Relations in 1980*, pp. 218–19.

49. Arafat's reaction was venomous. See *FBIS*, Daily Report, Middle East and Africa, 20 April 1981, A9. The initial PLO reaction may be found in *FBIS*, Daily Report, Middle East and Africa, 5 June 1980, A4–7. The PLO's attitude has not changed. See the remarks of Faruq Qaddumi on the occasion of Guilio Andreotti's visit to Amman in January 1985 in *FBIS*, Middle East and Africa, Daily Report, A2–3.

50. For three accounts, see 'Secret Mart Paper Urges Full Israeli Pullback in Two Years', *Jerusalem Post* (International Edition), 1–7 March 1981; 'The European Working Paper', *The Middle East*, no. 81 (July 1981), 33–4; and the *Washington Post*, 4 March 1981.

51. A good example is that of British journalist Michael Adams. See his article, 'Reagan "Encouraging Israelis to Pass the Point of No Return" ', *The Guardian*, 15 March 1981, 8.

52. See 'Palestine Liberation Organization', *Background Brief* (London: Foreign and Commonwealth Office, May 1981).

53. *New York Times*, 7 August 1984, D1.

54. Though clearly an American project, the European participants in the MNF, especially the French, often spoke about it as if the Americans did not even exist. See Prime Minister Pierre Mauroy's remarks to Parliament, *FBIS*, Western Europe, Daily Report, 11 October 1983, K8–9.

55. This is discussed more fully in Adam M. Garfinkle, 'Sources of the al-Fatah Mutiny', *Orbis*, vol. 27, no. 3 (Fall 1983), 614–17, and see also Sicherman, 'Europe's Role in the Middle East', *Broker or Advocate?* pp. 817–22.

56. Even what remained of UNIFIL as of March 1985 appeared to Israel to be doing the same thing. Israel's preemptive 'iron fist' strategy against Shi'ite attacks in the wake of its withdrawal toward the international border ran up against UNIFIL, particularly the French contingent. At one point Israeli soldiers physically removed French soldiers who obstructed their access to a Shi'ite village. Later, in a Knesset subcommittee debate, Defence Minister Yitzhak Rabin astonished his colleagues by saying openly: 'They, the French, are the biggest bastards.' Quoted in *FBIS*, Daily Report, Middle East and Africa, 17 February 1985, 17.

57. For some detail here, see Sicherman, 'Europe's Role in the Middle East', p. 820. For a characteristic European remark urging the 'merger' of the Fez and Reagan Plans — as supposedly implied by the EEC Venice Declaration — see the remarks of the Italian foreign minister, Emilio Colombo in *FBIS*, Daily Report, Western Europe, 16 May 1983, L4. Colombo's remarks are also quoted in Sicherman, 'Europe's Role in the Middle East', p. 823.

58. See the reportage in Thomas L. Friedman, 'America's Failure in Lebanon', *New York Times Magazine*, 8 April 1984, 36.

59. See 'Italy', *The Economist*, vol. 292 (7353) (4 August 1984), 37–8, and 'Bettino Craxi', *Encounter*, vol. 61, no. 4 (December 1983), 43–4.

60. See, for example, Craxi's remarks to the Tunisian periodical *Al-Amal*, reprinted in the Italian periodical *Avanti*, and carried in *FBIS*, Daily Report, Western Europe, 1 September 1983, L1. See also the two articles by Dino Frescobaldi on Andreotti's views in *Corriere della Sera*, 23 and 24 December 1983, and Andreotti's remarks in Amman reported in *FBIS*, Middle East and Africa, 7 January 1985, F3–4.

61. The account in 'Craxi's Middle East Initiative', *Foreign Report*, no. 1857 (31 January 1985), 5–6, appears to be essentially correct on this. But see especially Andreotti's comments before the Italian Lower House Foreign Affairs Commission on 12 December 1984, noted in *FBIS*, Western Europe, Daily Report, 13 December 1984, L1. See also *FBIS*, Middle East and Africa, 7 January 1985, F4.

62. Private communication from Jordanian officials in Washington.

63. It was a brief period between the announcement of a Hussein-Arafat

'agreement' and the very conditional approval of the deal by the PLO Executive Council. The stipulation that there be an all-Arab delegation and that all the other Arab states accept the bargain too, was a transparent cave-in to the fear of Syria and its long-armed secret police force. Clearly, a deal between the king and Arafat will be a serious one only when part of the bargain allows for the transfer of PLO headquarters from Tunis to Amman. This does not mean that the 11 February 1985 meeting was without any significance. As part of a longer process leading, perhaps, to a joint Jordanian-Palestinian diplomatic programme, it could be of some importance. Later that month, the atmosphere was kept serious by an Egyptian initiative aimed at starting up direct talks. See Thomas L. Friedman, 'Seeking Peace in Mideast', *New York Times*, 17 March 1985, 1, 12.

64. *Foreign Report*, 31 January 1985, also mentions intra-EEC pressure for restraint.

65. 'Craxi and Peres Meet; No Mideast Plan Seen', *New York Times*, 19 February 1985, and see *FBIS*, Daily Report, Western Europe, 19 February 1985, L2–3.

66. *FBIS*, Daily Report, Western Europe, 19 February 1985, L3. Craxi's opposition to an international conference on the Middle East was diametrically the opposite of what Andreotti had told King Hussein the previous month. See *FBIS*, Middle East and Africa, Daily Report, 7 January 1985, F4.

67. *FBIS*, Daily Report, Western Europe, 28 February 1985, L2.

68. The phenomenon was investigated by Edward Sapir. See *Language: An Introduction to the Study of Speech* (New York: Harcourt Brace, 1955).

69. I have advanced suggestions along these lines. See my 'America and Europe in the Middle East', 643–8.

PART THREE

THE LEBANESE AND IRAN-IRAQ CRISES: PERIPHERAL
BUT RELATED CONFLICTS

7 PEACE IN LEBANON

R. D. McLaurin

The author wishes to express his gratitude to his colleague Paul A. Jureidini, whose uniquely keen insights on Lebanon appear throughout this chapter. So long, closely, intensively and productively have the two of us dealt together with the issues of Lebanon, that it is not possible to separate our ideas.

Introduction

Perhaps the only phenomenon more unremitting than violence in Lebanon is the literature on the subject. Relatively little of this literature focuses on the subject of 'peace in Lebanon', and most of that is titled in the interrogative rather than the declarative form. The intermittent raising and obliteration of Lebanese and other aspirations for peace in Lebanon have been so regular that anyone attuned to developments in that fractious part of the world must recognize peace will not come easily to, as it has not arrived quickly in, Lebanon. As the concluding section of this chapter should make clear, if we were to discuss candidly only the chances for peace in Lebanon, the subject could perhaps be exhausted in less space than this introductory paragraph has already consumed. One of the most astute observers of Lebanon has commented,

> The cascading violence in Lebanon has — over the span of nearly ten years — confounded all but the most recalcitrant optimists, while it has swelled the pessimists' ranks. As the situation has gone from bad to worse and from worse to seemingly worst, spectators and participants alike have learned to be skeptical about even the dimmest rays of hope. Thus, only a fool would venture any specific hopeful prediction as to the future of Lebanon, or even the possibility that Lebanon has a future.[1]

And this from a Lebanophile!

Rather than considering only the *likelihood* of peace in Lebanon,

159

this chapter will address the requirements, domestic and regional, for such a peace. However, responsive understanding of these requirements depends naturally upon the assessment of the causes of the violence that has besieged Lebanon and the Lebanese for almost precisely one decade. Because the interpretations of these causes vary widely, it is only fair that we begin *our* interpretation, for the reader who disagrees about the causes is unlikely to accept the conclusions. Consequently, the chapter consists of three substantive parts. The first is a brief review of the historical background to the violence in Lebanon. The second is an analysis of what may be called the motive forces, or the dynamic, driving the present situation inexorably forward (or, some would insist, atavistically backward) toward fundamental change. On the basis of the two preceding sections, then, the final part will address requirements for a viable peace in Lebanon.

Background to the Violence in Lebanon

Lebanon's Viability

Lebanon is a Third World state. By this truism is meant both more and less than it may appear. On the one hand, Lebanon shares with *most* other Third World states the characteristics that its political independence is young; that its administrative and political institutions (e.g. government ministries) are not well rooted in, and are therefore to some extent peripheral to, day-to-day life; and that the political, economic and social culture has remained, or at least remained until 1975, to a great extent hidden, active, and not effectively transformed by these new and alien institutions.[2] On the other hand, Lebanon is *not* a new country or society, and the much maligned Lebanese 'identity' has real roots in history and culture.

To claim, as Syrians are wont to do, that Lebanon is a part of Syria is as much a misreading of history[3] as is the claim by some over-zealous Zionists that the northern border of Israel should lie well inside what is now Lebanon.[4] Lebanon was a part of *geographical Syria*, it is true, but geographical and political Syria have no more in common than geographical and political Micronesia, geographical and political Morocco, or geographical and political America. The Federated States of Micronesia are in geographical Micronesia; the Maghreb Kingdom (or Morocco) is in the geographical Maghreb; America is in geographical America. But the former is in each case an entity distinct from the latter. Is El Salvador part of political 'America' merely because it is located in geographical America? Is Lebanon part of political Syria simply because it lies in what once was geographically called Syria? In point of historical fact, the *political* entity of Lebanon has a much clearer and incontrovertible pedigree than the *political* entity of Syria. Lebanon is distinct in political history, even if its historical political borders are not precisely those of contemporary Lebanon. Certainly, if we jump 150 years backwards, the Lebanon of 1835 bears a much closer resemblance to today's Lebanon than the America of 1835 does to today's America. Note, now, we are discussing *political* history and not mixing geographical and political concepts.

We dwell on the history and identity of Lebanon for a reason. Those who aver that Lebanon's violence derives from its inauthenticity, from its lack of history or identity are mistaken, just as mistaken as those who assert that violence in Lebanon has been the rule not the exception. There is no country in the region save Egypt, Turkey and Iran that can point to a longer history as distinct political entities, none save Egypt to a history less marred by violence, and none at all to a longer cultural distinction.[5]

But what of Lebanon's much analyzed divisions? Again, there is not a country in the Middle East, not one, without minorities, whether they be religious, ethnic, racial or tribal.[6] Syria has far deeper and more numerous divisions than Lebanon. We are not arguing that primordial loyalties of whatever provenance are unimportant, any more than we suggest that the shallow roots of the country's institutions or the arbitrariness of its borders are insignificant. Yet these factors are insufficient conflict explanations by themselves, as any American, living in a country of even more numerous minorities and far more arbitrary boundaries, should understand. By any of the means we have considered, or all, Lebanon matches up quite well against other regional states. If these be the criteria for authenticity, and if on their bases Lebanon be judged inauthentic, then surely only Egypt in the Middle East has any claim to authenticity.

Our intent here is to suggest that some of the most widely accepted arguments about the causes of conflict in Lebanon are at least questionable and certainly inadequate. If their proponents honestly applied these so-called explanations to all the Middle East, then conflict in Lebanon should be judged the least likely, or put differently, almost all the Middle East should long before have been charred by internal conflagrations for more destructive than that of Lebanon. Manifestly, neither is the case. Moreover, while most of the other countries of the Arab world have endured one oppressive form of tyranny or another in the aftermath of sovereignty, Lebanese society was libertarian. We cannot say it was an egalitarian society, a concept that remains unrealized, in any case, but that it was relatively free cannot be gainsaid. To such an extent, in fact, that many Lebanese of all stripes have suggested 'too much freedom' to be the cause of Lebanon's conflict. If the polity were inherently unviable, then, with such an open system, it should have collapsed decades ago.

A variety of approaches could be used to evaluate Lebanon's 'viability'. Snider[7] has employed quantitative techniques. I suggest that another form of empiricism may be in order. The survival from the beginnings of recorded history to the present day of a distinct society in the land called 'Lebanon' and its cultural, not to mention economic, productivity over those millenia — these factors must surely be weighed in the balance of history.

The thesis of conflict advanced here is that the course of violence in Lebanon is neither social nor economic, but political; that it is a product of Lebanese and regional myopia; and that the violence has endured long enough and produced such a degree of anomic chain-reaction that the requirements for a peaceful solution cannot be satisfied without additional violence — if at all. We hope our thesis, at least this part of it, is invalidated by the onward march of a more pacific history.

What Was Lebanon?

The boundaries of the modern state of Lebanon returned the historic Lebanese coastal plain to 'Mount Lebanon', as the nearer to the sea of Lebanon's two principal parallel mountain ranges, the Lebanons and anti-Lebanons, is called. It joined Beirut to this polity, as well as the northern area, Tripoli and the 'Akkar. Finally, the valley between the two mountain ranges, a rich agricultural land called the Beqa'a, was also made a part of Lebanon. In the country that resulted there was no sectarian or class majority, only a number of minorities. It is imperative to note that though these minorities are religious, the differences among them are political, not religious. There is no religious war in Lebanon, but there are conflicts among various groups whose identity is to a great extent defined by sectarian affiliation.[8]

The largest of Lebanon's minorities at the time modern Lebanon was established was the Maronite Christians, based in Mount Lebanon where they were a clear majority. The Maronites had a long history of close ties to France, but many have chosen to forget that the creation of Greater Lebanon was anything but universally popular among the Maronites. Why, many of them argued, should we be a minority, even if the largest, among others, when we would be a clear majority in the old Lebanon (Mount Lebanon)? Although the Maronites are concentrated in the Metn and Kisrawan north and northeast of Beirut, they were also substantial in numbers in the Shuf and were found in virtually every part of Lebanon.[9]

The second-largest minority was the Sunni Moslem community, and this was the only community with near-uniform views: virtually all opposed the creation of Lebanon separate from Syria. The Sunnis, who otherwise were part of the Sunni Arab majority in Syria, were the only group to *become* a minority in Lebanon. The Sunnis have traditionally predominated in the coastal cities of Tripoli, Sidon and Beirut (i.e. what is now West Beirut), but also were numerous in the 'Akkar and Iqlim al-Kharrub.

The once third-largest minority,[10] which is today the largest in terms of those Lebanese actually residing in Lebanon,[11] was the Shi'a Moslem community. In the last 500 years, the Shi'as have predominated in two areas — the south, including the city of Tyre, and the Beqa'a Valley (especially around Baalbekk and Hermil). The south was shared with the Christians, but few Sunni Lebanese inhabited the area. Shi'a and Druze have not found it possible to live together, so that Druzes in the south were virtually unknown, and Shi'as in the Shuf tended to live in villages that were either all Shi'a or Shi'a-Christian. The Shi'as were, along with the Druzes, the most feudal and the most tribal of Lebanese communities. In view of unquestioned Sunni supremacy in 1920, less heed was given their views than perhaps should have been. Since 1926, the Shi'as have been as nationalistic as the Maronites, for they could always aspire to a major role in Lebanon, but would be completely subordinated in a Sunni Syria and in the predominantly Sunni Arab world.[12]

The next largest minority is the Greek Orthodox Christian community. Unlike the Maronites who were so concentrated in Mount

Lebanon, the Greek Orthodox, the remnants of the original Christian church in the Middle East, are spread far and wide in the eastern Arab world.[13] Their mentality tended to be more accommodationist than the Maronites, since *resistance* to Islam was seen as a threat to the survival of the community.[14] The Greek Orthodox as a whole were not as enthusiastic about Lebanese independence as some, cut off as they were from the bulk of their community, but felt more secure in a pluralist Lebanon than in a Sunni Syria.

The Druzes are fewer in number than the Greek Orthodox, and perhaps even than the Greek Catholics,[15] but their role in modern Lebanese history has been important, for they controlled the largest part of Lebanon for centuries, centuries in which they lived mostly at peace with their Christian countrymen. The Druzes were divided over the separation of Lebanon and Syria.[16] An intensely closely knit community,[17] the creation of Lebanon cut them off from other Druzes. However, they were far more secure in Lebanon than in Syria or Palestine, especially as those in Lebanon are almost wholly concentrated in the mountainous Shuf. Although considered in Lebanese political terms part of the Moslem community, the Druzes' faith incorporates elements clearly at odds with some of the most central tenets of Islam.[18] Druze social order and political leadership are highly traditional.[19]

The Greek Catholics, whose number is about the same as that of the Druzes, inhabit several areas of Lebanon as a minority, but predominate only the Beqa'a Valley town of Zahle and its immediate environs.

Numerous other sectarian groups reside in Lebanon, but only one has anything near the political importance of those discussed. The small 'Alawi community has been enlarged through immigration from Syria, encouraged by the Syrian government, and now numbers perhaps 40,000. Although the number is insignificant (about 1.3 per cent of the total Lebanese population), the 'Alawis are important because of Syria's support. The ethnic Armenian community, divided among at least three religions, is clustered in Beirut. At its height, this community may well have been as numerous as the Druzes.

Contrary to popular belief, Lebanon has a written constitution, and one that has proven relatively flexible in its interpretation and implementation over the years. More well known, undoubtedly because of its uniqueness, is what is often called the 'unwritten constitution' of Lebanon, the 'National Pact', a historic compromise that was a security guarantee to the Christian community in order to secure Christian support for Lebanese independence from France. The idea that the Christian preponderance in administration and the Maronite presidency were based upon the 1932 census is fallacious; they were earnests to the Christian community that Lebanon's independence and the security of the Christian community in the resulting state were to be permanent, the former not merely a transition to union in a Syrian or pan-Arab state, the latter not merely a transition to submersion in the Islamic world. The problem with the political system is not that it failed to work, for it certainly outperformed any other in the Arab world. Rather, it is that the system perpetuated, and in fact contained the elements to accentuate, confessionalism, rather than providing an effective transition to larger loyalties. Because the system was *based upon*, rather than merely reflecting, the sectarian realities of Lebanese politics in 1932, major change was too threatening to be acceptable, and the system could not adapt to the political, social and economic changes that confronted the country. As Tueni has cogently and with well-placed irony pointed out, the written constitution proved to be eminently more adaptable than the unwritten constitution.[20]

Under the National Pact, the head of state was to be a Maronite; the head of government, a Sunni; and the head of the Chamber of Deputies, a Shi'a. These three positions, all called 'presidencies' in Arabic, were to be relatively close in power, but in more-or-less descending order of importance as given. In fact, the head of state (or 'president' in English) has been predominant much of the time; the head of government (or 'prime minister') was seen as a number 'two'; and the head of the parliament was third in prestige. Note the Druzes, barely 6 per cent of the population today, perhaps 7 per cent in 1943, were, by virtue of community size, not included in the top three posts. However, the army chief of staff is always a Druze, and the deputy head of the Chamber of Deputies is Greek Orthodox.

Another national institution bears mention in view of its contemporary importance — the Lebanese Army.[21] From its inception, the army has been seen as the symbol of Lebanese independence. However, the Lebanese made a fateful decision in the early years. Afraid of a strong army's potential threat to the only real Arab democracy, even more concerned lest the presence of a powerful army be perceived a threat by either of Lebanon's two more powerful neighbours, and loath to divert resources to the military sector, the Lebanese felt, probably accurately for some years, that a small army was enough to deter aggression against them.[22] In the late 1940s and even the early 1950s, Lebanon's terrain may well have made this true; certainly, no Arab force could project *sustained* military power beyond its borders. But as the arms race in the Middle East accelerated, the unwillingness of the Lebanese to augment their army at the very least to the proportional degree necessary to maintain credible deterrence was to have serious repercussions.[23]

Finally, we cannot fail to mention the influx into Lebanon of Palestinians, whose national tragedy has affected so much of the region's modern history. Into Lebanon many fled, and were welcomed, welcomed by Christian and Moslem alike,[24] another element destined to drastically reshape Lebanese history.

We are naturally influenced by the drama of the present to reinterpret the past. But the bitter and profound divisions of the present were unknown in the past, and the crisis of 1958, which has been more recently seen as the precursor of 1975, was far from that. We could argue that 1958 was a precursor to later events in Lebanese *regional* relations, but even the most cursory review of the alliances of 1958 discloses a panorama in which sectarian differences were much subordinate, though related, to other questions. Moreover, while current reconstructions posit that the army was not used, or as some put it with heavy but misplaced irony, that the army's role of doing nothing was legitimized in 1958,[25] in fact the army intervened in literally hundreds of incidents. And without a single, recorded episode of splitting along confessional lines did it do so! Could the army have been used to settle the overall issue in 1958? Should it have been so used? The answers to these questions are unclear even to the present day.

The roots of the 1975 violence may be several, but it is clear that the precipitating factor was the Palestinian role in Lebanon. From 1948 until 1967 Palestinian refugees lived in Lebanon in great numbers, some in refugee camps that became refugee cities, others in and among the Lebanese, while still others became Lebanese citizens. Throughout this period the Lebanese never resented the presence of the Palestinians among them. Incidents were few and minor, because over those two decades the Palestinians did *not* intervene in any significant way in Lebanese internal affairs. However, the PLO Phoenix that rose from the ashes of the 1967 war infused a new spirit in the Palestinian movement, a new dedication in its struggle against Israel, and a new approach to dealing with Arab states. PLO leaders and increasing numbers of individual Palestinians demanded that everything be subordinated to the Palestinian struggle.[26] No Arab could be fulfilled, no Arab people could achieve any worthwhile objectives, it was argued, until Palestinian rights triumphed. On this basis, the PLO constructed the armed struggle to be employed against Israel from Arab land.

Existing Arab governments individually took a jaundiced view of this development, because Palestinian raids into Israel resulted in Israeli reprisals against the territory of the state from which the raid had come, and these reprisals were generally much more destructive and sanguinary than the original raid. Egypt and Syria clamped down effectively on the guerrillas in their own territory and prevented raids. Yet they and other Arab governments insisted that the PLO must be enabled to carry out the 'armed struggle' fantasy — from Jordan and Lebanon. Eventually, the threat to the order in Jordan grew too great, and in a brief but bloody crackdown by the army, the guerrillas were driven from Jordan. They fled, many to Syria, and from there large numbers infiltrated into Lebanon. Suddenly, the guerrillas that had already in 1969 clashed[27] with the army — and even then the guerrillas were supported directly and indirectly by the Syrian government, which sent its Saiqa units into battle in eastern Lebanon[28] — were a considerable military force.

Clashes between the army and the Palestinian guerrillas occurred again in 1971 and yet again in 1973. In each instance the clashes were terminated by a compromise that further legitimized the Palestinian role and presence, that provided more time for Palestinian armament, and that firmly persuaded the Christians and many Moslems, especially the Shi'as, that a showdown was near.[29]

The Palestinian problem paralyzed the Lebanese government. It also dramatically exacerbated latent sectarian differences. While the PLO itself did not 'take sides' in sectarian rivalry, in fact large numbers of individual Palestinians and some of the more ideological Palestinian groups did. Moreover, the Palestinians increasingly assumed the position of 'guardians' of the Sunni community, creating an attraction to many Sunnis. The inability of the army to stop Israeli reprisals (which is to say the unwillingness of the Lebanese Army to see itself destroyed for the Palestinian cause) became a rallying point of opposition to government.[30] Ironically, in view of PLO efforts to stay outside the fighting, but appropriately in view of their role, the incidents that opened the conflict in 1975 erupted between the Kata'eb Party and Palestinian elements.

We shall eschew a discussion of the events and trends in the conflict from 1975 to 1982, especially as this task has been ably performed by others.[31] The key changes that bear heavily upon our own subject include: (i) the expulsion of Palestinians from their camps east of the Green Line; (ii) the entry of Syria into the conflict, initially behind the scenes in support of the Palestinians and their Lebanese allies, then overtly on the side of the Lebanese government; (iii) the remarriage, or re-engagement of the Syrians and Palestinians, that followed Sadat's trip to Jerusalem; (iv) the establishment of a surrogate Israeli militia under the late Saad Haddad and the Israeli intervention of 1978; (v) the internationalization of the conflict through the Zahle confrontation which became the missile crisis which in turn led to a Palestinian-Israeli cease-fire; (vi) the Israeli invasion of 1982; and (vii) the failure of the 1982 crisis to produce a stable order in Lebanon.

Motive Forces and Change Factors

In this section we shall consider some of the dynamics behind the current situation in Lebanon. Certainly, different analysts would list different factors, but most would probably agree, or could be persuaded to agree on some combination including such internal considerations as social change, generational change, demographic change, and the rise of religious extremism; and such external considerations as the continuing Arab-Israeli problem, the specific Syrian-Israeli rivalry, and the Palestinian issue.

Internal Factors

The internal factors are essentially social-change issues. While all may be considered social change, we should note that under this rubric are subsumed several types — viz. generational, demographic and fundamentalist.

Social Change Prior to 1982. Every sectarian group in Lebanon has experienced a dramatic change in its circumstances, and all but the Sunnis can be said to have experienced some substantial degree of social revolution. The Sunni community, urban, established and (especially in Beirut) middle class, was characterized by the antithesis of a revolutionary predisposition. No group in Lebanon was less oriented toward revolution than the Lebanese Sunnis. (Ironically, it was principally among this group that the Palestinian revolutionaries, as well as the other Palestinians, established themselves. Little wonder that the only Lebanese Sunni militias were mere tools of the PLO rather than militant revolutionaries.[32])

The most notable social change in the Christian community took place among the Maronites, whose traditional upper-class leadership was close to the higher Maronite clergy. The rapid growth of Maronite *suburban* communities around the edges of east Beirut in areas like Ain ar-Rummaneh and Sin al-Fil created a lower and lower middle class resentful of their domination by the traditional leadership in society and church. It was from among this group that Bashir Gemayel recruited heavily for his Lebanese Force (LF) militia, and it can be said that the force that emerged under Sheikh Pierre Gemayel's youngest son was the single, greatest threat to the traditional leadership and even to the growing lower-class party led by his father.[33]

Bashir Gemayel incarnated *two* forms of change — generational as well as class. Lebanon's peculiar government form had led to rigidity not only in institutions but also in leadership. For all intents and purposes, the country's consociational democracy precluded replacement of traditional political figures, so that a profile of Lebanon's 1975 leadership startlingly resembled the independence-era leadership. Camille Chamoun, Pierre Gemayel, Kamal Jumblatt, Saeb Salam, Rashid Karame, Kamal Asa'ad, Suleiman Frangieh, Majid Arslan — almost every major national political figure in 1975 was also a political figure of some standing at independence. Meanwhile, two generations of would-be replacements laboured in frustration. Some of the younger political aspirants were the scions of the established political families (for example, Arslan and Jumblatt among the Druzes; al-Khoury and Edde among the Maronites; as-Solh and Karame among the Sunnis; al-Asa'ad and Hamadeh among the Shi'as), some the sons of the 'new' (i.e. independence era) political elites (e.g. Chamoun, Gemayel and Frangieh among the Maronites; Salam and Sa'd among the Sunnis); and a few new to the relatively closed Lebanese political arena. All were excluded by the club of Lebanese political 'godfathers' to a greater or lesser extent.

At about the time that many Maronites were moving to the eastern Beirut suburbs in the 1960s and 1970s, the late Kamal Jumblatt was embarking on a strategy to alter the political structure and patterns of the Druze community and to broaden the straitened political options open to Druze leaders. Historically, Druze political leadership had been closely tied to, though distinct from, the reclusive community's religious hierarchy. The credentials of the principal families — the Atrash in Syria and the Arslan in Lebanon — were based on tribal structure. Two basic divisions or tribal branches encompassed Lebanon's Druzes — the Jumblattis and the Yazbakis. From each of those branches one family emerged as leader — the Jumblatts and the Arslans, respectively. Of these two, the Arslans were traditionally the more important, enjoying a higher status within the tribal structure, but the personal stature of Kamal Jumblatt was significant and extended beyond Lebanon.

The existence of two alternatives among Lebanon's Druze leadership was not only a function of the two clans, but was as well a product of Druze political custom which was always to maintain some participation in *both* of the primary political currents competing for the country's support — Israel versus Syria, Lebanese nationalism versus Arab nationalism, capitalism versus socialism, left versus right, and so forth. On most issues of principle, then, Druzes could be found on both sides. The cynical might call this opportunism, but in fact the phenomenon represented the community's survival instincts, the primal drive of every sectarian minority in the Middle East.[34] Nor did the 'antagonistic' Druze political leaders pursue their divergent objectives without regard for each other. Intra-communal linkages among the Druzes have always been strong, even when kept invisible to outsiders.

Jumblatt's vision exceeded the traditional scope, however. He sought to forge links with other, non-Druze groups that would enable him to overcome the power of the religious hierarchy, the upper masha'ekh, including the sheikh al-Aql, over Druze politicians, to transcend the historic limits of Druze leadership by forming a truly national base, thereby forcing the upper masha'ekh of the community to support him. (Nor, it should be added, was Jumblatt willing to accept the 1943 National Pact's limitations on the Druze political role — and therefore on his own — by the 1970s.) The principal vehicle he established to carry out this strategy was the Progressive Socialist Party, though the PSP was merely the hub of a series of interlocking organizations from the local to the national level, organizations aimed at garnering Moslem and Christian support to add to his Druze base, organizations like the Lebanese

National Movement (LNM) and the National Progressive Forces, many of which supported and were supported in turn by the Palestinians. While it can hardly be argued that Jumblatt's initiatives represent a true social revolution, they did constitute an unprecedented threat to the traditional leadership, and have led to a fundamental change in the Druze order increasing the power of the lower masha'ekh.[35]

During still the same period, political novelties were also beginning to affect the most quiescent of Lebanon's major communities, the Shi'as. The least politically mobilized and the poorest of the major groups, the Shi'as by the 1970s were probably already the largest as a result of their unusually high fertility rate and of the return of many Shi'as from overseas, especially Africa. Several factors affected the Shi'as. First, the influx of Palestinian guerrillas and the increase in guerrilla raids against Israel affected them because these activities were based in the south, one of their two principal areas. Secondly, Israeli reprisal raids on the south, raids designed specifically to mobilize the Shi'as against the Palestinians, struck Shi'a areas, driving a people particularly attached to its land into 'exile' south of Beirut and creating several large Shi'a slums near the Palestinian camps there. Thirdly, a rather bizarre Iranian mullah, Musa Sadr, arrived on the Lebanese scene in 1959, soon emerging as a major force in mobilizing Lebanon's Shi'a community to improve its lot — and its share of political power. 'Imam Musa' was initially to come to Tyre, but found the tribal Beqa'a amenable to his efforts. He later began to concentrate on the south, a region of greater political importance. He established Amal, an organization that advanced Shi'a interests and came, following his mystery-shrouded disappearance in 1978, to symbolize as well as to politically mobilize the Shi'a community.[36]

Although the ground was clearly fertilized by the inadequacy of government attention to the Shi'as over many years and alienation toward their leaders, the rising political consciousness of the community can be attributed to the animosity that developed toward the Palestinian guerrillas; the turbulence caused by Shi'a displacement from the south; the leadership of the enigmatic Sadr, and even more, his disappearance which made him a martyr; the erosion of the ability of traditional Shi'a leaders to operate effectively in the complex Lebanese political system as a result of the paralysis induced by the violence; and the success and impact of the Iranian revolution. This last contribution introduced a new and volatile element to the Shi'a social revolution, particularly after the Israeli intervention in 1982. The size of the community, which by the 1970s clearly enjoyed a plurality in Lebanon, highlighted the need to bring the Shi'as more fully into the political and economic system.

Prior to 1982 the Shi'a movement focused on improving the lot of the community; de-legitimizing and replacing the traditional Shi'a leadership; and reducing or eliminating the Palestinian occupation. These foci resulted in strange alliances: Shi'a covert co-operation with Israel grew, and demands for government and particularly Lebanese Army presence grew apace.

Social Change After 1982. The events and aftermath of the 1982 war altered much of the direction of social change. In the Christian community the war placed Bashir Gemayel and his revolutionary Lebanese Forces in the driver's seat — temporarily. The assassination of Bashir led to the capture (or re-capture) of the LF by the Kata'eb Party, first through Pierre Gemayel's neutralization of Bashirist elements, then, following his death, by the pressure brought to bear by Amin Gemayel through alliances established between 1982 and 1984. By late 1984 the LF was in danger of expiring, unable to mobilize the Christian community because it could identify neither enemy nor friend nor cause, prevented from doing so by the Kata'eb. Sheikh Pierre's death led the president to undertake quickly a move to control the party, and he succeeded, but a party controlled by the president could no longer effectively even suggest that it represented a kernel of opposition views. The Lebanese government represented the traditional interests and ways of doing business in Lebanon.

Underneath the surface of the Christian community, the attitudes favourable to change, attitudes wakened, mobilized, and almost brought to power by Bashir Gemayel, remained. Meanwhile, opposition to government policy along sectarian lines was also universal within the community. To the Christians of the 'heartland' there was a Druze canton established in full autonomy, Minister Walid Jumblatt allowing to be carried out only those activities of the national government he wished in his own community's interest; a Shi'a zone in the south, where Minister Nabih Berri represented as best he could the divided views of his community; a Syrian area of occupation; and an Israeli area of occupation. In each of these regions the government's fiat was carried out only if and to the extent the local leadership deemed desirable. By contrast, all elements of the government, and at least one occupier, had significant influence over what transpired in the Christian area. The government was perceived to be a Syrian vassal. The only focal point for the frustration of the community over this perceived situation was the Lebanese Forces, but the LF leadership appeared to be working closely with the government, especially after late 1984.

It is in this context that the new Christian Decision Movement (CDM) should be seen. The movement unquestionably represents the virtually unanimous view within the Christian community of the heartland, and irrespective of sect. It is unclear to what extent it represents the views of the other geographically discrete communities — e.g. Zahle, Jazzin and so forth. The leadership of the Movement revolves around several individuals close to Bashir Gemayel — Elie Hobeiqa, Samir Ja'ja, Solange Gemayel (Bashir's widow), Fadi Frem, Karim Pakradouni and others. It is interesting to note that while many of the leaders of this group have close ties to Israel, former President Suleiman Frangieh, himself close to Syria, did not condemn the movement, and indeed took the same stand as the CDM leaders on a number of specific issues giving rise to the movement.

A large part of the Druze community supported Bashir Gemayel for president in 1982 as well. Druze and Shi'a as well as Christian votes had elected him president. The Jumblatts were at the modern nadir of their political power in 1982. However, the assassination of Bashir, the lack of LF support for Amin, the death of Majid Arslan, Israeli determination to 'punish' Amin, and the Syrian determination to block American efforts in Lebanon restored Walid Jumblatt, who in the spring and summer of 1983 had been virtually without power in his community, to almost sole leadership of the Druze — but at great economic cost to the community.[37] The economy of the Shuf was built on the foundation of Christian-Druze co-operation and juxtaposition. When, as a result of the Mountain War of 1983, the Christians were driven from the Shuf, the economy collapsed. Moreover, Walid found it impossible to follow in the footsteps of his father. Instead, rhetoric notwithstanding, he returned to the role of paramount Druze leader. His PSP, always predominately Druze, became exclusively so when the most mercilessly pursued Christians in the Mountain War were those of the PSP and its LNM allies, the Syrian Social Nationalist Party (SSNP) and Communists. Walid had never garnered the support of the young, middle-class Druze.[38] After 1983 there was no alternative to Jumblatt, but waiting in the wings, waiting for him to err, were middle-class technocrats and businessmen, on the one hand, and the lower masha'ekh, especially the powerful masha'ekh of the Hasbayya region.[39]

Community survival — always the key to understanding politics in the Levant — was also a principal consideration in Druze behaviour. Only two centuries ago the Druzes ruled most of modern Lebanon. By 1982 they may have been a minority, even in the Shuf. Unlike the Shi'as and many Sunnis, the Druzes tend to be monogamous. Moreover, unlike the Shi'as and Maronites, they generally have small families, an anomaly among mountain peoples. It is due to these factors and some Druze emigration that their respective proportion of the Lebanese population has declined, probably to about 6 per cent. By contrast, the rapid growth of the Shi'as has exerted political pressure to re-divide the Moslem power balance in the latter's favour, an especially threatening development in view of the historically bad blood between the two groups. The Druze response to this complex of challenges has been to establish a separate Druze canton. This is the essence of the campaign Walid Jumblatt has been waging along the Lebanese coast, for such a canton desperately needs a maritime outlet.

The Shi'a movement prior to 1982 was characterized by an apparent unity that derived more from decentralization of control, prominence of adversary, and generality of objectives than from substantive consensus. The prolonged Israeli occupation after 1982; the growing influence of fundamentalist elements as a result of intermittent Syrian support, government insensitivity, and Israeli repression (and as a result too of a general increase in frustration that fed extremism in *all* religious groups throughout the Middle East); the shunting aside of the traditionalist Shi'as; the inclusion of Amal leader Nabih Berri in the government at a time when he was unable to either accelerate Israeli departure or realize other Shi'a demands; and the lack of control or leadership that seemed to characterize Amal's ranks — all these factors contributed to the fragmentation of the Shi'a community in the period after 1982. In these circumstances, local leaders, especially religious leaders, took an outsized importance, and while none seemed eager to surface at the national level (i.e. to repeat Berri's error), the emergence of a confessional class of local mullahs, something new to the Lebanese Shi'a community, further propelled the sectarian and fundamentalist nature of Shi'a political mobilization in the period after 1982.[40]

Even the Sunnis were deeply affected by the social ferment after the 1982 war. Although the earlier Sunni so-called 'revolutionary' groups, virtually all of which were secular, even in Tripoli, a city always until 1980 more in tune with the conservative Syrian Sunni heartland of Homs, Hama and Aleppo,[41] espoused revolutionary rhetoric, they were usually only the tools of foreign powers and enjoyed no real popular base. Even the Sunni communities of Beirut, the Iqlim, and Sidon were anything but unhappy to see the departure of the PLO and Syria.[42] Nevertheless, for the first time after 1980 the Sunni communities began to give some evidence of extremism — predictably that of the right. In every case this extremism has been and remains a response to a serious threat to community interest; in every case this threat is neither Christian nor Israeli.

The first Sunni area to manifest the new trend was, not surprisingly, Tripoli. There a Sunni fundamentalist movement emerged in reaction to the rapidly growing 'Alawi community, the great bulk of which was transplanted from Syria. Together, Yasser Arafat's PLO and the fundamentalist Tawhid movement under Sheikh Said Sha'aban fought the 'Alawis and their Syrian supporters. When Arafat was ousted from Tripoli, Sha'aban continued the battle as best he could alone. Increasingly, he enjoyed the support of the entire Sunni population.

In Beirut, the Sunnis were threatened by the Druze militia and, especially, the Shi'as who by 1983 had become the dominant factor in West Beirut. Too late did the Sunni community recognize the magnitude of the threat, and Amal and the PSP refused to permit the formation of any Sunni militia.[43] By 1983 growing Sunni fundamentalism was also in evidence in Beirut.

Of Sunni dominance in the three great coastal cities — Tripoli, Beirut, Sidon — little endures. Tripoli remains predominantly Sunni, but political power must be divided with the 'Alawis, at least as long as 'Alawis control Syria and the latter remains in Lebanon. There are probably more Shi'as than Sunnis in West Beirut today, and all demographic change there is one-sided, with Shi'as constantly moving into neighbourhoods once Sunni or Sunni-Greek Orthodox. Already, the real power derives from the barrels of Amal's guns, however diverse their aim. Finally, no one knows the relative population of the communities in Sidon, but recent events[44] suggest that there too Shi'as are the real power, and certainly demographic change is in their favour.

On one plane, at least, change *is* being effected. The older leaders are passing from the scene. Amin Gemayel now leads the government; Walid Jumblatt, the Druzes; the youthful group at the head of the LF (the CDM), the Christians; and a host of new faces, the Shi'as. Only among the Sunnis is the pre- and early independence era leadership still in place, but new faces are appearing there too. (Ironically, the Sunnis of Beirut had in the Maqassed the only national institution for bringing in new communal leadership.) What has changed in *every* community is the ability of a leader to 'deliver' his constituency, one of the pillars of consociational government. It is predictable as a result that a variety of new leaders will emerge, and it is likely that they will be leaders with military or militia experience. When violence is the language of politics, leaders establish their legitimacy with the appropriate speech.

Like most Middle East politics, the face of politics in Lebanon is theatre and bears scant resemblance to the body of politics. The Druze community leaders condemn 'feudalism', 'cantonization', and Israel, but in practice are more feudal, fight more effectively for a canton, and collaborate more closely with Israel than the leaders of any other community. Shi'a leaders 'support' the Druze in word, while combating them in deed. Christian leaders talk about sacrifice and worry about profits. The president speaks of a 'new Lebanon', but has attempted to restore the old, at least as much as possible, under the circumstances. Sunni leaders — seeing the erosion of their position in Lebanon — who have historically weakened Lebanon by using their Arab world links against the interests of all the other communities, are now vehement nationalists.

Yet a serious resolution to these demographic, generational and sectarian problems cannot even be undertaken. Not because they are too complex, but because they are all pre-empted by the role of external powers in Lebanon.

External Factors

External change factors have played a seminal role in creating Lebanon's current predicament and constitute perhaps the most immediate and undeniable set of constraints as present. We shall consider three external variables — the Arab world, the

Palestinians and the Israeli-Syrian conflict.

The Arab World and Lebanon. Lebanon's relationship with the rest of the Arab world has always been *sui generis*. The country's historic links to the West, its long-established cosmopolitan identity, its openness to ideas foreign to the Arab world — all these characteristics have set the Lebanese apart and have, periodically, inspired Arab distrust of the Lebanese. In candour, it must be said as well that the size and vigour of Lebanon's Christian community has also created tension in an Arab world that is overwhelmingly Moslem. Lebanon's membership in the Arab League should have quashed Arab reservations about Lebanon's legitimacy, and in the legal sense this was true (except to some degree in Syria). Yet Lebanon's 'difference' remained something of a magnet for problems in the Arab world.

The 1943 National Pact on which Lebanon was established balanced external as well as internal divergencies. Whereas the Sunni community looked predominantly toward the Arab world for its identity and linkages, the Christians, especially the Maronites, looked Westward. The principle that was inculcated in the National Pact was that neither Lebanon's occidental nor its oriental inclinations should be allowed to compromise the country's sovereignty or either of the diverse sets of real and existential interests that these inclinations engendered. For all intents and purposes, Lebanon was neutralized by these proscriptions.

Jureidini has cogently pointed out that the Arab world into which Lebanon was born was a very different Arab world from today's. There was no Israel; the Arab states were all Western-oriented; there was no superpower rivalry; no Arab state was powerful enough to really project force beyond its borders against another Arab state. The creation of the state of Israel added a new actor that had not accepted Lebanese neutrality. The emergence of anti-Western Arab governments and the ideological revolution of the 1950s and 1960s meant that Lebanon's social-economic philosophies and ties to the West were now questioned, and in fact constituted grounds to deny or disregard Lebanon's 'neutrality'. A growing Soviet role added external pressure. And a regional arms race in which Lebanon did not participate soon left Lebanon vulnerable to either neighbour's military pressure.[45]

After 1958 Lebanon, trying to adapt to the new circumstances, moved somewhat further from the West and endeavoured to make its peace with the 'positive neutralists' of the Arab world. In the process, which lasted until 1975, Lebanon suffered political marginalization both in the Arab world and in the West, thereby losing its traditional friends; Lebanon never did secure the support of those the country courted, thereby retaining its antagonists; and Lebanon alienated Israel, thereby creating an enemy it could ill afford. The truth is, after 1948, Lebanon's neutrality was no longer acceptable in the Arab world; and Lebanon's unique nature meant any attempt to exit the conflict with Israel would *not* be supported by Lebanon's fellow Arab governments.[46] The Arab record on Lebanon is a sad one — replete with broken promises, double-dealing, and outright subversion, when it is not characterized principally by apathy.

The Palestinians and Lebanon. Perhaps the best example of the Arab world's ambivalence toward Lebanon is the experience with the Palestinians who have themselves known Arab betrayal on more than a few occasions.

No Arab country welcomed the Palestinians more graciously or fully than Lebanon in 1948, when 150,000 Palestinian refugees poured into the country.[47] A measure of Lebanon's relative peace and its comfort with the National Pact is that the inherent threat to the sectarian balance was perceived to be secondary to the need to welcome the refugees, despite the fact that the vast majority of refugees were Moslem.[48]

During the period between the first and second Arab-Israeli wars, the large Palestinian refugee populations in Lebanon lived side by side with the Lebanese without incident. It was in the aftermath of the second war (the 1956 Suez War), however, that various Arab governments, especially Egypt and Syria, began to use the Palestinian problem and the Palestinians as an arm of their own foreign policies. From the inception of this phenomenon, Lebanon was victimized by Palestinians acting on behalf of non-Palestinian foreign interests.

The manipulation of Palestinians by Arab governments was only a part of the picture. In the 1960s a number of Palestinian groups moved toward ideological extremism both in the sense of the political spectrum and in the sense of apotheosizing the Palestinian problem. The moderate states — primarily Jordan and Lebanon — in which Palestinians were living, were beset by two distinct challenges: Palestinians who insisted that revolution in the Arab world was the first and necessary precondition to the realization of Arab and Palestinian objectives, and those who openly subordinated all Arab and 'regional' (i.e. national) interests to the interests of the Palestinian movement.[49] By the late 1970s, in the humiliating and bitter aftermath of the 1967 'setback', it was politically unacceptable to oppose or constrain the true heroes of the Arab world, the Palestinian guerrillas. Ironically, the strong (Egypt, Syria) were able to completely constrain and control the guerrillas, but no other Arab state accepted that the weak (Jordan and Lebanon) should do so.

As early as 1969 Syrian military personnel were intervening in Lebanon as, and in conjunction with, Syria's 'house' Palestinian guerrilla group, Saiqa.[50] Later, Syria's opposition to Palestinian motives and activities led to the direct intervention of Syrian armed forces. Although the Lebanese government welcomed Syria's invasion at the time, later attempts to secure the withdrawal of what became an only slightly disguised occupation force failed.[51] Syrian co-operation with and attacks on the PLO in Lebanon alternated, and in 1983 Syria used its presence in Lebanon to support an 'internal' Fatah rebellion against the established leadership of Yasser Arafat. This initiative led to an 'internal' Palestinian war on Lebanese soil that cost the lives and property of many Lebanese.[52]

After 1976 there were two occupiers, for the PLO had already established itself as such in the south, where PLO personnel seized homes, property and people, acting as a law unto themselves. The raids into Israel never posed a serious military threat to the latter, but did provoke Israel's retaliatory airstrikes that devastated the south, driving tens of thousands of Shi'as off their land.[53] The PLO also developed a curious and close relationship to the Moslem communities, especially the Sunnis, in several cases.

Palestinian raids led to the establishment of a local militia in the south under the command of the late Saad Haddad, to Israel's invasion of 1978, to Israeli support of the Haddad militia,[54] and eventually to the Israeli invasion of 1982.[55] After the 1982 war, Israeli forces occupied most of southern Lebanon, before withdrawing from the Shuf in the fall of 1983, from the area between Beirut and the Awwali in 1984, and from most of the south in 1985. While the Israeli government has announced (and accelerated) a programme to withdraw completely from Lebanon, virtually no one believes the withdrawal will be functionally or geographically complete.

Almost incredibly, few Palestinians are prepared to concede responsibility for a large part of what befell Lebanon. Leaving aside the 1975–6 fighting, and even the combat among Lebanese after that, the PLO exploitation of Lebanon has certainly been a principal factor in the violence in that country. And it is quite predictable that Palestinian involvement in inter-Arab politics will extend that past truth into the future, as it is that should armed Palestinians return to southern Lebanon even greater devastation will follow in their wake. This is a criticism of the PLO from the point of view of Lebanese nationalists — Christian, Moslem and Druze — only, not from another point of view; for it is apparent that an inherent conflict exists between what is in the interests of existing Arab states and what many Palestinians believe to be in the interest of Palestinian nationalism.

Israel, Syria and Lebanon. Borders are imaginary lines with real implications. Individual Israelis and Syrians have always had reservations about Lebanon's borders. In Syria many questioned the legitimacy of the Lebanese state as constituted in 1943 distinct from Syria.[56] In Israel many questioned the legitimacy of the Lebanese state for other reasons.[57] Both suffered Lebanese sovereignty, but grudgingly. When events allowed them to take actions that undermined this sovereignty, even if that was not the intent behind the specific actions, neither hesitated to do so.[58] Both initially worked through Lebanese agents, both were pushed into military intervention, both used their occupations to create new political facts, and both have long since abandoned any pretence or intention of respecting Lebanese sovereignty.

History has shown that under a given set of circumstances Israel can dominate most of Lebanon, but not all. Given Israel's clear-cut military superiority over Syria, these circumstances involve Israeli public opinion and peace on the Egyptian front more than any other factor. Israeli opinion does not now permit such an extensive Israeli empire in Lebanon, and is unlikely to permit it for the foreseeable future.

History has shown that under a given set of circumstances, such as those prevailing today, Syria can dominate most of Lebanon, but not all. While Israel is more powerful, there are Lebanese and Israeli constraints on the extent of Israeli control, constraints that do not apply to Syria. However, Israel's military predominance precludes the extension of Syrian control to the southernmost part of Lebanon — or to any part Israel is willing to fight to keep away from Syria.

The line of demarcation between the Lebanese spheres of influence of Israel and Syria is variable. To the extent both actively pursue maximizing the size of their spheres, *soi-disant* 'internal' conflicts will rage in Lebanon, for both Israel and Syria act through agents.[59] To the extent one of the two is prepared to allow the other to have maximum permissible territory, 'internal' peace, meaning merely the absence of hostilities, may predominate. And if both subordinate Lebanon to other interests, violence or peace may prevail depending upon technique. That is, if Israel and Syria reach a tacit accord, as between 1976 and 1981,[60] such violence as erupts will be largely a function of other conflicts. If, by contrast, they simply turn to other problems, leaving Lebanon to 'stew', as it were, substantial violence will follow as surrogates of the external powers fight for their own ends and with the belief that their masters will step in to protect them if their position deteriorates too much.

One of the most common errors made by analysts of the Lebanese conflicts has been the presumption that surrogates were the same as puppets. There are many surrogates in Lebanon, and indeed most important groups have worked with or for a variety of external sponsors. However, in most cases these groups *already* existed as valid actors on the Lebanese scene. Even astute and careful analysts have applied the term 'puppet' to Lebanese such as the late Saad Haddad, to the current prime minister, Rashid Karame, the Gemayel brothers, to Camille Chamoun, to Suleiman Frangieh, to Walid Jumblatt, to Nabih Berri, and so forth *ad nauseam* at one time or another.[61] It is unnecessary to join the issue for the Gemayels, Chamoun, Frangieh, Jumblatt or Berri, since all have co-operated with several external actors and worked openly against the interests of their most prominent outside supporters at some time. But even Karame is, and Haddad was, valid Lebanese. Both represented a segment of opinion, both were the recipients of external support, and each appears to have acted for the most part in accordance with his own interests and values. Neither was created by his external supporters,[62] and both have been used by them.

Thus, when the Druzes, for example, are not subject to too much pressure by Israel or Syria, they may act on their own behalf. To the extent the LF is able to operate outside such pressure from Damascus or Jerusalem, it will do the same. It is important to recognize that whereas a tacit agreement between Israel and Syria can reduce or even eliminate such violence in the short run, the other option of a free hand cannot, with all the social change pressures we have discussed, have this result.

Not that the Lebanese hate each other. Not that nationalism is unknown. Not that they fail to resent the intervention of outside powers or place little value on life. Rather, the institutions and processes necessary to adaptation have been stifled as a consequence of the internal conflict, the imposed violence, and the continuing occupations of Lebanon, such that today no one knows what Lebanon is, what the ground rules are, what the expectations are, or what the relative power of the diverse communities and other aggregate identity groups is. For analysts who believe that political shares are based on perceived power, the result of this anarchic situation should hardly be surprising — violence to determine relative power, to establish ground rules, to ascertain and shape expectations.

We must remember, too, that 'Lebanon' exists physically only in the cartographic sense; it is not permitted to exist in any other by Israel and Syria. The cross-border activities of the 1960s gave rise to open military intervention in the 1970s. By the latter half of the 1970s, the eastern and northern border had little meaning to Syria, the southern no more to Israel. Both crossed Lebanese frontiers at will to carry out military, economic, and political actions. By the 1980s, after a succession of demands and pronouncements by the two antagonists, each indirectly 'recognized' the special security interests of the other in Lebanon, and both took pains to express, directly or through mouthpieces, their recognition of each other's needs.[63] Note the implications. Israel not only crosses Lebanon's borders at will but concedes to Syria the same right; Syria acts on a parallel course. The frequency and magnitude of the disregard of Lebanese sovereignty have long since inured the international community, which tolerates and indeed anticipates continued disregard, to future violations. The Lebanese themselves, irrespective of their yearning for the return of Lebanese government authority, must look to Israel and Syria to meet their daily needs. For years, Lebanese of the Beqa'a have been forced to turn to Syria to respond to those needs; Lebanese of the south, to Israel.

There is not the slightest suggestion that Syria will treat Lebanon as sovereign. Syria's implantation of an 'Alawi colony around Tripoli and the endeavour to legitimize that colony by providing it a specified number of seats in the Chamber of Deputies show 'Alawi intentions as regards Tripoli's future. And certainly there is little prospect of the withdrawal[64] of Syrian forces from Lebanon as long as 'Alawis rule in Syria. Lebanon is the only feasible route for large numbers of 'Alawis to return to the 'Alawi heartland if control in Damascus is lost. Tripoli's incorporation *de facto* or *de jure* into Syria will provide much better port facilities. The Lebanese economic potential to serve and service Syria has long been an object of Syrian interest.[65]

There is not the slightest suggestion that Israel will treat Lebanon as sovereign. After the chastening political experience of the Lebanese affair, Israeli leaders have apparently concluded that, absent Israeli pressures (that are not politically feasible for domestic reasons), the government in Beirut will remain responsive to Syria, therefore hostile. Consequently, the intent appears to be to establish layered security — a belt of Lebanese territory along the Israeli-Lebanese frontier that will be subject to heavy Israeli control, whether exercised through surrogates or requiring frequent military excursions; a strip to the northeast that will be, in effect, a Druze canton; and a mobile Israeli military force inside Israel itself to make such forays into an area between the Druze canton, the sea and the security strip.[66] It is striking that most Lebanese do not understand why Israel has encouraged the Druzes to create a canton at this time. Such a canton, controlled by a people with whom Israel has always enjoyed close and co-operative relations at the *sub rosa* level, is clearly a rational and understandable outcome of the 'security' dilemma.

Both Israel and Syria, then, have sowed the seeds for even greater derogation of Lebanese sovereignty in the future, indeed, for the dismantling of the Lebanese state.

The Requirements for a Viable Peace in Lebanon

If this were a perfect world, one could consider as most important among the requirements for a peace in Lebanon the purely *Lebanese* issues, leaving aside or, at the very least, deferring until those issues are resolved, the external considerations. But then, if this were a perfect world, we would not be considering the

requirements for peace in Lebanon against the backdrop of a sanguinary conflict vortex that has already consumed between 100,000
and 150,000 lives and caused damage that will require over
$US25,000 million of reconstruction.[67] The hard realities are that
the Lebanese currently enjoy very little freedom of action at the
community, regional or national level, and none at all in certain
matters. Despite the wisdom of journalistic pundits, the external,
not the internal, problems are driving the Lebanese conflict as this
is written. We must therefore first consider those elements in
arriving at, or rather in aspiring for, a recipe for conflict-
resolution.

External Requirements

There are essentially five outcomes to the Lebanese conflicts at the
international-status level. They are the following:

● Lebanon becomes a Syrian vassal, or part of Syria.
● Lebanon becomes an Israeli vassal.
● Lebanon is partitioned between Israel and Syria.
● Lebanon disintegrates.
● Lebanon's sovereignty is restored.

As we have already indicated, neither of the first two outcomes is
likely. Neither neighbour under foreseeable conditions can be
expected to control *all* of Lebanon. Although some Lebanese and
Syrian leaders have recently resurfaced the first option in the guise
of a federal union,[68] and although such a union could indeed even
be proclaimed, there is no practical possibility that, even in this
case, Syria can extend its effective control to the south of Lebanon,
or even into the Shuf. To endeavour to do so does not risk realizing
the first option, but, rather, encourages the third (partition) or
fourth (disintegration).

Partition cannot be as easily discounted, if for no other reason
than that Lebanon has been 'temporarily', 'flexibly', and *de facto*
partitioned for years. Southernmost Lebanon could be looked
upon by Israel as a buffer, and Israel would likely try to completely
control that buffer. Syria's primary interests lie in Tripoli and the
Beqa'a, but the Syrian government would or could derive
numerous benefits from annexing Beirut as well. There can be little
doubt for anyone aware of Syrian activities around Tripoli that the
Syrians, or at least the 'Alawi government of Syria, is bent upon

complete control of that port and its *de facto*, if not *de jure*, annexation by Syria.[69] Similarly, as long as the 'Alawis remain in power in Damascus, control of the Beqa'a is vital to community interests.

Israel's determination to prevent attacks on and shelling of northern Israel from Lebanese territory is the motivation behind control of the south of Lebanon. While many have averred that Israel has long been interested in annexing that part of Lebanese territory south of the Litani, and certainly there are and have been for some time Israelis so motivated, there is little evidence to support such a thesis and much to invalidate it. Less clear is the question of *control*, however, for Israel's water needs are great, and the waters of the Litani and Hasbani Rivers have certainly not gone without notice in Israel. Indeed, there have been numerous assertions that Israel has been diverting, or has made preparations for the diversion of, these waters.[70] Whether for security or natural resource purposes, Israeli domination of the extreme south will continue, and if Syria were to take the lead by annexing parts of Lebanon, Israel might 'extend security administration' over the south, slowly moving toward its annexation.

The region that defies partition is the Shuf. The Druze community is subject to greater Israeli than Arab political influence, but plays the Arab role and is plainly an Arab population. It is probable that neither Israel nor Syria could tolerate annexation of the Shuf by the other.

The disintegration of Lebanon, by which we mean its disappearance as a single entity and replacement by two or more smaller polities, and perhaps in combination with the annexation of parts of Lebanon by Israel and Syria, cannot be excluded either. The gulf separating the Lebanese from one another has never in history been as great as it is today. The yearning to reconstitute a sovereign Lebanon, a desire that cuts across all communities, is to a great extent an artifact and a fantasy, for agreement on what such a Lebanon should be is less easy today than even a year ago. Moreover, recent events, the most important ones again imported from outside, have had a chilling effect on Lebanese national unity. Let us consider briefly some of the elements of the disintegrative current.

● *Homogenization or territorialization.* One of the problems associated with partition or cantonization has been the heterogeneous nature of most of Lebanon, each region having one or more minorities. In 1975–6, however, the Christian heartland lost its non-Christian element. In 1983 the Shuf lost its non-Druze element. Christians have left Tripoli. The exclusivist Shi'as' creeping annexation of West Beirut and Sidon continues, and a new exodus of Christians and Sunnis from many areas of the south is already underway. The sectarian map of Lebanon is beginning — and, contrary to widespread assumptions, for the first time — to take on a distinctly territorial appearance.[71]

● *Powerlessness.* The Lebanese are few and weak, but this is not a novelty; so have they always been. What has changed is the degree of inter-communal co-operation. The Lebanese triumphed over outsiders in the past *only* when communities co-operated with each other against external forces. When they broke ranks they became pawns of the more powerful external forces. Today, each community is working with outside powers, usually only to survive, but in the process weakening ever more both the bonds of unity and the common and reciprocal interests in a shared future. Each is so weak it sees power only in alignment with the strong outsider rather than its weak compatriots, intentionally overlooking what each knows well — that alignment with powerful foreign interests is always made on *their* terms and at one's own expense.

● *Leadership vacuum.* The consociational political style was based on quasi-feudal Lebanese political culture. The social revolution that sustained violence has effectively eliminated all but a few vestiges of that system, but did not replace it with any other means of legitimizing leaders save through violence. The result is that no community or region today has leaders who can 'deliver' their people, who can duplicate the kind of historic compromise consecrated in the 1943 National Pact.

Disintegrative forces are ubiquitous in the Middle East, and in south Asia and Oceania as well. They may well arise in Africa and southeast Asia, though likely not with the same vigour in the near term.[72] So, Lebanon is not alone. Rather, it is only the most publicized victim of a growing pathology. It is the catalytic effect that foreign powers have had — and, of course, characteristic of Lebanon's *laissez-faire* tradition, the weakness of the Lebanese central government — that magnified the power of disintegrative forces in Lebanon.

Any of the first three options could restore internal 'peace' to

Lebanon, but at the cost of Lebanon's independence and existence, and even then only temporarily, i.e. as long as the power of external force compelled acceptance of political institutions and behaviour. Neither Israel nor Syria is likely, and no Lebanese party is able, to perpetrate this forced 'peace', but peace there would be. Even now, Israel and Syria can control, and do influence, such internal violence as reigns in Lebanon. This paper does not address such a so-called 'peace', a peace that amounts to the loss of everything Lebanon stands for, and, therefore, to the end of what makes Lebanon worth saving.[73]

It is apparent that any conflict resolution prescription or 'peace plan' would be inappropriate in the event Lebanon is partitioned between Israel and Syria, or is thus partitioned in combination with the emergence of a Druze mini-state in the Shuf. Similarly, since a peace plan is presumably to forestall fragmentation, the fourth option is equally to be disregarded. Consequently, the ideas developed below are based upon a reassertion of Lebanese sovereignty and the re-establishment of Lebanon's independence from both its larger and covetous neighbours.

Internal Requirements

Tragically, we believe that no solution can be found to Lebanon's problems without yet more violence. Only internal upheaval in Syria will reduce Syria's erosion of Lebanon's separateness. It is, in truth, difficult to see *any* circumstance in the near or medium term that could have the same effect on Israel. Even if both neighbours were to restore their respect for Lebanese sovereignty, however, the result would certainly bring renewed *internal* violence. Pluralist countries tend to cohere under two different, and in many respects opposite, conditions. The first is that one group imposes unity (not uniformity); the second is that independent groups negotiate as equals to give up sovereignty in favour of unity. In American experience, the second model is reflected by the Constitutional Convention period, and the first after the war between the states.

When Bashir Gemayel was elected president he profited from the support of Israel and the United States, to be sure, but he also fielded by far the most powerful indigenous military force in Lebanon, and enjoyed almost complete support, and the unquestioned leadership, of the Christian community.[74] At that time Walid Jumblatt and Majid Arslan could speak for the Druzes; Amal's leadership, for a Shi'a community much less fragmented than at present. Today, leadership is weaker in all communities, and that which was accepted in 1982 is no longer so. Shi'a aspirations in Sidon, West Beirut, the Shuf and Lebanon are now clear, and the Druzes and Sunnis, much more than the Christians, fear them. The Druze card in the Shuf has been played, and the Iqlim al-Kharrub, key to the emergence of a viable Druze mini-state, has laid bare the magnitude of the conflict between Druze and Shi'a aspirations. The cynical Israeli attempt in 1983 to use the Shuf to teach Amin Gemayel a lesson backfired, strengthening the president by weakening his competitors and potential competitors — Dany Chamoun, whose base was the south and the Shuf, the Lebanese Forces who 'lost' the Shuf, and senior Christian officers of the Lebanese Army who did likewise. The president relied on his traditional Kisrawan and Metn Kata'eb support, but ultimately alienated himself from those bases and of necessity turned to and depended on Syria. There are no leaders of unified communities; the closest is certainly Walid Jumblatt, who, however, depends upon continued violence, upon Syrian support, and upon meeting the minimum demands of the community's pro-Israel religious leaders. The communal leadership required to compromise short of additional violence is absent.

Intermittently since the conflict first erupted in Lebanon in 1975, and frequently since the emergence of Bashir Gemayel and the election of his brother, various groups have called for national reconciliation in Lebanon. Although different parties clearly mean different things by the phrase 'national reconciliation', everyone recognizes that the Lebanese political system must find new modes of adaptation to changing demographic, political, economic and social realities. In particular, the traditional Maronite-Sunni alliance, which has been the centrepiece of the Lebanese political system since independence, must either accept some fundamental changes, particularly from the plurality Shi'a community, or must allow for the alteration of specific structures and institutions.

In this section we have dealt with the problem of the reconcilia-tion of sectarian demands 'unrealistically' — i.e. as an internal issue. We address and assess these demands from *Lebanese* Sunni, Shi'a, Druze, Maronite and other Christian viewpoints. Let there be no doubt that all Lebanese parties in fact favour reconciliation. The majority of all sects favour co-existence and even co-operation across confessional divisions. Despite the blood that has been spilled, there can be no doubt that most Lebanese still prefer

'Lebanon' over any feasible alternative.[75]

Issues

Lebanese views on reconciliation and reform[76] involve a plethora of issues, eleven of which will be considered here. These eleven concern six themes — the scope of Lebanon, government structure, separation of powers, centralization, representation and political orientation. Specifically, the primary issues are

1. scope in Lebanon — Grand Liban (Greater Lebanon) vs Mont Liban (Mount Lebanon);
2. government structure — the institutions of government and the relationship of these institutions to each other;
3. separation of powers — the allocation of power to the different branches of government and to the different elements of the executive, specifically as between the president and the prime minister;
4. centralization — the power of the central government both *vis-à-vis* the various regions of the country and *vis-à-vis* the various sectarian groups;
5. representation — the representation of sectarian groups in government (whether through allocation of offices by sect or otherwise), and the question of whether or to what extent secularism will be an objective or characteristic of government;
6. political orientation — the determination of the role of Lebanon in the regional and larger worlds in which the country must survive.

Practically, then, these six themes involve eleven issues — the size of Lebanon, government institutions, the role of the central government in security and foreign affairs, the power of the central government with respect to geographical subdivisions, the central government's power *vis-à-vis* Lebanon's sects, the role of the armed forces in internal security, the geography of the subdivisions, confessionalism as a principle, the means to protect vital interests of the sects in practice, the relationship of Lebanon to its immediate neighbours (Israel and Syria) in terms both of defence and foreign policy, and Lebanon's position *vis-à-vis* the Arab world and the West.

It must be understood that one can deal with the issues discretely as below, but that in fact they are interdependent. That is, the precise position of any group on any one subject is affected by its (and others') views on other subjects. For example, how Shi'as feel about the power of the prime minister *vis-à-vis* the president, or whether there should be a bicameral legislature depends very heavily upon whether the position of prime minister remains one allocated to the Sunnis.

Rival Philosophies for Lebanon's Restoration. The rise of the Lebanese Shi'as has created polarity in the conception of a new Lebanon. The choice is basic and inevitable between 'Grand Liban' and 'Mont Liban' concepts. This is a choice that has not been made by any major Lebanese leader, a choice all communities believe must come from the Maronites.

The dichotomy arises as a result of the demographic puissance and political mobilization of the Lebanese Shi'as and the resulting threat perceived by the Druze and Sunni communities, and to a lesser extent the Christian,[77] pressures to which we have already adverted. The Druzes and Sunnis would feel much more secure in a Republic of Mount Lebanon, i.e. in a republic that excluded the Beqa'a, parts of the south, and conceivably even Tripoli (though here the Sunnis part company with the others). The relatively stable community shares of population in such a Lebanon would, it is argued, reduce friction. Moreover, while the Sunnis and the Sunni-Druze partners would clearly be subordinate to the Christians, they would have a role superior in power, stability and security to what both Sunni and Druze fear will be their lot in the emerging Lebanon. The Druzes would control the Shuf; the Sunnis, their traditional cities. Both would look to each other and the Christians as allies against Shi'a expansion.

By contrast, the Greater Lebanon option, which assumes continuation of a Lebanon of 10,452 square kilometers (4,035 sq. miles), suggests a Christian-Shi'a partnership, or at least a commitment to accord the Shi'as a greater role more reflective of their numbers and power. At present, Druze and Sunni leaders are trying to block this possibility by publicly aligning with the Shi'a and privately talking with, and trying to establish a commitment from, the Christians, i.e. the Maronites.

Government Structure. The principle issues with respect to the structure of the government concern the nature of government institutions and their relationship to each other. Currently, Lebanon has a combination presidential-ministerial form of government in which the president is the chief executive but the prime minister is the head of government. The government has varied over time, including technocrats on some occasions, political leaders on others. Traditionally, the president is seen as the chief decision-maker, but claims have often been made with a view to increasing the prime minister's power,[78] and in fact, at various times the prime minister has been the critical decision-maker *in some domains*. The unicameral Chamber of Deputies (parliament) has the legislative function, but a formal system of checks and balances does not exist.

Sunni, Shi'a and Druze communities would prefer to see a strengthening of the prime minister's office and responsibilities *vis-à-vis* those of the president. By contrast, all Christian sects tend to see the maintenance of a strong president as necessary to an effective Lebanese government, if the country remains unitary in nature (see below). Shi'as favour a stronger prime minister, but would be far more adamant in this position if the prime minister were, or even could be, a Shi'a.

Some thought has been given to the concept of a bicameral legislature in recent years, and indeed the decision to move in that direction was made during the Lausanne Conference. Generally, the purpose of such an initiative is seen as being the creation of a prestigious new position for a Druze. The greater advantages of such a legislature, advantages that might be quite significant for communities such as the Druze, the Greek Orthodox, the Greek Catholic, and other small sects if a second house had some important blocking capability such as the US Senate, do not seem to have been widely considered.

Separation of Powers. The unitary Lebanese government has not in the past looked to the concept of 'separation of powers' as a technique to control the amount of power in any single branch's hands, even though it is certainly true that the Chamber of Deputies has powers not granted to the executive and vice versa. Still, the debate over the prime minister's powers as against those of the president reflects at least a minimal awareness of the importance of a separation of powers to all Lebanese communities. Similarly, the role of the Chamber of Deputies, which is now quite limited though still important in areas such as budgetary authority, remains an area for potential adjustment of various sects' fears and aspirations.

Again, no single community has asserted a clear view with respect to the increase, decreases, or modification of the *powers* of the Chamber. (Strong views have been advanced relative to its composition.) In the event government structures become an active subject of consideration among the communities, it is likely all will develop strong views on the role and powers of the Chamber.

By contrast, the role of the army is and has been for many years a very active subject of debate and discussion. Historically, the Christian community has favoured a strong army and has supported the role of the army as the ultimate guarantor of internal security, while the Moslem communities and the Druzes have sought to dilute the army's power in principle and to oppose its use for internal purposes. (Moslem and Druze communities favour a greater gendarmerie role in internal security and a lesser army role. It should be noted that the Shi'a and even the Sunnis have often requested a greater army presence in specific areas.) It is unlikely that these views will soften in the short term, although changes taking place in the composition, leadership, training, equipment and primary mission of the army, as well as its challenge to Israel in the south in 1985, may have a long-term impact on all communities.

Centralization. Some of the principal proposals put forth to resolve a variety of the domestic problems besetting Lebanon involve decentralizing the control currently exercised by the government in Beirut. Under a variety of rubrics such as 'decentralization', 'devolution', 'federation', 'confederation', 'autonomy', and others, the concept of local self-government has been proposed as a means of defusing distrust toward a central government that either in the present or in the future may treat one's identity group adversely.

The concept of decentralization relates directly to those of government structure and representation. That is, each community views with favour decentralization to the extent it lacks power or control of the central government.

● The Druze community, which does not enjoy leadership of any major element of the government, but which controls a substantial and clearly identifiable geographic area, has for some time been attracted to decentralization. Indeed, recent events have given the Druze community *de facto* autonomy in the Shuf.
● The Maronite community was less interested in this approach as long as the alternative worked, but is much more likely to accept it

today. (Some within the community have long favoured such an idea.) The other Christian faiths, except the Greek Orthodox in the Kura, do not have substantial areas in which they predominate. However, territorialization of the confessional map has altered their views to some extent for the present, and created a broad spectrum of accord within the Christian heartland. In this context, the Christian Decision Movement creates an autonomous regime in the Christian heartland similar to the Druze autonomous zone in the Shuf.

● Sunnis at one time were credited with greater territorial domination than they now enjoy. Decentralization along regional lines would be especially difficult for the Sunni community, since it would share Beirut with the Christians (in the East) and Shi'as (who in fact outnumber Sunnis in Beirut now), Tripoli with the 'Alawis, and Sidon with the Shi'as.

● By contrast, the Shi'a community clearly predominates in large areas of the country, including most of the south and the Beqa'a Valley, and is a major factor in Sidon and Beirut. In the case of the Shi'as, decentralization offers the possibility of much greater control over their destiny, since the current leadership position allotted to a Shi'a (president of the Chamber) is not particularly powerful except to block legislation. Government control even now is relatively limited in all Shi'a areas. However, the Shi'a community is very concerned about decentralization for two reasons — financial (see below) and geographical. The emergence of the Druze canton has split the Shi'as into three non-contiguous areas, a development with ominous overtones in view of the uncertain future of a unified Lebanon.

Decentralization need not be along geographic lines only (although confessional territorialization probably assures this). That is, various types of issues may be treated in different ways. Personal-status issues, for example, could be relegated to muhafizat (or other jurisdictional) control, while foreign affairs and defence remain the province of the central government. Indeed, in this sense most governments provide for differential types of responsibilities. At the same time, it must be pointed out that decentralization does not necessarily relieve and may in fact exacerbate the problems of religious coexistence Lebanon has encountered — unless of course territorialization continues. In those issues that devolve upon local governments, what protects the autonomy or rights of the local minorities?

Nor is this the only problem with decentralization, for although it is true that the Shi'as would like to have greater control of the south, for example, it is also true that they would not like revenues to be divided on the basis of region of origin. Yet if the Christians, for example, produce a disproportionate share of state revenues, they see no reason for such revenues to be devoted to areas in which they have no influence over governance or over the treatment of their co-religionists. This problem has become considerably more complex as a result of population movements that have taken place since 1983.

Representation. The representation issue concerns the geography of the subdivisions of the Lebanese state, the sectarian or secular nature of government, and the specific sectarian (or secular) positions identified for each group.

How Druzes or Shi'as or Sunnis or Maronites or others will be represented is a question clearly related to government structure and centralization. How, for example, will the lines be drawn in the Shuf, which has traditionally had both Christian and Druze representation?

Whether Lebanese government is to be sectarian is another important issue. If positions — executive and legislative both, as well as administrative (civil service) — are to be allotted on the basis of sect, then geographical predominance is important; but no less important is overall community size. But the issue is: should the government be so divided? Is it necessary or desirable? We have already pointed to the nadir of inter-communal trust, but the institutionalization of sectarianism may perpetuate or further enflame this distrust. If there is a high degree of decentralization such that local governments deal with personal-status issues and the like, highly contentious between sects, is there still a need for the central government to remain confessionally identified?

Civil service appointments are also currently allotted by sect. This is a divisive and probably an indefensible practice, since it institutionalizes patron-client relations in an area where it is least necessary and where the cost in terms of administration development and modernization — the development of a meritocracy — is highest.

Finally, and specifically, if the government remains a confessional one, which sects should be allotted which posts? Although there seems to be general agreement that a Christian (probably a Maronite) should remain president, there is no consensus about the prime ministry, about the composition of the cabinet, about the structure or leadership of the Chamber, or with respect to control of the security forces.

Most Westerners believe Lebanon must ultimately move toward a secular form of government. And in fact there has been at various points, most recently in the late 1970s and early 1980s, substantial intellectual support for secularism, at least over the long term. Earlier, the appeal of the SSNP, the Ba'th and Communist Party reflects once again some base of attraction to secularism. At the same time, it must be said that this base — at least as far as any short-term move toward secular government is concerned — has probably diminished substantially as a result of the bitterness, fear and distrust created by the violence of the past decade. However, even to the extent there is support for secularism, whether in the short or long term, the pervasive fear of secularism is also a reality of capital significance.

In principle, many people favour government deconfessionalization but not necessarily secularization. Deconfessionalization means ending the system of confessional ratios and appointments, but retention of different personal-status rights and education by sect. Whether deconfessionalization should apply to such positions as the presidency is still a subject of debate, and depends to some degree on the powers associated with specific offices. Secularism in Lebanese government is a victim of the conflict. Christians do not believe that the Moslem communities will accede to secularization of personal-status issues, and the Christian argument has been that confessional government is therefore inevitable. This reasoning is only in part a rationalization for the maintenance of a system of government long believed to protect the most vital Christian interests. Sunnis and Shi'as are increasingly attracted to deconfessional government, as long as personal-status matters are not secularized.

Although there is substantial debate about the identification of specific religious positions in the event of changes in national government, and some talk about moving toward a 'Moslem' (instead of Sunni) prime minister, growing debate has tended to push people toward preservation of something very close to the traditional allocation. The concrete proposals at the Lausanne Conference reflected minimal tinkering with the existing system, changes that added even more protections to the existing ones.

Political Orientation. Finally, there is the question of the external political orientation of Lebanon. Tactically, today this question must be answered in terms of its conceptions of Israel and Syria, but in the broader sense it has to do with the relationship of Lebanon both to its immediate regional environment and to its larger environment beyond the region. Manifestly, such a question cannot fairly be answered until foreign forces have left the country.

Many Lebanese favour the principles contained in the National Pact — i.e., that Lebanon should not permit itself to be drawn into regional squabbles and should therefore remain neutral both regionally and globally. The National Pact cautioned against too close a linkage with the West, and against any regional organization or pole that might subordinate Lebanese sovereignty. All communities favour Lebanese sovereignty today, but clearly the Sunnis continue to look to the Arab world (especially Saudi Arabia and Syria), while the Christians look to the West (and in time of threat when the West does not appear to attend to their appeals, to Israel). Lebanon is an Arab country whose future is indissolubly linked to the Arab world, but the last decade should have made it perfectly clear that Lebanon can only survive to live that future if it preserves its independence from its powerful neighbours and does not enter as a party into their quarrels. One can perhaps also conclude what few have said to date, viz., that the existence of Lebanon may well depend upon normalization of relations with *both* Israel *and* Syria.

Directions for Conflict Resolution

Whether Lebanon will be given a chance to exercise options to select its future is at present dubious. Since government at the national level retains no real room for manoeuvre, and since local parties (principally sectarian groups) are anything but free to co-operate, even if they chose to, Lebanon is no longer an independent actor. Thus, whether Lebanon as we have known it *has* a future lies in others' hands.

If one is to postulate, for the sake of conflict resolution, that greater decision-making capacity will eventually devolve upon Lebanon, it appears at present that such capacity will in fact lie in the hands of those who dominate the virtually autonomous regions within Lebanon — the Christian heartland, the Shuf, and West Beirut and the south. There is very little indication that the north, the Beqa'a, or the extreme southern part of Lebanon have any practical chance of playing a constructive or independent role in the shaping of future Lebanon.

If Christian leaders representing what we shall call Mt Lebanon (i.e. essentially, the CDM or some later incarnation), Druze leaders representing the Shuf, and Shi'a leaders representing West Beirut and the south, arguably with the participation of Sunni leaders of West Beirut, were to endeavour to put the Lebanese Humpty Dumpty back together again, what kinds of arrangements, if any, could satisfy their *Lebanese* concerns and aspirations? That is the question to which we now turn.

Despite the inter-communal distrust, the gap between communities over the nature of government and national status is not as great as eight years of war suggests. When rhetoric is pushed aside, each community is seeking power not unlike that sought by the thirteen original American states in the Constitutional Convention — a veto power to protect the vital interests of the community. At the same time, it is clear that the levels of distrust and antipathy are far greater, as is the acceptability of trafficking with foreign powers, than was the case in late eighteenth-century America. Christian perceptions of a near-monolithic Moslem threat, Sunni fears of being overwhelmed by the Shi'a demographic tidal wave, Druze particularism, and Shi'a resentment over past neglect are a combustible admixture.

Yet when minimum positions along the dimensions we have discussed are considered, substantial agreement emerges, and there is flexibility among groups across a surprising number of issues. The proposal advanced below is, therefore, only one of several approaches that may be feasible, recognizing the interdependence of several of the issue areas as we have indicated above. It is not the structures that are significant; it is the essence of the commitment of government to protect the vital interests of each segment of this plural society.

A key point in contention is the monopoly of force available to the state which, given the traditional power of the Maronites, has been seen increasingly (and inaccurately) as a tool of the Christians. Ironically, and for a variety of reasons, no single community opposes a strong army, *as long as its mission is defence of the national territory*. Nor have strong objections been raised about the

Internal Security Forces, since this group is commanded by a Sunni. Moslem and Druze communities favour, and Christians would not seem to violently oppose, the strengthening of the regionally based gendarmerie to serve internal security purposes. The principle of the gendarmerie should be local control of local problems.

The proposal of confederation is impractical. Lebanon is not Switzerland, and its location and strategic value to neighbouring countries do not permit of the luxury of such a degree of decentralization. Moreover, confederation — the Swiss example notwithstanding — has consistently failed over time, even in much more appropriate circumstances than those of contemporary Lebanon. Even federalism has had a rocky history, generally most successful in countries where the constituent elements have previously enjoyed independence and are therefore accustomed to administering their own affairs — that is, in cases where federal units are *giving up* rather than *acquiring* greater power.

There appears no reason to believe that an essentially unitary government is unworkable in Lebanon. What is necessary is to endow the communities with the power to prevent the government from acting against the vital community interests. Not so much that it would do so; rather, the intent is to provide confidence-building measures to each community to facilitate overcoming its fears.

In practice, however, contemporary developments suggest that if Lebanon should be reconstituted as a sovereign state it will most likely move toward confederal or loose, federal form. This is the message of recent developments in the Shuf and Mt. Lebanon, whose communities are determined to limit the degree a national or external authority can impose on local authorities or interests.

A federal system for Lebanon may be the best compromise between the force of current events and the requirements of preserving public social order. A federal government of a number of districts could provide for federal foreign affairs and defence responsibilities, as well as development planning; some taxation, transportation, and communications activities; and justice. Other areas (e.g. agriculture, labour, commerce, education) might be subject to district control. Ideally, all major religious groups, including the Greek Orthodox and Greek Catholics, should dominate at least one district, through gerrymandering, if necessary.

Lebanon's confessional system of government has had the

unintended effect of increasing rather than decreasing sectarian divisions. Still, given current tensions, it is wholly impractical to propose total deconfessionalization of Lebanese politics. Instead, a system that recognizes confessional pressures without reinforcing them, that reduces their ubiquity, is desirable. The Moslem and Druze communities will in any case not consider secularization of personal-status laws, and Christians insist upon governmental structures to protect their own vital interests. These are both non-negotiable positions. In light of these demands, we believe a gradual process could still be developed to shift protection of vital interests to structures and away from functions. This may have the effect over time of reducing the salience of sectarian aspects to non-sectarian issues while providing the institutions to build greater co-operation. A representative two-stage process might envisage:

Stage One
A new president may be elected by the existing Chamber. The president could be a Maronite. His prime minister could be a Sunni, and the president of the Chamber could remain a Shi'a. The LAF commander could be a Greek Orthodox, the FSI commander, a Druze.

The president could then dissolve the Chamber and call for national elections for a new, bicameral parliament to be composed of a Chamber of Delegates and a National Assembly. Although representation in the Chamber of Delegates would be by district, the sects would have such representation that a ratio of 5 Shi'a; 5 Maronite; 4 Sunni; 3 Greek Orthodox; 2 Druze; 2 Greek Catholic; 1 other Christian, will be maintained. The number of delegates would be firm and fixed perpetually, as would the ratio. The National Assembly would be representative of districts, with each member representing about 30,000 people. Members would be directly and democratically elected. Prior to the election of a National Assembly, a census could be conducted under international supervision. In the past a census has been impossible for political reasons, but the superior power of the Chamber of Delegates and sectarian identification of specific offices could reduce the opposition to such a census.

Sectarian ratios would be abolished in the civil service and army, but rigorous examinations and other objective standards for recruitment, promotion and assignment by merit would be employed. The recent erosion of power of the senior 'patrons' is a propitious moment to move Lebanese administration in the right direction and away from patron-client relations.

The president of the Chamber of Delegates would be elected by the Chamber, but would have to be a Shi'a in the first stage. The president of the National Assembly would be elected by the Assembly, but would have to be a Druze in the first stage.

All national legislation would have to be approved by both chambers of parliament. No legislation, however, could be enacted without the approval of the president. Presidential rule by decree would be limited both functionally and temporally. The president would not be able to dissolve parliament except in a declared national emergency.

Treaties would have to be approved by a 60 per cent majority of the Chamber of Delegates. The LAF commander would be confirmed by the Chamber; the FSI commander, by both branches.

Stage Two

In the second phase, the president who would have to be a Christian, would be elected by the Chamber of Delegates. (After his term, presidents would be popularly elected.) He would call for parliamentary elections. The Chamber of Delegates' president would have to be a Moslem, but the National Assembly president could be of any denomination. The prime minister, selected by the president, could be of any sect except that of the president, and would have to be approved by 60 per cent majorities in both branches of parliament.

Beirut could be called the 'capital district'. It could consist of up to four districts for parliamentary purposes, but could for administrative purposes be governed by a Capital District Government. The president could serve as governor of Beirut, but the district government might consist of a ten-person board (2 Greek Orthodox, 2 Maronites, 2 Shi'as, 2 Sunnis, 2 at-large), which could elect a chairman who could, under the auspices of the governor, have responsibility for day-to-day administration of the Capital District.

Conclusion

There is no suggestion in the above proposal that government structure or system is the cause of Lebanon's problems. We do believe that confessional government has confessionalized non-sectarian issues, and in any case social change has eroded the foundations of consociational government. If Lebanon survives — and the survival question is likely to be a function of external variables more than internal ones — its democratic traditions will have to find expression in a remodelled administrative structure in which meritocracy replaces patron-client relations and gerontocracy; in which communal interdependence dominates independence; and in which the voice of politics is expressed through voting rather than violence.

No specific set of structures, including that delineated above, can protect countries against themselves. Tragically, yet more traumatic events are probably necessary to save Lebanon. Moreover, to such a degree has Lebanese sovereignty eroded that only violence can restore it, and violence that seriously affects both Israel and Syria. If by some miracle yet unseen, some cataclysm unwanted, Lebanon manages to survive, political institutions to give voice to the essential pluralism that has long symbolized the nation and its people are not lacking. Should this rebirth of Lebanon occur, however, it is to be hoped that the Lebanese will have learned from the terrible toll the conflicts have exacted, that sizeable identity groups in any country turn to another country as an internal ally only at their peril.

Notes

1. Augustus Richard Norton, 'Harakat Amal' in Edward E. Azar *et al.*, *The Emergence of a New Lebanon: Fantasy or Reality?* (New York: Praeger, 1984), p. 162.

2. Cf. R. D. McLaurin, Don Peretz and Lewis W. Snider, *Middle East Foreign Policy: Issues and Processes* (New York: Praeger, 1982), pp. 6–7.

3. Jean-Pierre Péroncel-Hugoz, *Une Croix sur le Liban* (Paris: Lieu Commun, 1984), pp. 56–9; Annie Laurent, 'Syrie-Liban: les faux frères jumeaux', *Politique étrangère*, XLVIII, 3 (automne 1983), 591–600.

4. See Leslie Schmida, *Keys to Control: Israel's Pursuit of Arab Water Resources* (Washington, DC: American Educational Trust, n.d.), p. 4; John Norton Moore (ed.), *The Arab-Israeli Conflict* (3 vols, Washington, DC: American Society of International Law, 1974), III, p. 47. More recently, see, e.g., 'Ne'eman Wants Annexation of Southern Lebanon', *The Jerusalem Post*, 22 February 1985, 2, wherein southern Lebanon is demanded as part of historic Eretz Yisra'el.

5. Abdallah Bouhabib, 'Clarifying Lebanon's History', *New York Times*, 18 January 1984, and 'Lebanon, the United States and the World', *World Affairs Journal*, forthcoming; Philip K. Hitti, *Lebanon in History from the Earliest Times to the Present* (New York: St Martin's, 1967), passim.

6. See Laurent Chabry and Annie Chabry, *Politique et minorités au Proche-Orient* (Paris: Maisonneuve & Larose, 1984); and R. D. McLaurin (ed.), *The Political Role of Minority Groups in the Middle East* (New York: Praeger, 1979).

7. Lewis W. Snider, 'Perspectives on Lebanon's Political History: The Not-So-Precarious Republic' in Edward E. Azar *et al.*, *Lebanon and the World in the 1980s* (College Park, Md.: University of Maryland, 1983), pp. 27–50.

8. It should be noted that Lebanon had had boundaries quite similar to its present ones in earlier periods, such as under Fakhreddin II and Bashir II. The most detailed treatment of the post-World War I process of creating Lebanon's boundaries is in Meir Zamir, *The Formation of Modern Lebanon* (London: Croom Helm, forthcoming), which, however, takes a more conflictive view of Lebanese history than do we. On the last point in the text, see also Wadi Haddad, *Lebanon: The Politics of the Revolving Doors* (Washington, DC: 'Washington Papers', Georgetown University Center for Strategic and International Studies, forthcoming).

9. On Christian views, see Paul A. Jureidini and James M. Price, 'Minorities in Partition: The Christians of Lebanon' in McLaurin (ed.), *The Political Role*, Chapter 7.

10. Until the Crusades, Shi'as constituted the majority of Lebanese.

11. The census of 1932 counted Lebanese not resident in Lebanon, including those that had lost their Lebanese citizenship. The practice of including citizens out of the country for electoral or other administrative purposes is not unusual; it is standard practice, including in the United States. Clearly, non-citizens are *not* normally counted. Even leaving aside this latter category, however, Christians would probably outnumber Moslems if non-resident nationals were included in a census today. By contrast, Moslems predominate among residents. The most careful study of contemporary demography in Lebanon is probably Joseph Chamie, *Religion and Fertility: Arab Christian-Muslim Differentials* (Cambridge: Cambridge University Press, 1981).

12. Chabry and Chabry, *Politique*, pp. 137–8.

13. Betts.

14. Hitti, *Lebanon*, pp. 254ff.

15. Hratch Bedoyan, 'The Policies Pursued by the Druze Political Leadership in Lebanese Internal Politics', *Haliyyat*, 26 (Spring 1982), 12; Helena Cobban, 'Lebanon's Chinese Puzzle', *Foreign Policy*, 53 (Winter 1983–84), 35; McLaurin (ed.), *The Political Role*, p. 276.

16. Bedoyan, 'The Policies', p. 13; Walid Khalidi, *Conflict and Violence in Lebanon: Confrontation in the Middle East* (Cambridge, Mass.: Harvard University Center for International Affairs, 1979), p. 35.

17. Peter Gubser, 'Minorities in Isolation: The Druze of Lebanon and Syria' in McLaurin (ed.), *The Political Role*, p. 125.

18. Cf. Gubser, 'Minorities', passim; Philip K. Hitti, *The Origins of the Druze People* (New York: Columbia University Press, 1928).

19. Bedoyan, 'The Policies', passim; Gubser, 'Minorities', passim.

20. See Snider, note 7 above, for data on comparative political performance. Tuéni's point is made in Ghassan Tuéni, *Une Guerre pour les autres* (Paris: Lattès, 1985), p. 58.

21. Little has been written on the Lebanese Army. See Adel Freiha, *L'Armée et l'état au Liban* ('Army and State in Lebanon') (Paris: Librairie Générale de Droit et de Jurisprudence, 1980); Yves Pierre Ely, 'L'Armée libanaise', unpublished thesis, Université Jean Moulin, Lyon, 1984; Fuad Lahhud, *Maisaat jaysh lubnan* ('The Drama of the Lebanese Army') (Beirut: n.p., 1977). A short history is found in R. D. McLaurin, 'Lebanon and Its Army: Past, Present, Future' in Azar *et al.*, *The Emergence*, Chapter 5.

22. J. C. Hurewitz, *Middle East Politics: The Military Dimension* (New York:

Praeger, 1969), pp. 390ff.

23. Amine Gemayel, 'Lebanon and Its Role: The Price and the Promise', *Foreign Affairs*, LXIII, 4 (forthcoming, Spring 1984).

24. Péroncel-Hugoz, pp. 101–3.

25. See the IDF journal, *Maarachot*, September 1982, for a description of the Lebanese Army's history in terms of 'conflict avoidance'.

26. Rashid Khalidi lucidly summarizes:

[T]here was an inevitable contradiction between the *raison de révolution* of the Palestinian resistance and the *raison d'état* of every one of the regimes in the Arab countries where it operated. This contradiction was aggravated because the resistance was trying to draw the Arab world into a confrontation with Israel, something which these regimes did not want. Finally, in the case of Lebanon, the unique sectarian balance of the country's political system was upset by its presence . . .

Rashid Khalidi, 'The Palestinians in Lebanon: Social Repercussions of Israel's Behavior', *Middle East Journal*, XXXVIII, 2 (Spring 1984), 255–6. Walid Khalidi trenchantly observed that 'The concurrent halos of martyrdom and championship surrounding the Palestinian revolution exerted a powerful fascination over the Moslem masses and radicals of Lebanon'. He adds that the Jordanian experience persuaded the Palestinians they should never again remain apart from the masses. 'If the Lebanese Moslem and leftist waters were crying for the Palestinian fish to jump into them, the Palestinian fish were not going to play coy'. W. Khalidi, *Conflict and Violence*, pp. 80–1.

27. The 1969 confrontations led to the Cairo Accord. See Kamal S. Salibi, *Crossroads to Civil War: Lebanon 1958–1976* (Delmar, NY: Caravan, 1976), pp. 42–6. A more detailed treatment of the clashes, and one that discusses the Syrian role, is found in Paul A. Jureidini and William E. Hazen, *Six Clashes: An Analysis of the Relationship Between the Palestinian Guerrilla Movement and the Governments of Jordan and Lebanon* (Kensington, Md.: American Institutes for Research, 1971).

28. Jureidini and Hazen, *Six Clashes*, passim.

29. Salibi, *Crossroads*, p. 69.

30. McLaurin, 'Lebanon and Its Army', pp. 91–2.

31. The conflict in Lebanon has by 1985 produced an extraordinary volume of literature. On the overall conflict in Lebanon see Marius Deeb, *The Lebanese Civil War* (New York: Praeger, 1980), which deals with the 1975–6 period; Khalidi, *Conflict and Violence*, a fine essay that sketches the development of the conflict through 1978; Antoine Khuwayri, *al-harb fi lubnon 1976* (3 vols., Jounieh: al-bulusiyyeh, 1976), a detailed study of events in the critical year of 1976; Salibi, *Crossroads*, a good historical introduction to the fighting in 1975–6. More general, more ambitious analyses are available in Ghassan Tuéni, *Une Guerre*; Haddad, *Lebanon*; and Karim Pakradouni, *La Paix manquée: le mandat d'Elias Sarkis, 1976–1982* (Beirut: Fiches du Monde Arabe, 1983). International aspects of the conflicts in Lebanon are addressed in P. Edward Haley and Lewis W. Snider (eds), *Lebanon in Crisis: Participants and Issues* (Syracuse: Syracuse University Press, 1979); Annie Laurent and Antoine Basbous, *Une Proie pour deux fauves? Le Liban entre le lion de Juda et le lion de Syrie* (Beirut: ad-Da'irat, 1983); Itamar Rabinovich, *The War for Lebanon 1970–1983* (Cornell: Cornell University Press, 1984); Ze'ev Schiff and Ehud Ya'ari, *Israel's Lebanon War* (New York: Simon & Schuster, 1984); Adeed I. Dawisha, *Syria and the Lebanese Crisis* (New York: St Martin's, 1980); as well as Haddad, *Lebanon*, Pakradouni, *La Paix*, and Tuéni, *Une Guerre*. Military details of the combat are covered in the following works:

(a) 1975–81: Paul A. Jureidini, James M. Price and R. D. McLaurin, *Military Operations in Selected Lebanese Built-Up Areas, 1975–1978* (Aberdeen Proving Ground, Md.: US Army Human Engineering Laboratory, 1979); R. D. McLaurin, *The Battle of Zahle* (Aberdeen Proving Ground: US Army Human Engineering Laboratory, forthcoming).

(b) 1982: Trevor Dupuy and Paul Martell, *Flawed Victory: The 1982 War in Lebanon* (Dunn Loring, Va.: HERO Books, 1985); Richard A. Gabriel, *Operation Peace for Galilee* (New York: Hill & Wang, 1984); Schiff and Ya'ari, *Israel's Lebanon War*; Phillip P. Katz and R. D. McLaurin, *Psychological Operations in Urban Warfare: The Lessons from the 1982 Middle East War* (Aberdeen Proving Ground: US Army Human Engineering Laboratory, forthcoming); McLaurin with Paul A. Jureidini, *The Battle of Beirut* (Aberdeen Proving Ground: US Army Human Engineering Laboratory, forthcoming); McLaurin, *The Battle of Tyre* (Aberdeen Proving Ground: US Army Human Engineering Laboratory, forthcoming); McLaurin, *The Battle of Sidon* (Aberdeen Proving Ground: US Army Human Engineering Laboratory, forthcoming).

32. Even the Lebanese Arab Army, founded by junior Sunni dissident officers, acted largely as a tool of non-Lebanese. It was unable to rally and sustain the support of the bulk of the Sunni (much less Shi'a) officers and men of the Lebanese Army. Yet, it came closer to being a 'Sunni' militia than any other.

33. Cobban, *Lebanon's*, pp. 37–40; Paul A. Jureidini and R. D. McLaurin, 'Social Change and Political Change in Lebanon', unpublished manuscript.

34. Bedoyan, 'The Policies', pp. 12–13; Gubser, 'Minorities', passim.

35. Jureidini and McLaurin, 'Social Change'. For the several 'hats' Jumblatt (and most other Lebanese leaders) wore during the 1975–6 period, see William E. Hazen and Paul A. Jureidini, *Lebanon's Dissolution: Futures and Consequences* (Alexandria, Va.: Abbott Associates, 1976), especially the figures. Tuéni's *Une Guerre* can be read with great profit for insights into Druze political culture.

36. See Marius K. Deeb, 'Lebanon, Prospects for National Reconciliation in the Mid-1980s', *Middle East Journal*, XXXVIII, 2 (Spring 1984), 268–73; and especially the several excellent studies by Augustus Richard Norton: 'Harakat Amal' in Azar *et al.*, *The Emergence*, Chapter 7; 'Harakat Amal' in *Religion and Politics* (Political Anthropology Annual III, New Brunswick, New Jersey: Transaction, 1984); 'Political Violence and Shi'a Factionalism in Lebanon', *Middle East Insight*, III, 2 (1983), 9–16; 'Making Enemies in South Lebanon: Harakat Amal, the IDF, and South Lebanon', ibid., III, 3 (1984), 13–20; 'Occupational Risks and Planned Retirement', ibid., IV, 1 (1985), 14–18; and 'Shiism and Social Protest in Lebanon' in Juan Cole and Mikki Keddie (eds), *Shiism and Social Protest* (New Haven: Yale University Press, forthcoming). Pakradouni, *La Paix*, provides an interesting portrait of Musa Sadr.

37. Jureidini and McLaurin, 'Social Change'; Deeb, 'Lebanon', pp. 276–8; Paul A. Jureidini and R. D. MacLaurin, 'Lebanon After the War of 1982' in Azar *et al.*, *The Emergence*, p. 27. The Shuf is historically built on an economic interdependence of Christian and Druze. The 'Mountain War' created an economic crisis of unprecedented proportions in the Shuf, and to date only large infusions of Libyan aid have helped assuage the resulting problems.

38. Jureidini and McLaurin, 'Social Change'.

39. Ibid.

40. Ibid.; Norton, 'Making Enemies'; Augustus Richard Norton, 'Instability and Change in Lebanon', *American-Arab Affairs*, 10 (Fall 1984), 86.

41. Tripoli's close psychological linkage to conservative Sunni areas of Syria was given as a reason not to include Tripoli in modern Lebanon. See Meir Zamir, 'Smaller and Greater Lebanon: The Squaring of a Circle', *Jerusalem Quarterly*, 23 (Spring 1982), 85–91.

42. See Augustus Richard Norton, 'The Political Mood in Lebanon', *Middle East Insight*, II, 5 (1983), 9, and 'Israel and South Lebanon', *American-Arab Affairs*, 4 (Spring 1983), 27; and Rashid Khalidi, 'Problems of Foreign Intervention in Lebanon', ibid., 7 (Winter 1983–4)', 24–6.

43. Attempts in 1984 to reconstitute a viable Murabitoun were overcome by force of arms, primarily by the Druze militia, PSP.

44. In the aftermath of Israel's withdrawal from Sidon, a large Shi'a demonstration erupted there and one that was beyond the power of Amal or the government to control. Although a large proportion of the demonstrators were transported from the Shi'a suburbs of Beirut, the purpose of the demonstration, which turned violent in its later stages, was to demonstrate the ability of the Shi'a community to dominate Sidon if it so willed.

45. Paul A. Jureidini, 'Lebanon's Regional Policy' in Azar *et al.*, *The Emergence*, pp. 208–9.

46. Ibid.

47. See Péroncel-Hugoz, *Une Croix*, Chapter IV. While Rosemary Sayigh, in her useful book, *Palestinians: from Peasants to Revolutionaries* (London: Zed, 1979), provides many quotations showing ill will toward the Palestinians, these incidents are believed to be atypical of 1948. It is interesting that all such examples she quoted reflected Moslem (probably mostly Shi'a) problems with the influx of Palestinians. The Christian church donated lands to the refugees, and a large proportion of the community was devoted to promoting the interests and cause of, or in giving succour to, the Palestinians.

48. As Rashid Khalidi puts it, 'Palestinians enjoyed a higher degree of autonomous control over their own affairs than any of their compatriots have since the beginning of the British mandate in Palestine'. ('The Palestinians', p. 255.) However, this was after the Cairo Agreement of 1969. Prior to that agreement, Lebanese Army G-2 exercised careful monitoring and extensive control over the camps. Palestinians living outside the camps, largely middle class and more educated, did enjoy substantially greater freedom than in any other Arab country.

49. Haddad, *Lebanon*; R. D. McLaurin, 'The PLO and the Fertile Crescent' in Augustus R. Norton (ed.), *The International Relations of the PLO* (Carbondale: Southern Illinois Press, forthcoming).

50. Haddad, *Lebanon*; Jureidini and Hazen, *Six Clashes*.

51. Haddad, *Lebanon*; Pakradouni, *La Paix*.

52. Adam Garfinkle treats what he views as the precursors of this episode in 'Sources of the al-Fatah Mutiny', *Orbis*, XXVII, 3 (Fall 1983), 603–41. The sceptical may be forgiven if we see in this 'mutiny' or 'internal revolt' the continuity of policy of a very 'external' actor — Syria — still determined to 'capture' and exploit the PLO.

53. It was a clear element of Israeli policy to create Shi'a resentment toward the PLO, and this policy was successful.

54. There are those (e.g., Johnathan C. Randal, *Going All the Way: Christian Warlords, Israeli Adventurers, and the War in Lebanon* [New York: Viking, 1983], passim, and George W. Ball, *Error and Betrayal in Lebanon* [Washington, DC: Foundation for Middle East Peace, 1984], pp. 27–8) quick to point out that as early as the 1950s Israeli leaders had sought to create a Saad Haddad. In fact, despite the almost prophetic words of Ben Gurion as recorded in Prime Minister Moshe Sharett's diaries (see Livia Rokach, *Israel's Sacred Terrorism* [Belmont, Mass.: Association of Arab-American University Graduates, 1980], pp. 24–30), the concepts suggested in the 1950s and those attempted in the 1970s were quite different.

55. In fact it was not so much PLO raids that led to 1982 as it was a combination of IDF concern over the PLO artillery build-up, the triumph of a group determined

to close the PLO chapter, and a linkage between the PLO in Lebanon and Likud aims in the West Bank. See Schiff and Ya'ari, *Israel's Lebanon War*, passim; Shimon Shiffer, *Opération Boule de Neige* (Paris: Lattès, 1984), pp. 91–145; and Efraim Inbar, 'Israel and Lebanon: 1975–1982', *Crossroads*, 10 (Spring 1983), 67.

56. All Israeli government spokesmen and officials have made it quite clear that Israeli control of a 'border strip' (presumably similar to that occupied by the Haddad militia in the past) will continue indefinitely. While this strip will not be annexed to Israel officially, it will operate under the complete control of some kind of Israeli-supported security force. Resettlement patterns abetted by Israel have led some to the conclusion that Israeli leaders are trying to regroup Christians in this border strip so that a maximum number of villages there will be Christian.

57. In his famous speech of 20 July 1976, Syrian President Hafez al-Assad avowed that 'through history, Syria and Lebanon had been one country and one people. The people in Syria and Lebanon have been one through history'. Abdel Halim Khaddam has made similar comments on numerous occasions. Moreover, those involved in the highest levels of political activity and diplomacy in Arab circles indicate that, notwithstanding Syrian pledges to withdraw totally from Lebanon, the highest levels of the Syrian government have made quite clear their determination to completely control, and perhaps eventually to annex, the Tripoli area and the Beqa'a, as well as to inextricably link the Lebanese to the Syrian economy.

58. See note 54 above.

59. Contrary to widespread views, the agents are not clearly divided. Israel has worked closely with the Christian Lebanese Forces, the Druze PSP, Shi'a Amal, and certain Sunni families at different times. Syria has also worked closely with the Kata'eb Party (overwhelmingly Maronite) and the Syrian Social Nationalist Party (Maronite, Greek Orthodox, Shi'a), with Sunni groups such as the Lebanese Arab Army, with the Druze PSP, and of course with Amal.

60. The agreement on acceptable Syrian roles and deployments in Lebanon must certainly be seen as a tacit accord — at the very least. See Inbar, 'Israel and Lebanon', passim Haley and Snider, *Lebanon in Crisis*, and Pakradouni, *La Paix*, for example.

61. There are of course some Lebanese 'puppets', Lebanese whose political *existence* is a function of foreign powers and whose direction is completely determined by those powers. The most obvious examples are some elements of the Syrian Social Nationalist Party (which in its heyday was a centre of intellectual independence but most of which has now come completely under the control of the Syrian government) and the Syrian-oriented Ba'th Party in Lebanon.

62. It is quite fashionable in some Arab and anti-Israeli circles to paint Haddad as a creation of Israel. That he owed his importance and his militia's survival to Israel cannot be doubted, but Haddad's arrival and role in the south was at the outset very much a function of internal Lebanese politics, and Saad Haddad remained in close touch with certain political circles in Mt Lebanon throughout his years in the south.

63. For Syria, this occurred first in 1976 as a by-product of Syrian intervention. By acceding to Israeli conditions on the terms and limits of Syrian forces deployed in Lebanon, Syria certainly acknowledged Israel's security interests. Accepting Israeli surveillance overflights was a further element of this acknowledgement. Following the Lebanese Chamber of Deputies' rescinding of the 17 May accord, Syria again recognized Israel's security interest in affirming Damascus's willingness to see achieved security arrangements that would facilitate IDF withdrawal. For its part, Israel may be said to have tacitly accepted Syria's security interests in agreeing to the 1976 Syrian intervention, but numerous leaders were much more explicit on the point in 1983 following the Mountain (Shuf) War.

64. We are not discussing force reduction here. It is quite conceivable that Syrian forces may be reduced in Lebanon for any of a variety of Syrian reasons.

65. It is not likely after the Hamah massacre of 1982 (see Fred Lawson, 'Social Bases for the Hamah Revolt', *MERIP Reports*, 110 [November–December 1982], 24–8) that any 'Alawis will choose to move toward the Latakia area along the main road that runs through Homs and Hamah.

66. The southernmost part of this multi-part *cordon sanitaire* may prove somewhat problematical. The danger recognized today in Israel is that the cycle of violence between Israel, on the one hand, and the Shi'as of southern Lebanon, on the other, may be approaching the level where a final withdrawal will be inadequate to arrest it. Thus, there is the danger of Lebanese extremism. Second, Israelis are concerned that Palestinians may well re-enter the south, notwithstanding the strong and adverse reaction that may be anticipated from the Shi'as. What kind of border strip will provide adequate 'security' then? Some speculate that Israel will 'create' an all-Christian border zone. Will this not further antagonize the Shi'as? Will such a strip offer adequate protection against rocket attacks?

67. Gemayel, 'Lebanon and Its Role'.

68. See the remarks of 'Asim Qansuh, secretary-general of the (Syrian) Ba'th Party in Lebanon, carried over Voice of Lebanon on 3 March 1985 (reprinted in *FBIS*, 4 March 1985, G6.). On 25 February 1985, *as-Siyasah*, a Kuwaiti daily, reported that a plan for a loose union of Lebanon and Syria had been developed and was being studied by leaders in both Damascus and Beirut. In the weeks that followed, Amin Gemayel did in fact 'sound out' individuals within the Christian community about their attitudes. He encountered staunch resistance, and indeed the Christian Decision Movement emerged rapidly during this period.

69. Cf. note 41 above.

70. Schmida, *Keys*; John K. Cooley, 'The War Over Water', *Foreign Policy*, 54 (Spring 1984), 22–3.

71. See also Joseph Maila, 'Liban, violence et précarité', *Études*, CCCLXII, 2 (février 1985), 151–2.

72. Paul A. Jureidini and R. D. McLaurin, 'Political Disintegration in Contemporary Politics', *International Interactions*, XI, 2 (1984), 167–92; and Lewis W. Snider, 'Political Disintegration in Developing Countries: Theoretical Orientation and Empirical Evidence', ibid., 137–66.

73. Some reflections of the same idea may be evident in the remarks by Abdallah Bouhabib, Lebanon's ambassador to the United States, in Chicago, Illinois, on 2 March 1984.

74. The only exceptions were the Zgharta-area Christian community and some of those Maronites and Greek Orthodox resident in predominantly Moslem areas.

75. Haddad, *Lebanon*.

76. Gemayel, 'Lebanon's Role'.

77. Christian concerns clearly reflect *religious* rather than political fears, an unusual circumstance in Lebanon. See, e.g. Péroncel-Hugoz, *Une Croix*, passim, who eloquently reflects these fears. Also, we refer to the dominant Christian community whose immediate security is not really threatened by the Shi'as, but individual Christians in the south and the Beqa'a (Zahle) feel much more threatened.

78. Haddad, *Lebanon*.

8 TOWARDS RESOLVING THE IRAN-IRAQ CONFLICT

Fariborz Rouzbehani

In September 1980 Iraq launched an invasion against Iran, initiating a protracted armed conflict longer than World War I and the most devastating since World War II. It marked yet another event in the history of a long-standing rivalry between Iranians and Arabs. To be sure, there are local historical, cultural, socio-economic and religio-political reasons for this on-going antagonism. Nevertheless, post-colonial and current rivalries within the international political system have also been major factors.

In the following analysis, the history of the Iranian-Arab rivalry in general, and the Iranian-Iraqi conflicts in particular, will be reviewed. The environment in which this history has evolved will also be examined. Here, the emphasis is to analyze the problems facing both Iran and Iraq, not only in light of the history of their long conflict but also in the context of Cold War politics. Any resolution of the conflict, of course, will be conditioned not only by internal factors but also by external variables in the international political system.

The study will avoid what has been termed 'factor monism', i.e. the tendency to explain, describe or predict international relations phenomena only in terms of one or a few variables.[1] Instead, a multidimensional approach will be adopted to capture the salient issues and complications of the Iran-Iraq conflict. The dimensions include a look at Iranian-Arab political history to reveal the nature of an ambivalent relationship between the two nations. A survey will be made of the evolution of significant treaties dealing with border disputes leading up to the current war which, of course, will also be examined. The political structures in Iran and Iraq will be analyzed as they bear upon this conflict. Finally, the effects of external inputs from the Cold War will be discussed.

Iranian-Arab History: Ambivalent Relationship

Geographical proximity had long encouraged extensive interaction

208

between the Iranians and Arabs. The advent of Islam in the seventh century AD, however, brought a new look to the relationship. It created a pronounced antipathy on the one hand and empathy and concord on the other. The new relationship had both cultural and political implications.

When the Arabs invaded Iran in 636 AD, the Persian Empire crumbled within a short time and the Iranians came under the tutelage of the conquering Arab Moslems. Nevertheless, while the Iranians were Islamized they were never Arabized. Within one century of the Arab occupation, the Iranians revolted against the Umayyads, albeit unsuccessfully, except for an assertion of Iranian cultural identification, the genesis of Iranian nationalism.[2] Interest in pre-Islamic Persian history and civilization became rallying points for freedom from Arab rule. The fact that these uprisings were crushed by the conquerors only added fuel to an already strained Iranian-Arab relationship.[3]

Under the Umayyad and Abbassid Caliphates, Iranians were treated as second-class citizens. Arab persecution of Iranians was common during these periods, which became known in Iranian nationalist rhetoric as 'the Arab racist rule'.[4] Simultaneously, diverse minor theological sects emerged in Islam of which Shi'ism was the largest. This development also proved to be, of course, an important input into the Iranian-Arab relationship.

Nevertheless, despite the tensions and intense animosity between Iranians and Arabs, certain benefits emerged from their interaction in the Islamic community of the faithful. The Iranians played an important role in it and, of course, their contributions to Islamic civilization produced a strong sense of pride. Later, after minor Iranian dynasties rose up to govern Iran, a certain ambivalence continued to affect the Iranian-Arab relationship. Some Arabophile tendencies were there as well as vestiges of past animosity, although they were nearly erased when the Turks, Mongols and Tartars invaded Iran. In 1501, when Shah Ismael Safavi founded his dynasty and regarded himself as the first Iranian national sovereign since 641 AD, he shaped Iran's future: he declared Shi'ism its official religion and an integral part of Iranian nationalism. Yet while he promoted the unique Persian characteristics of his nation — to combat the Sunni Ottoman Turkish Empire — he himself claimed descent from the Prophet Mohammad, an Arab.[5]

Heretofore, Shi'ism had not been an integrated part of Iranian culture; it had been only one aspect of the Islamic experience in Iran. Indeed, when Shah Ismael proclaimed Shi'ism the state religion, Arab Shi'i scholars had to be imported to promote the faith *en masse* among the Iranians. The conversion of the majority of the Iranians to Shi'ism marked a turning point in the history of Islam in Iran.[6] Iranian national consciousness and Shi'ism, which also had an early history of oppression, joined forces against the Sunni Ottoman Turks in the sixteenth century. It was the beginning of a new era of Islamic disunity and Shi'i-Sunni antagonism.

Conflicts in the border areas were an early manifestation in the Persian Gulf of the differences. The most significant controversy in these territorial disputes was over the Shatt al-Arab waterway.[7] Although the dispute goes back to earlier history, the seventeenth century was the beginning of intense power struggles over the Shatt al-Arab between the two dominant empires, the Sunni Ottomans and Shi'i Iranians.

The two sides relied heavily upon tribal allegiances in the region of Mesopotamia (modern Iraq) for their claims in resolving their border conflicts. As time passed, other issues have arisen which have made settlement of the differences more complex. In the meantime, of course, the political order had evolved. What had been border disputes between the Ottoman and Iranian empires became disputes between the British and Russian empires and finally, in the contemporary scene, conflicts between Iran and Iraq.

Controversy over the sovereignty of the Shatt al-Arab waterway has produced many agreements, among which six international treaties stand out. It was only when no decisive military victory could be achieved that the disputants sought political solutions. The Treaty of Zuhab was enacted in 1639 between the Ottoman Empire and the Iranians. When it became ineffective in 1823, the first Treaty of Erzerum was signed. With the advent of British and Russian imperialism in the area, the second Treaty of Erzerum was signed in 1847. Subsequently, with British and Russian involvement, the Protocol of 1913 became the new basis for demarcation of the boundaries. When this treaty failed to satisfy the parties, Iran and Iraq signed the Iraq-Iran Frontier Treaty in 1937 which Iran abrogated in 1969. Still seeking to obtain an effective means of resolving the dispute, the Algiers Treaty of 1975 was signed, only for Iraq to abrogate it in 1980.

The 1639 Treaty of Zuhab

After indecisive battles between Iran and the Ottoman Empire over Iraq (Mesopotamia), and after each had occupied it for a short period of time, both Iranians and the Ottomans decided to seek a political solution to the frontier dispute. They signed the Treaty of Zuhab in 1639. The question of jurisdiction over the entire frontier, including the Shatt al-Arab waterway, was resolved on the basis of the allegiance and loyalties of the indigenous inhabitants of the frontier zone. However, this proved only to be a temporary containment of the dispute. The provisions of the treaty had not taken into consideration the aspirations of the indigenous populations.

Concerned with their own interests, of course, they shifted their loyalties whenever it was deemed necessary. Additionally, the terms of the treaty were not clearly defined and those relating to the Shatt al-Arab waterway remained vague. The result of this flawed treaty was further border conflict.

The First and Second Treaties of Erzerum

Inconclusive wars between the Ottoman Empire and Iran over the borders and sovereignty of the Shatt al-Arab continued in the eighteenth and well into the nineteenth centuries. In 1823 the first Treaty of Erzerum sought to bring a resolution to the border conflict by relying on the 1639 Treaty and other agreements as a basis of this new accord. The end result was a treaty that suffered from the same ambiguities that had marked the earlier agreements.

In 1847 the second Treaty of Erzerum attempted to rectify the previous lack of clarification. By this time the Russian and British empires had begun their penetration of the region. In addition to what the Iranians and Ottoman Turks expected to gain from this treaty, the British and Russians had their own interests in mind. Each party had to move against complicated designs and, in the end, the second Treaty of Erzerum served the growing British and Russian interests in Iraq (Mesopotamia) and Iran to the extent that the parties to the conflict were no longer in control and the imperial powers of Britain and Russia were dictating events. Harbour and anchorage rights were granted to Iran, while the Shatt al-Arab was awarded to the Ottoman Empire without clear marks and indications on the course of the border. This rendered the treaty as ineffective as previous ones.[8]

The 1913 Protocol of Constantinople

Not satisfied with the second Treaty of Erzerum, Iran repeatedly sought to renegotiate the provisions pertaining to the sovereignty of the Shatt al-Arab. Iran desired joint ownership of the waterway with the Ottoman Turks, but Britain and Russia were rivals in their influence over the area, and it was not until the signing of the 1907 Anglo-Russian Convention, wherein northern Iran was divided into the Russian sphere of influence and southern Iran became a British zone of influence, that they took an interest in resolving the conflict. The manoeuvring of British and Russian negotiators, each reaffirming their own interests in the dispute, resulted in the signing of the 1913 Protocol of Constantinople and the Procès-Verbaux of the Delimitation of Frontiers Commission of 1914. Among Britain, Russia, Iran and Turkey, the status of the Shatt al-Arab remained as it was in the 1847 Treaty of Erzerum, but most other border issues and demarcation issues were agreed upon. A Delimitation Commission representing the four powers involved was appointed according to the Protocol to establish boundary marks. The commission's work came to an end upon the commencement of World War I.[9]

The 1937 Iraqi-Iranian Frontier Treaty

The political conditions of World War I and its consequences led to the creation of new states which joined those with clear historical identity. Iraq was among those newly created states, with British sponsorship. Such British interest carried the weight in future negotiations over the sovereignty issue of the Shatt al-Arab. Prior to the 1937 treaty, Iran had argued that the previous treaty was illegal because Iran had not agreed to the provisions of the second Erzerum Treaty of 1847, which was the basis of subsequent agreements and reflected the self-serving designs of the British Empire and Imperial Russia.

Political manoeuvring and border clashes once again brought the contending parties to negotiations which culminated in the 1937

Iraqi-Iranian Frontier Treaty. The sovereignty of the Shatt al-Arab continued to belong to Iraq although, for the first time, Iran was granted a 4-mile anchorage zone in addition to the previously granted harbour and anchorage rights. It was also stipulated that the usage of the waterway would remain unhindered by both parties.[10] Soon, as was the case in the past, the passage of time and the arrival of new political conditions and different interpretations of the treaty rendered it as ineffective as those signed before. World War II presented both Iran and Iraq new challenges. Iran found itself well into the Western camp led by the United States, and by becoming signatories to the Baghdad Pact of 1955, both Iran and Iraq became part of a Western alliance to contain Soviet expansionism. Iranian-Iraqi relations within this period, although not cordial, were not based on belligerency, and the issue of the sovereignty of the waterway was handled contractually. This did not mean that the problems had been resolved, but that a *modus vivendi* had been achieved.

In 1958 a new regime replaced the monarchy in Iraq, and a new chain of events began to beset that country. Iraq withdrew from the Baghdad Pact and proclaimed itself fully in charge of its destiny. The relationship with Iran took a new turn for the worse. Whatever previous arrangements and contractual agreements had been achieved were jeopardized. The new government of Abdul Karim Qassim and Shah Mohammad Reza Pahlavi's government raised claims and counterclaims. Iran demanded half the sovereignty of the Shatt al-Arab and Iraq accused Iran of expansionist designs. However, Iraq lacked the military power to effect policy. In 1968 Iraq again underwent a change when the Arab Ba'th Socialist Party came into power. Hostilities between the two countries increased, and in April 1969 Iran unilaterally abrogated the 1937 treaty.

The Iraqi Ba'th regime, perhaps because of its political and ideological orientation, launched a campaign to change the *status quo* and power structure of the Persian Gulf region. The relationship between Iraq and the Soviet Union, particularly after the 1972 Soviet-Iraqi Friendship Treaty, threatened the Iranian government and the United States, which also had a vital interest in maintaining the *status quo* and stability of the region. To curb the spread of Iraq's radical ideas in the area, both Iran and the United States sought to keep Iraq occupied at home. To this end, Iran under Shah Mohammad Reza Pahlavi and the United States under Richard Nixon, supported the Kurdish secessionist movement in

Iraq. With outside support, the Kurds, who form 20 per cent of the Iraqi population, posed a formidable challenge to the government of Iraq. In turn, Iraq attempted to offer similar support to Iranian minorities against the central government, particularly the Arabs of Khuzestan, but to no avail since these minorities did not constitute a challenge to Tehran.

Faced with the direct military confrontation with Iran or a negotiated settlement of existing problems, Iran opted for the latter. During a summit of OPEC in March 1975, the Shah of Iran and Saddam Hussein, then Vice President of the Revolutionary Command Council of Iraq, held two meetings which resulted in an agreement to resolve all existing problems between the two countries.

The 1975 Algiers Treaty

For the first time in the history of the dispute, the two sovereign states of Iran and Iraq seemed to have worked out an equitable settlement of their differences. The contracting parties decided to honour the 1913 Protocol of Constantinople and the 1914 Procès-Verbaux of the Delimitation of Frontiers Commission with respect to their frontiers. The fate of the Shatt al-Arab waterway and its jurisdiction were settled on the basis of the *Thalweg*, an established principle in international law. According to this provision, the border was to be marked in the middle (*Thalweg*) of the Shatt al-Arab channel. Iran and Iraq additionally agreed to cease infiltration and subversive activities in each others' country.

The provisions of the Algiers agreement (see Appendix, p. 226ff.) led to the 1975 treaty of international boundaries and good-neighbour policies, effecting a *quid pro quo* arrangement in which Iran promised to desist from aiding the Kurdish secessionists and Iraq agreed to share the sovereignty of the Shatt al-Arab. It also signalled a message to Baghdad that Iran would not tolerate anti-*status quo* regimes at its doorsteps and had the capability to destabilize them if it chose to do so. The Iraqis understood and acquiesced in these agreements, but begrudged the circumstances under which the 1975 treaty was signed. They were later to contend that they had signed under duress and would have refused had they had the opportunity. Circumstances changed with the advent of the Islamic Revolution in Iran in 1979 and Iraq abrogated the

1975 treaty and invaded Iran.

It is evident that the two contending parties signed agreements for the most part only under duress from the other. Obviously, the Shatt al-Arab problem always has remained despite the agreements. Iranians were not content with the first five treaties, and Iraqis were unhappy with the last one. These treaties were instruments to peace provided there was a state capable of enforcing them. It tends to confirm the thesis of certain theorists that a preponderance of power must exist on the side of *status quo* forces. Otherwise, those who are unhappy with the *status quo* are sorely tempted to go to war to change it.[11]

Iraq obviously perceived the Iranian power struggle triggered by the revolution as the propitious moment to restructure its own disadvantageous relationship with Iran. A successful military invasion of Iran would logically have at least three favourable results: first, it would destabilize the Islamic regime in Tehran leading to the overthrow of the Khomeini government; secondly, it would allow Iraq to reclaim sovereignty over the entire Shatt al-Arab and perhaps also the entire province of Khuzestan; and thirdly, it would mark the beginning of Iraqi hegemony in the Persian Gulf and a prominent position in Arab politics.

Many reasons were cited by Iraq for the invasions: *inter alia*, Iraq blamed Iran for the 'exportation of her revolution' to the Shi'i population of Iraq and interference in Iraq's internal affairs. But this was only the surface excuse. Iraq was aware of its internal problems, particularly its vulnerability to the Shi'i Moslems whom the government had largely ignored. Iraq also knew that the Iraqi Shi'i counterparts in Iran had overthrown the powerful secular government of the Shah and that the same fate could befall the Iraqi leadership. Therefore, President Saddam Hussein seized this rare opportunity to strike at the Iranians and save himself and his secular government and, at the same time, to restructure the imbalance of power in Iraq's favour.

The War

On 22 September 1980 Iraq invaded Iran with the purpose of occupying the province of Khuzestan, besieging and capturing the major cities within that province. The campaign, if successful, could destabilize the regime in Tehran and offer an opportunity to the Iranian opposition, with whom Saddam Hussein was in contact, to move against Khomeini. At the very least, it would force the Tehran government to renegotiate the frontier dispute and send a strong signal to Tehran that Iraq was a new force in the region with which it must contend.

Somewhere, however, there had been a miscalculation. The Iranians were more resilient than expected, and despite fierce fighting, the likes of which had been rarely seen since World War II, the Iraqis were only able to capture the port city of Khoramshahr and were otherwise denied the anticipated conquest of Khuzestan. Iraq declared that it had limited aims: to regain full sovereignty of the Shatt al-Arab; to stop Iran from interfering in Iraq's internal affairs; and the return of the islands of Abu Mosa and the Tunbs at the mouth of the Persian Gulf near the Strait of Hormouz. (Iraq claimed the islands belong to the Arabs, while Iran had maintained that the islands were Iranian territories.) If Iran were to accept these conditions, Iraq would withdraw its forces. Iran refused.

Meanwhile, internal developments in Iran took a positive turn for the clerical government and its Islamic Republican Party. The war, which had come to be known as 'the imposed war' (*jange tahmeli*), had a stabilizing effect, enabling the regime to consolidate its strengths against the opposition. The first Iranian president, Abol Hassan Bani-Sadr, was ousted in 1981 amid disagreements with the Islamic Republican Party. The Mojahedeen, an opposition group, was effectively silenced, and the regime was able to eliminate other opposition groups as well.

Between the time of the invasion and May 1982, the war had become stalemated. The Iraqis were unable to score any decisive victory beyond the capture and control of Khoramshahr. Finally, after its domestic opposition had been quelled, Iran was prepared to seize the initiative in the war. In May 1982 it broke the stalemate and liberated Khoramshahr and captured a large number of Iraqi soldiers. Other Iranian campaigns against the occupying forces were equally successful. Startled by the turn of events, Saddam Hussein declared his willingness to negotiate peace and, for the first time, the Gulf Cooperation Council, realizing the danger of a spillover of the conflict, began to encourage negotiations. It spoke of creating a Gulf Reconstruction Fund to pay war reparations to Iran. However, the Iranians, with the upper hand, wanted revenge. Iran refused to negotiate unless Iraq met its conditions:

1. The removal of Saddam Hussein from power;
2. the withdrawal of all Iraqi forces from Iran and the recognition of the 1975 treaty;
3. repatriation of Iranian Iraqis to Iraq; and
4. war reparations for Iran.

From this period forward, Iran began a campaign aimed at creating circumstances within which the above conditions could be met. Since Iraq had invaded Iran, security of its borders became a major Iranian concern. Iraq had to be kept at a distance. To this end, the Tehran government took the war into Iraqi territory. The assault against Iraq, begun with the Basra offensive in September 1982, was designed to secure Iran's border as well as to pressure Iraq into accepting Iran's conditions for peace.

The ensuing strategies and counter-strategies, offensives and counter-offensives, campaigns and counter-campaigns translated into one question for most outside observers: 'At what price, victory?' However, for Iran it was obvious that Iraq's willingness to negotiate (expressed in 1982) already spelled victory. Therefore, Iran stubbornly insisted upon its four preconditions for negotiations. Although the price in human sacrifice had been horrendous, Iran continued its offensives into Iraq.

For its part, Iraq experimented with a variety of strategies, including chemical warfare, to pressure Iran into negotiating peace. Iraq's 'tanker war', part of its general strategy from the beginning, escalated when Iraq acquired the Super Étendard Exocet system from France in late 1982. It was intended to inflict serious economic damage by attacking Iran-bound oil tankers. Iraq also believed that this strategy would widen the war against Iran, thus forcing Iran to the bargaining table. It failed. Iran developed a counter-strategy, attacking tankers bound for Kuwait and Saudi Arabia, Iraq's economic life-support system. Both Kuwait and Saudi Arabia had given massive support to finance Iraq's war efforts against Iran. The message was unambiguous: if Iran's ability to export its oil was obstructed, others in the Persian Gulf would suffer the same fate.[12]

Iraq's strategy was not tactically successful, nor was Iran's, except as a counter-threat to Iraq's attacks. The attacks failed to sink the tankers and the crude oil was usually salvaged. The increased war-risk insurance premiums on shipping were merely offset by discounts on the price of crude. Kuwait made provisions to replace any crude loss without charge, and the Saudis provided air cover for ships bound to Saudi Arabia.[13]

Iraq's next strategy, air attacks on Iran's civilian-population centres, also failed to bring Iran to the negotiating table. In March 1985 Iraq upgraded its attacks to inflict massive civilian casualties in all major Iranian cities to bring popular pressure on Iran to negotiate peace. But Iran still did not buckle under. Instead, it initiated its own counter-attack against Iraq's major cities. The much smaller Iranian air force was not used as an attack force; it could be used better in defence. Iran employed Scud surface-to-surface missiles. Each time the Iraqi planes bombed an Iranian city, Iran retaliated with a missile. The war continued. It was another stalemate.

There were a couple of other constants. First, Iraq continued to send signals that it was ready to negotiate, adding that it would treat the 1975 treaty as a point of departure if Iran agreed to comprehensive peace negotiations. Secondly, Iran stubbornly insisted upon its four preconditions, albeit somewhat modified.[14] The most notable modification was in the condition that Iraqi forces withdraw from Iran. Now that Iran held Iraqi territory which she considered more strategic (e.g. the Majnoon Islands) than the territories held by Iraq, Iran no longer insisted upon an Iraqi withdrawal.

Special Factors Affecting the Peace Process

To be sure, the earlier treaties must be taken into consideration in any peace negotiations. Nevertheless, the current conflict and the domestic political systems of both states, not to mention the international political system within which this conflict is being played out, are quite different from the past.

Both countries are in the early stages of political development. Both invoke a particular ideology, the Ba'th credo in Iraq and Islamic fundamentalism in Iran. There are limitations upon flexibility and manoeuvrability in resolving international conflicts since the foreign relations of each, like their domestic politics, are structured within a constrictive ideological framework.

The current Iraqi political system is based upon a Revolutionary Command Council, which is the supreme political as well as legislative body of the country. Saddam Hussein, President of the Republic, is a member of the Council, under whose leadership the war with Iran is being conducted and foreign policy is being formulated. A national assembly also plays a legislative role, but the real power lies with the Socialist Arab Ba'th Party headed by Saddam Hussein. Party doctrine is based upon Arab nationalism (secular) with three significant functions:

1. The creation of a united Arab entity;
2. independence from external hegemony; and
3. the practice of an Arab version of socialism.[15]

Specifically in the area of foreign policy, Iraqi doctrine perceives the world as a potential multipolar order in which Iraq is capable of playing an influential role. In fact, it envisages a regional role for the Iraqi Ba'th Party under the tutelage of Saddam Hussein, resembling Nasser's Arab nationalism in the 1950s and 1960s. In 1979, when Saddam Hussein assumed the presidency, he felt that the time was ripe to assume his historical role in the area.[16] Typical of self-appointed 'men of destiny', of course, he has become pretty absolute in his leadership, in effect, heading a one-man decision-making system. The Iranian system under Khomeini is not dissimilar.

When the Shah was overthrown in the Iranian revolution, an Islamic government was established which proclaimed that its legitimacy — and sovereignty — were derived ultimately from God. To be sure, the Islamic government is a constitutional system. Nevertheless, the system is essentially theological. The laws are derived, for example, from the Koran, the Hadith, and the traditions of the Shi'i Imams which are, of course, also interpreted by theologians, the ruling clergy.

As the architect of the concept of the direct hierocratic rule in the absence of the Hidden Imam, Ayatollah Khomeini spoke of validity of the *valayat-e faqih* (religious guardian-jurisprudent) concept. According to this concept, the temporal rulers are illegitimate and the Islamic community can best be served by *mojtahids* (learned Shi'i scholars who render *ijtihad*) who are also *fuqaha* (jurisprudents) for they are the sole interpreters of the rule of God in the absence of the divinely guided *Mahdi* (Hidden Imam). In essence *valayat-e faqih* places sovereignty under the exclusive control of the clergy.[17]

The foreign-policy formulation in Iran is under the exclusive governance of the ruling clergy headed by Ayatollah Khomeini.

According to this world view, the international system as constituted currently is unacceptable, and consequently a new Islamic world order must be established. Thus, the call for Islamic universalism with its centre in Iran and the Iranian Islamic government as the model for the Islamic community, becomes an active part of foreign-policy formulation. The propagation of this brand of Islamic ideology abroad is obligatory.[18]

Both leaders perceive the other as a threat to their respective legitimacy and survival. Therefore, with antipathetical one-man foreign-policy decision-making in both countries — and given Iranian Islamic universalism versus Iraqi Arab nationalism — there are obvious limitations to the peace process. This is the downside.

It is obvious that despite extraordinary bloodshed, human suffering and economic loss, both countries and their political systems have survived, displaying almost incomprehensible resilience to the destructive war. Since the strategies of both seem flawed in that neither side can attain a military victory, perhaps they may ultimately see the futility of this bloody contest. This is the upside for the peace process.

The East-West struggle, of course, also spills over into this conflict. When Iran was part of the Western alliance in the Middle East, the United States sought to destabilize Iraq through Iran. The policy was rigorously pursued until the Iranian revolution, which not only Iraq welcomed but so did its ally, the Soviet Union. Indeed, the USSR had high expectations in Iran when the latter broke its ties with the United States after the revolution. However, Iran perceived both superpowers with suspicion. It viewed the Soviet occupation of Afghanistan with particular disfavour to the end that the Soviet Union found itself in much the same position as the United States in Iran's opinion.

Nevertheless, neither the United States nor the Soviet Union could leave Iran alone, since the war, regardless of its origins, could have benefits for them. As for the Soviets, the war would bring them closer to Iraq since the latter depended heavily upon Soviet arms. In the American case, the war could so preoccupy Iran that it would preclude it from radicalizing the Persian Gulf. Moreover, it would also remove Iraq from the Arab-Israeli conflict, in which the United States has a vested interest in the peace process. Finally, both of these mono-industrial (oil) nations must rely on others to wage the war, not to mention, to rebuild after it. The combatants now procure armaments from the superpowers for cash, albeit indirectly from America.

In essence, the major Cold War powers look upon the region strictly within the context of Cold War politics and their own interests. Neither the United States nor the Soviet Union perceives the Iran-Iraq war as a destabilizing threat to their sphere of influence. According to a Staff Report of the United States Senate Committee on Foreign Relations, the Iran-Iraq war does not pose a threat of superpower confrontation. According to it, stability can be maintained so long as there is 'no victor, no vanquished' in the war.[19] Pursuing this policy, the United States abandoned its position of 'neutrality' and had 'tilted' towards Iraq in an effort to assure the continuity of the war of attrition: 'The U.S. has taken a number of steps to shore up Iraq, including what the report [The Foreign Relations Committee Staff Report] describes as "vigorous support" for an arms embargo against Iran.'[20] The end result is that Iran is not winning the war due to a worldwide arms embargo against it; and Iraq is not losing due to massive arms supplies from the Soviet Union and France.[21] A victory by either side could have a destabilizing effect, threatening American interests.

Ironically, the Soviet Union pursues the same 'no-victor no-vanquished' policy regarding the war. Therefore, earnest efforts are made to keep the Iraqis in their camp while making sure that Iraq will not be strategically victorious. If an Iraqi victory should become a reality, the power mosaic of the region will be dangerously altered. The closest Soviet ally, Syria, Iraq's foe, will suffer if Iraq should win this war, a possibility the Syrians would not like to contemplate. The Soviets, although in alliance with Iraq, are also concerned about alienating Iran. An Iraqi victory is likely to jeopardize the already suspicious Iranian-Soviet relationship, and the Soviets are not anxious to harm their future interactions with Iran.

Conversely, the Soviets do not want to see an Iraqi defeat. The Soviet Union's maintenance of a foothold in Iraq is strategically a significant part of their overall foreign policy in the Middle East. An Iranian victory would cause strain on the cautious attitude that Iraq has towards the Soviet Union. If Iran should be the victor, the Soviets believe they too will suffer. Such a victory would probably undermine the Soviet activities in Afghanistan and could also be dangerous among the Moslem populations of the Soviet central Asian republics with whom the central government has a very cautious relationship. Thus, the Soviet Union, not unlike the United States, must pursue an active policy of 'no victor, no vanquished' in the Iran-Iraq war.

Given these facts, both Iran and Iraq must take into serious consideration that the war is not being conducted in a vacuum. Therefore, a military solution is out of the question. It is self-destructive. However, they can control its resolution, if they wish.

Towards Peace

It is clear that the Iranians and Iraqis, particularly the Iranians, remain committed in their dispute to ideological concerns and saving face. Indeed, the commitment is so deep that to abandon it now may pose serious internal problems. For both sides, the war has had a stabilizing effect on the domestic political scene. In Iran, Khomeini was able to eliminate the opposition, and in Iraq, Saddam Hussein achieved the same objective, even to the point of neutralizing a potential Shi'i uprising. Nevertheless, due to the severity and length of the war, its continuation could become a major destabilizing factor in both countries.

Iran faces a serious dilemma. War propaganda has become such an integral part of the Iranian Islamic ideology that it cannot be ignored in any move toward peace with Iraq. In effect, any gesture toward peace may become a major destabilizing force. Therefore, if the Khomeini government moves in this direction, it may well perforce publicly announce a 'no peace' position, while privately it pursues a 'no war' policy. Iraq is less vulnerable since it has sought a negotiated end to the war since 1982.

It is worthwhile at this point to examine Iran's preconditions for negotiations to see whether they are as formidable a block to peace now as they appeared to be when Iran first issued them:

1. *Withdrawal of all Iraqi forces from Iran.* As noted earlier, this was no longer an issue once Iran had captured Iraqi territory, which in Iran's eyes was more strategic than the Iranian territories held by Iraq.

2. *Recognition of the 1975 treaty.* In its bid for a negotiated peace, Iraq has referred to the 1975 Algiers Treaty which, among all of the treaties of the past, may be the most equitable. (See Appendix.) In effect, this does not appear to pose an obstacle to the peace process.[22]

3. *Repatriation of Iranian Iraqis.* The Iraqis have so far ignored Iran's condition that the Iraqi refugees (Iraqis of Iranian

extraction) now living in Iran be repatriated to Iraq. But then Iraq has not objected to it either. Therefore, this condition is probably not a serious deterrent to the initiation of the peace process.

4. *War reparations for Iran.* Khomeini's demands have ranged from $150,000 million to $350,000 million. Without offering these sums, the Gulf Cooperation Council has spoken on a number of occasions of creating a Gulf Reconstruction Fund to encourage Iran to negotiate peace. Although the offer in its original format is no longer outstanding, another version might be forthcoming if it brought peace to the region. In any case, this is a negotiable issue.

5. *Condemnation of Iraq as the aggressor.* It is interesting to note in this regard, that Iran has begun to give conflicting, yet encouraging, signals that it wants to work within the United Nations to resolve the conflict, provided it is willing to recognize Iran's grievances.[23] Iran would seek the same sort of condition of the Organization of Islamic Conference, of course, if it were involved. Either organization could work out the verbal niceties to please both sides.

6. *Removal of Saddam Hussein from power.* This is the most difficult precondition, of course, since it is obviously highly unlikely that he would agree to his own removal. The assumption throughout this analysis has been, naturally, that Haddam Hussein and Ayatollah Khomeini would be the negotiators in any peace process. However, given time and the pattern of sudden change of leadership in the Middle East even this condition may not be insurmountable.

In conclusion, two levels of conflict resolution are possible: (i) at the local level between Iraq and Iran themselves, or (ii) at the international level. Direct negotiations between Iraq and Iran for a peace treaty would certainly be most fruitful. However, given the cost of this war on both sides in human life and other resources — not to mention their diametrically opposed ideologies — resolution of this conflict in the near future appears unlikely, even impossible, at this level.

Therefore, if any attempt at all is made to negotiate a settlement, it will probably be made at a higher level, in the UN or some other international forum — but then only to be abrogated again down the road by Iraq or Iran because the outstanding issues were not finally resolved by them but by others who, of course, also served their own interests at their expense. While old soldiers in the Middle East pass away, their disputes rarely do.

Notes

1. See Willard A. Beling (ed.), *The Middle East: Quest for an American Policy* (Albany: State University of the New York Press, 1973), p. vii.

2. Hamid Enayat, 'Iran and the Arabs' in Sylvia G. Haim (ed.), *Arab Nationalism and a Wider World* (New York: American Academic Association for Peace in the Middle East, 1971), p. 14.

3. Ibid., p. 14.

4. Ibid., p. 14.

5. Ibid., p. 17.

6. John O. Voll, *Islam: Continuity and Change in the Modern World* (Boulder: Westview Press, 1982), p. 83.

7. Peter Hunseler, 'The Historical Antecedents of the Shatt al-Arab Dispute' in M. S. El Azhary (ed.), *The Iran-Iraq War* (New York: St Martin's Press, 1984), pp. 9–10.

8. Ibid., pp. 11–12.

9. Ibid., pp. 12–13.

10. Ibid., pp. 14–15.

11. Theodore A. Couloumbis and James H. Wolfe, *Introduction to International Relations: Power and Justice*, 2nd edn (Englewood Cliffs: Prentice-Hall, Inc., 1982), p. 177.

12. Thomas Stauffer, 'The War Iran Must Escalate', *Middle East International*, no. 227 (15 June 1984), 14–15.

13. *Christian Science Monitor*, 29 August 1984.

14. *The Times*, 14 September 1984.

15. Ahmad Yousef Ahmad, 'The Dialectics of Domestic Environment and Role Performance: The Foreign Policy of Iraq' in Bahgat Korany and Ali E. Hillal Dessouki (eds), *The Foreign Policies of Arab States* (Colorado: Westview Press, 1984), pp. 156–8.

16. Ibid., pp. 157–9.

17. For a detailed discussion of the concept see Imam Khomeini, *Valayat-e Faqih: Hokomat-e Islami* (Tehran: Amir Kabeer Press, 1981).

18. R. K. Ramazani, 'Khmmayni's Islam in Iran's Foreign Policy' in Adeed Dawisha (ed.), *Islam in Foreign Policy* (Cambridge: Cambridge University Press, 1983), pp. 17–18.

19. *Christian Science Monitor*, 29 August 1984.

20. Ibid.

21. Ibid.

22. Glen Balfour-Paul, 'The Prospects for Peace' in M. S. El Azhary (ed.), 'Iran-Iraq War', p. 136.

23. *Kayhan Airmail Edition*, 22 May 1985.

Appendix

Algiers Declaration of 6 March 1975 Joint Communiqué Between Iraq and Iran

During the meeting in Algiers of the Summit Conference of the Member Countries of OPEC and on the initiative of President Boumedienne, His Majesty the Shahinshah of Iran and H. E. Saddam Hussein, Vice President of the Revolutionary Command

Council of Iraq, held two meetings and had lengthy discussions on the subject of relations between the two countries.

These meetings, which took place in the presence of President Boumedienne, were marked by great frankness and a sincere wish on both sides to reach a final and permanent solution to all the problems exisiting between the two countries.

In application of the principles of territorial integrity, the inviolability of borders and non-interference in internal affairs, the two contractual parties have decided:

1. To effect a definitive demarcation of their land frontiers on the basis of the Protocol of Constantinople, 1913, and the procès-verbaux of the Delimitation of Frontiers Commission of 1914.
2. To delimit their fluvial frontiers according to the Thalweg line.
3. Accordingly, the two parties will restore security and mutual trust along their common boundaries, and hence will commit themselves to exercising a strict and effective control over their common boundaries with a view to putting a definitive end to all acts of infiltration of a subversive character no matter where they originate from.
4. The two parties also agreed to consider the arrangements referred to above as integral elements of the comprehensive solution. Hence any impairment of any of their components shall naturally be contrary to the spirit of the Algiers Agreement.

The two parties will remain in permanent touch with President Boumedienne who will offer, in case of need, the fraternal assistance of Algeria to implement the decisions which have been taken. The parties have decided to re-establish traditional ties of good neighbourliness and friendship, particularly by the elimination of all negative factors in their relations, the continuous exchange of views on questions of mutual interest and the development of mutual co-operation.

The two parties solemnly declare that the area should be kept free from any outside interference.

The Ministers of Foreign Affairs of Iran and Iraq met in the presence of the Algerian Foreign Minister on March 15, 1975 in Tehran to fix the details of work for the Joint Iraqi-Iranian Commission created to implement the decisions reached above by mutual agreement.

In accordance with the wishes of both parties, Algeria will be invited to all the meetings of the Joint Iraqi-Iranian Commission. The Joint Commission will draw up its timetable and workplan so as to meet, in case of need, alternatively in Baghdad and Tehran. His Majesty the Shahinshah has accepted with pleasure the invitation which has been conveyed to him, on behalf of H. E. President Ahmed Hassan El-Bakr, to make an official visit to Iraq; the date of this visit will be fixed by mutual agreement.

Furthermore, H. E. Saddam Hussein has agreed to make an official visit to Iran on a date to be agreed between the two parties.

His Majesty the Shahinshah and H. E. Vice President Saddam Hussein wish to thank particularly and warmly President Houari Boumedienne who, acting from fraternal and disinterested motives, has facilitated the establishment of direct contacts between the leaders of the two countries and, as a result, has contributed to the establishment of a new era in relations between Iran and Iraq in the higher interest of the future of the region concerned.

Algiers, March 6, 1975

Treaty Concerning the State Frontier and Neighbourly Relations Between Iran and Iraq

His Imperial Majesty the Shahinshah of Iran,

His Excellency the President of the Republic of Iraq,

Considering the sincere desire of the two Parties as expressed in the Algiers Agreement of March 6, 1975, to achieve a final and lasting solution to all the problems pending between the two countries,

Considering that the two Parties have carried out the definitive redemarcation of their land frontier on the basis of the Constantinople Protocol of 1913 and the minutes of the meetings of the Frontier Delimitation Commission of 1914 and have delimited their river frontier along the thalweg,

Considering their desire to restore security and mutual trust throughout the length of their common frontier,

Considering the ties of geographical proximity, history, religion, culture and civilization which bind the peoples of Iran and Iraq,

Desirous of strengthening their bonds of friendship and good neighbourliness, expanding their economic and cultural relations and promoting exchanges and human relations between their peoples on the basis of the principles of territorial integrity, the inviolability of frontiers and non-interference in internal affairs,

Resolved to work towards the introduction of a new era in friendly

relations between Iran and Iraq based on full respect for the national independence and sovereign equality of States,
Convinced that they are helping thereby to implement the principles and achieve the purposes and objectives of the Charter of the United Nations,
Have decided to conclude this Treaty and have appointed as their plenipotentiaries:

His Imperial Majesty the Shahinshah of Iran:
His Excellency Abbas Ali Khalatbary, Minister of Foreign Affairs of Iran.
His Excellency the President of the Republic of Iraq:
His Excellency Saddoun Hamadi, Minister for Foreign Affairs of Iraq.

Who, having exchanged their full powers, found to be in good form and due form, have agreed as follows:

Article 1. The High Contracting Parties confirm that the State land frontier between Iraq and Iran shall be that which has been redemarcated on the basis of and in accordance with the provisions of the Protocol concerning the redemarcation of the land frontier and the annexes thereto, attached to this Treaty.

Article 2. The High Contracting Parties confirm that the State frontier in the Shatt Al Arab shall be that which has been delimited on the basis of and in accordance with the provisions of the Protocol concerning the delimitation of the river frontier, and the annexes thereto, attached to this Treaty.

Article 3. The High Contracting Parties undertake to exercise strict and effective permanent control over the frontier in order to put an end to any infiltration of a subversive nature from any source, on the basis of and in accordance with the provisions of the Protocol concerning frontier security, and the annex thereto, attached to this Treaty.

Article 4. The High Contracting Parties confirm that the provisions of the three Protocols, and the annexes thereto, referred to in articles 1, 2, and 3 above and attached to this Treaty as an integral part thereof shall be final and permanent. They shall not be infringed under any circumstances and shall constitute the indivisible elements of an over-all settlement. Accordingly, a breach of any of the components of this over-all settlement shall clearly be incompatible with the spirit of the Algiers Agreement.

Article 5. In keeping with the inviolability of the frontiers of the two States and strict respect for their territorial integrity, the High Contracting Parties confirm that the course of their land and river frontiers shall be inviolable, permanent and final.

Article 6. (1). In the event of a dispute regarding the interpretation or implementation of this Treaty, the three Protocols or the annexes thereto, any solution to such a dispute shall strictly respect the course of the Iraqi-Iranian frontier referred to in articles 1 and 2 above, and shall take into account the need to maintain security on the Iraqi-Iranian frontier in accordance with article 3 above.
(2). Such disputes shall be resolved in the first instance by the High Contracting Parties, by means of direct bilateral negotiations to be held within two months after the date on which one of the Parties so requested.
(3). If no agreement is reached, the High Contracting Parties shall have recourse, within a three-month period, to the good offices of a friendly third State.
(4). Should one of the two Parties refuse to have recourse to good offices or should the good offices procedure fail, the dispute shall be settled by arbitration within a period of not more than one month after the date of such refusal or failure.
(5). Should the High Contracting Parties disagree as to the arbitration procedure, one of the High Contracting Parties may have recourse, within 15 days after such disagreement was recorded, to a court of arbitration.
With a view to establishing such a court of arbitration each of the High Contracting Parties shall, in respect of each dispute to be resolved, appoint one of its nationals as arbitrators and the two arbitrators shall choose an umpire. Should the High Contracting Parties fail to appoint their arbitrators within one month after the date on which one of the parties received a request for arbitration from the other Party, or should the arbitrators fail to reach agreement on the choice of the umpire before that time-limit expires, the High Contracting Party which requested arbitration shall be entitled to request the President of the International Court of

Justice to appoint the arbitrators or the umpire, in accordance with the procedures of the Permanent Court of Arbitration.

(6). The decision of the court of arbitration shall be binding on and enforceable by the High Contracting Parties.

(7). The High Contracting Parties shall each defray half the costs of arbitration.

Article 7. This Treaty, the three Protocols and the annex thereto shall be registered in accordance with Article 102 of the Charter of the United Nations.

Article 8. This Treaty, and three Protocols and the annexes thereto shall be ratified by each of the High Contracting Parties in accordance with its domestic law.

This Treaty, the three Protocols and the annexes thereto shall enter into force on the date of the exchange of the instruments of ratification in Tehran.

In Witness Whereof the Plenipotentiaries of the High Contracting Parties have signed this Treaty, the three Protocols and the annexes thereto.

Done at Baghdad, on June 13, 1975.

Abbas Ali Khalatbary   Saadoun Hamadi
Minister for Foreign Affairs   Minister for Foreign Affairs
of Iran   of Iraq

This Treaty, the three Protocols and the annexes thereto were signed in the presence of His Excellency Abdel-Aziz Bouteflika, Member of the Council of the Revolution and Minister for Foreign Affairs of Algeria.

(Signed)

Protocol Concerning the Delimitation of the River Frontier Between Iran and Iraq

Pursuant to the decisions taken in the Algiers communiqué of March 6, 1975,

The two Contracting Parties have agreed as follows:

Article 1. The two Contracting Parties hereby declare and recognize that the State river frontier between Iran and Iraq in the Shatt Al Arab has been delimited along the thalweg by the Mixed Iraqi-

Iranian-Algerian Committee on the basis of the following:

(1). The Tehran Protocol of March 17, 1975;

(2). The record of the Meeting of Ministers for Foreign Affairs, signed at Baghdad on April 20, 1975, approving, *inter alia*, the record of the Committee to Delimit the River Frontier, signed on April 16, 1975 on board the Iraqi ship *El Thawra* in the Shatt Al Arab;

(3). Common hydrographic charts, which have been verified on the spot and corrected and on which the geographical co-ordinates of the 1975 frontier crossing points have been indicated; these charts have been signed by the hydrographic experts of the Mixed Technical Commission and countersigned by the heads of the Iranian, Iraqi and Algerian delegations to the Committee. The said charts, listed hereinafter, are annexed to this Protocol and form an integral part thereof:

Chart No. 1: Entrance to the Shatt Al Arab, No. 3842, published by the British Admiralty;

Chart No. 2: Inner Bar to Kabda Point, No. 3843, published by the British Admiralty;

Chart No. 3: Kabda Point to Abadan, No. 3844, published by the British Admiralty;

Chart No. 4: Abadan to Jazirat Ummat Tuwaylah, No. 3845, published by the British Admiralty.

Article 2. (1). The frontier line in the Shatt Al Arab shall follow the thalweg, i.e. the median line of the main navigable channel at the lowest navigable level, starting from the point at which the land frontier between Iran and Iraq enters the Shatt Al Arab and continuing to the sea.

(2). The frontier line, as defined in paragraph 1 above, shall vary with changes brought about by natural causes in the main navigable channel. The frontier line shall not be affected by other changes unless the two Contracting Parties conclude a special agreement to the effect.

(3). The occurrence of any of the changes referred to in paragraph 2 above shall be attested jointly by the competent technical authorities of the two Contacting Parties.

(4). Any change in the bed of the Shatt Al Arab brought about by natural causes which would involve a change in the national character of the two States' respective territory or of landed property, constructions, or technical or other installations shall not change the course of the frontier line, which shall continue to follow the thalweg in accordance with the provisions of paragraph 1 above.

(5). Unless an agreement is reached between the two Contracting Parties concerning the transfer of the frontier line to the new bed, the water shall be re-directed at the joint expenses of both Parties to the bed existing in 1975 — as marked on the four common charts listed in article 1, paragraph 3, above — should one of the Parties so request within two years after the date on which the occurrence of the change was attested by either of the two Parties. Until such time, both Parties shall retain their previous rights of navigation and of use over the water of the new bed.

Article 3. (1). The river frontier between Iran and Iraq in the Shatt Al Arab, as defined in article 2 above, is represented by the relevant line drawn on the common charts referred to in article 1, paragraph 3, above.

(2). The two Contracting Parties have agreed to consider that the river frontier shall end at the straight line connecting the two banks of the Shatt Al Arab, at its mouth, at the astronomical lowest low-water mark. This straight line has been indicated on the common hydrographic charts referred to in article 1, paragraph 3, above.

Article 4. The frontier line as defined in articles 1, 2 and 3 of this Protocol shall also divide vertically the air space and the subsoil.

Article 5. With a view to eliminating any source of controversy, the two Contracting Parties shall establish a Mixed Iraqi-Iranian Commission to settle, within two months, any questions concerning the status of landed property, constructions, or technical or other installations, the national character of which may be affected by the delimitation of the Iranian-Iraqi river frontier, either through repurchase or compensation or any other suitable arrangement.

Article 6. Since the task of surveying the Shatt Al Arab has been completed and the common hydrographic chart referred to in article 1, paragraph 3, above has been drawn up, the two Contracting Parties have agreed that a new survey of the Shatt Al Arab shall be carried out jointly, once every 10 years, with effect from the date of signature of this Protocol. However, each of the two Parties shall have the right to request new surveys, to be carried out jointly, before the expiry of the 10-year period.

The two Contracting Parties shall each defray half the cost of such surveys.

Article 7. (1). Merchant vessels, State vessels and warships of the two Contracting Parties shall enjoy freedom of navigation in the Shatt Al Arab and in any part of the navigable channels in the territorial sea which lead to the mouth of the Shatt Al Arab, irrespective of the line delimiting the territorial sea of each of the two countries.

(2). Vessels of third countries used for purposes of trade shall enjoy freedom of navigation, on an equal and non-discriminatory basis, in the Shatt Al Arab and in any part of the navigable channels in the territorial sea which lead to the mouth of the Shatt Al Arab, irrespective of the line delimiting the territorial sea of each of the two countries.

(3). Either of the two Contracting Parties may authorize foreign warships visiting its ports to enter the Shatt Al Arab, provided such vessels do not belong to a country in a state of belligerency, armed conflict or war with either of the two Contracting Parties and provided the other Party is so notified no less than 72 hours in advance.

(4). The two Contracting Parties shall in every case refrain from authorizing the entry to the Shatt Al Arab of merchant vessels belonging to a country in a state of belligerency, armed conflict or war with either of the two Parties.

Article 8. (1). Rules governing navigation in the Shatt Al Arab shall be drawn up by a mixed Iranian-Iraqi Commission, in accordance with the principle of equal rights of navigation for both States.

(2). The two Contracting Parties shall establish a Commission to draw up rules governing the prevention and control of pollution in the Shatt Al Arab.

(3). The two Contracting Parties undertake to conclude subsequent agreements on the questions referred to in paragraphs 1 and 2 of this article.

Article 9. The Contracting Parties recognize that the Shatt Al Arab is primarily an international waterway, and undertake to refrain from any operations that might hinder navigation in the Shatt Al Arab or in any part of those navigable channels in the territorial sea of either of the two countries that lead to the mouth of the Shatt Al Arab.

Done at Baghdad, on June 13, 1975.

(Signed)

Abbas Ali Khalatbary   Saadoun Hamadi
Minister for Foreign Affairs   Minister for Foreign Affairs
of Iran   of Iraq

Signed in the presence of His Excellency Abdel-Aziz Bouteflika, Member of the Council of the Revolution and Minister for Foreign Affairs of Algeria.

NOTES ON CONTRIBUTORS

Willard A. Beling, King Faisal Professor Emeritus School of International Relations, University of Southern California, has published a number of books and articles on the Middle East.

Helena Cobban is an author and reporter specializing in the Middle East. Her publications include *The PLO: People, Power and Politics* (1984) and *The Making of Lebanon* (to be published in 1985).

Adam M. Garfinkle is Research Associate and Coordinator, Political Studies Program, Foreign Policy Research Institute, Philadelphia, PA. He has published a number of studies on the Middle East.

David E. Long is currently serving as officer in charge of the Near East and South Asia in the Office of Counter Terrorism and Emergency Planning in the Department of State. Previously he was a member of the Secretary's Policy Planning Staff, and before that was Chief of the Near East Research Division in the Bureau of Intelligence and Research. He has authored a number of studies on the Middle East.

R. D. McLaurin is a consultant, professor and author (eleven books) on the Middle East. He is a well-known specialist on the Levant.

Don Peretz is Professor of Political Science, State University of New York, Binghamton, and Director of its Southwest Asian-North African Program. He is the author of a number of studies on the Middle East and is a specialist on Israel.

William B. Quandt is Senior Fellow at the Brookings Institution. He was senior staff member, National Security Council staff (Middle East), in the Carter Administration. He is the author of a number of articles and monographs on the Middle East.

Fariborz Rouzbehani is a specialist on Iran and the Persian Gulf, which within the past year he has observed first-hand from both the Iranian and Arab sides.

Vladimir N. Sakharov, a Soviet-trained diplomat who defected to the West, is an author and lecturer on the Middle East, where he had served with the Russian KGB.

INDEX